HOW THE
BARBARIAN
INVASIONS

SHAPED THE MODERN WORLD

THE VIKINGS, VANDALS, HUNS, MONGOLS, GOTHS, AND TARTARS
WHO RAZED THE OLD WORLD AND FORMED THE NEW

THOMAS J. CRAUGHWELL

FAIR WINDS
PRESS
BEVERLY, MASSACHUSETTS

Text © 2008 Thomas J. Craughwell

First published in the USA in 2008
by Fair Winds Press, a member of
Quayside Publishing Group
100 Cummings Center
Suite 406-L
Beverly, MA 01915-6101
www.fairwindspress.com

12 11 10 09 08   1 2 3 4 5

ISBN-13: 978-1-59233-303-5
ISBN-10: 1-59233-303-6

Library of Congress Cataloging-in-Publication Data available
Craughwell, Thomas J., 1956-
    How the barbarian invasions shaped the modern world : The Vikings, Vandals, Huns, Mongols, Goths,
and Tartars who razed the old world and formed the new / Thomas J. Craughwell.
        p.   cm.
    Includes bibliographical references and index.
    ISBN-10: 1-59233-303-6
    ISBN-13: 978-1-59233-303-5
    1. Migrations of nations. 2. Middle Ages. I. Title.
    D135.C73 2008
    304.809--dc22

                                        2008000007

Photo research: Anne Burns Images
Cover and book design: Peter Long

Printed and bound in Singapore

CONTENTS

Introduction   8

Chapter 1

"THE BRIGHTEST LIGHT OF THE WHOLE WORLD IS EXTINGUISHED":

THE GOTHS SACK ROME, 410   14

Chapter 2

"THEY FILLED THE WHOLE EARTH WITH SLAUGHTER AND PANIC":

THE ARRIVAL OF THE HUNS, 369   36

Chapter 3

THE SCOURGE OF GOD: ATTILA THE HUN, c. 406–453   50

Chapter 4

KING OF THE LAND AND THE SEA: GAISERIC AND THE GLORY DAYS

OF THE VANDALS, 406–439   66

Chapter 5

AN EMPIRE OF THEIR OWN: THE VANDALS AND THE SECOND

SACKING OF ROME, 455   82

Chapter 6

THE GROANS OF THE BRITONS: THE ANGLE, SAXON, AND JUTE

INVASION OF BRITAIN, 449   98

Chapter 7

THE LONG-HAIRED KINGS: THE FRANKS, 270–511   114

Chapter 8

THE FIRST VIKING INVASION OF ENGLAND: THE SACKING OF

LINDISFARNE ABBEY, 793   128

Chapter 9

THE LAST KING: ALFRED THE GREAT, 849–899   144

Chapter 10

"FLOODS OF DANES AND PIRATES": THE VIKINGS IN IRELAND 795–980   158

Chapter 11

THE WASTELAND: THE VIKINGS IN THE FRANKISH EMPIRE, 820–911   172

Chapter 12

THE RESURRECTION OF HASTEIN: VIKINGS IN THE MEDITERRANEAN, 844–851   188

Chapter 13

THE BLOOD OF HEROES: IRISH AND VIKINGS AT THE

BATTLE OF CLONTARF, 1014   204

Chapter 14

THE END OF THE VIKING AGE: THE BATTLE OF STAMFORD BRIDGE, 1066   218

Chapter 15

VENGEANCE ON HER MIND: OLGA OF KIEV, c. 879–969   234

Chapter 16

THE PRINCE WHO MADE KIEV CHRISTIAN: VLADIMIR OF KIEV, 956–1015   248

Chapter 17

SPITTING ON THE EMPEROR: THE MONGOLS IN CHINA, 1215   260

Chapter 18

THE GOLDEN HORDE: THE MONGOLS IN RUSSIA, 1238–1240   274

Chapter 19

SACKS FULL OF EARS: THE MONGOLS IN EASTERN EUROPE, 1241–1242   288

Bibliography   304
Photography Credits   309
Index   310

INTRODUCTION

THE COUNTRIES OF ENGLAND, FRANCE, RUSSIA, AND CHINA are the result of the barbarian invasions. Moscow, Dublin, and Delhi are international centers of government, commerce, and culture because of the barbarians. Even the Europeans' unexpected discovery of the Americas can be traced back to the barbarians.

These claims may surprise readers. After all, the barbarians were rapists, killers, looters, destroyers of great cities, and ravagers of the countryside. And they were all that. They caused pain and destruction everywhere they went, but by examining their motives for rampaging across the territory of their neighbors we can see how they set off a string of events that resulted in the world we know today.

PREVIOUS PAGE:
MOUNTED ON
MAGNIFICENT HORSES,
A BAND OF BARBARIANS
APPROACH THE
WALLS OF ROME.

Popular culture has always preferred an image of the barbarians as hairy, half-naked wild men who swoop down on a village, slaughter the men, carry off the pretty girls, and send the local monks scampering for the hills. On the other hand, academic historians generally tend to shy away from the violent aspects of the barbarian invasions, preferring to discuss the trade routes opened up by the Vikings, or making the case that Rome never truly fell. Both points of view are true to a certain degree, yet both fail to offer a clear picture of the barbarians because each puts too much emphasis on only one facet of the story. The goal of this book is to find a middle way between two extremes.

A quick word about the term "barbarian." It comes from the Greek word *barbaros*, which refers to people who cannot speak Greek, meaning uncivilized outsiders.

A GREAT LIGHT IS EXTINGUISHED

One of the liveliest debates recently has raged over the question, "Did Rome fall to the barbarians?" The answer seems obvious—on August 24, 410, an army of Goths led by their king Alaric stormed into the city, subjecting the defenseless inhabitants to three days of looting, torture, and murder. Clearly, Rome fell.

Many professional historians point out, however, that the entire Roman Empire did not collapse in late August 410, and while Rome's provinces in western Europe were in for a rough time over the next few decades, Rome's provinces in the east, ruled by the emperor in Constantinople, flourished for centuries to come, virtually unaffected by the carnage and mayhem inflicted upon the west by the Huns, the Goths, the Vandals, the Franks, the Angles, and the Saxons. In other words, modern historians are trying to assure us that the sack of Rome in 410 was not the cataclysm we have been led to believe.

It's easy to be dispassionate at a distance of 1,500 years, but to the people who lived at the time of Rome's fall it seemed like the end of the world. "The brightest light of the whole world is extinguished!" lamented St. Jerome, the renowned translator of the Bible into Latin, and a man steeped in Roman culture who sheltered traumatized refugees from Rome in his monastery in Bethlehem.

In far-off Britain, a monk named Pelagius recorded that even in that remote province, "Everyone was mingled together and disturbed with fear; every household had its grief and an all-pervading terror gripped us." While in North Africa that great theologian and classical scholar, St. Augustine, began writing his greatest work, *City of God*, a meditation on the folly of placing one's trust in an earthly city when the only city that was truly eternal is found in heaven.

For the people of the Roman world, then, the fall of Rome to the Goths was a disaster. It struck at the heart of their civilization, it filled them with dread about where this barbarian group would strike next, it made them afraid

UTTERLY FEARLESS IN BATTLE, INTREPID ON THE OPEN SEA, AND MERCILESS TO ANYONE WHO RESISTED THEM, THE VIKINGS TERRORIZED WESTERN EUROPE FOR TWO HUNDRED YEARS.

that the only society they knew would be utterly destroyed—and if it were, how could they live in the coarse, violent world of the barbarians?

The fears of Jerome and Pelagius and countless others were well-founded. Within a century of the sack of the Rome, all of Rome's western provinces would be in the hands of various barbarian nations. The infrastructure of the empire crumbled: aqueducts no longer brought fresh water into the cities, no one performed the necessary routine maintenance on Rome's vast network of roads, the schools shut down, the libraries were trashed, and even the Latin language broke down, mutating into regional dialects that we know today as Italian, Spanish, Portuguese, Romanian, and French. It was truly a disaster, but over time, out of the ruins emerged modern Europe.

PIRATES AND MERCHANTS

For interested readers and researchers, there is no shortage of barbarian nations—the Alemanni, Magyars, Pechenegs, Sarmatians, and Gepids. The list is a long one. The purpose of this book, however, is to tell the stories of the most influential barbarian groups.

Every barbarian nation discussed in this book had a motive—often more than one—for invading its neighbors' territory. The Goths wanted revenge for years of mistreatment at the hands of the Roman emperors. The Vandals, who began as a weak, starveling band in the forests of Germany, wanted power, security, and respect.

The Vikings wanted the gold of the monasteries of the British Isles, not to hoard, but to hand out to their retainers. It sounds odd to say that the Vikings went to such trouble to steal things they planned to give away, but in Norse society the most admired man was the lord who dispensed gold and silver generously to the men of his war band—and the most honorable way to amass such treasure was to raid one's enemies.

In many ways the Vikings are the most interesting of the barbarian nations. They marauded from the northernmost islands of Scotland, to the Ukrainian city of Kiev, all the way to Pisa in Italy, and it is possible they even tried to raid the Egyptian port of Alexandria. Utterly fearless in battle, intrepid on the open sea, and merciless to anyone who resisted them, the Vikings terrorized western Europe for two hundred years.

Yet there was much more to the Vikings than mayhem. They were shrewd strategists who understood that a fragmented society such as the warring tribes of the Ukraine and Russia, or the petty kingdoms of England and Ireland, presented them with opportunities to pick off these tribes or kings one by one, establish themselves as the new rulers in the land, and then bring more Vikings in to colonize the country.

But settlement was only half of the Viking equation; they were also skillful, enthusiastic traders. From Kiev they used the Ukraine and Russia's network of rivers to carry furs, amber, and slaves to the markets of Constantinople and beyond. In return they received jewels, spices, and silk from Asia, which they sold in the market towns of Sweden and Norway. Archeologists excavating in Scandinavia have uncovered Moorish coins and even little figures of Buddha—striking evidence of the commercial reach of the Vikings.

In Ireland the Vikings found a society that was almost entirely rural and pastoral, whose entire economy was based on the barter system, and whose commercial ties did not extend beyond England, Scotland, and Wales. Considering the number of excellent bays and harbors along the Irish coast, the Vikings must have considered this a tremendous waste.

To remedy the situation, the Vikings founded Dublin, Wexford, Waterford, Arklow, Cork, and Limerick—the first cities in Ireland—all established as centers of international trade. To reach far-off markets, the Vikings taught the Irish how to build fine wooden ships. And to bring Irish merchants up to speed in the global marketplace, they introduced coins to the Irish economy.

TWO BARBARIAN KINGS

Every barbarian raid was led by a captain or a chief or even a king, yet in most cases the memory of these men died centuries ago. Attila and Genghis Khan are both the exceptions. Charismatic, daring, and relentless, both of these conquerors in their times astonished and terrified the world.

The fearsome reputation of Genghis Khan's Mongols spread so widely in the thirteenth century that fishermen in Denmark refused to put out to sea, afraid they might run into a Mongol fleet in the North Atlantic (actually, the

IT WAS SAID THAT GENGHIS KHAN HAD MADE THE SILK ROAD SO SAFE THAT A LONE WOMAN COULD WALK THE ENTIRE ROUTE CARRYING A FAT BAG OF GOLD AND NO ONE WOULD TROUBLE HER.

sea was the one place the Danish fishermen would have been safe—the Mongols never did learn the art of navigation).

Attila and Genghis shared an identical motivation: to make their poor, disunited, nomadic people a world power by merging them into an unstoppable fighting machine. Attila accomplished that original goal brilliantly. When he began, the Huns were desperately poor and often hungry. Within a few years the Huns' crude wooden carts were top-heavy with the loot from countless cities and towns, as well as chests brimming with tribute money paid to Attila by the Roman emperor. But what would the Huns do with all this wealth?

They had no tradition of farming or living in towns, and in spite of their successes on the battlefield, they showed no inclination to settle down in any of the lands they had ravaged. Even Attila could not imagine anything for his people other than a nomadic existence. Consequently, after Attila's sudden death, the Huns returned to the steppes of Asia, where they scattered, dissipated their wealth, and ultimately vanished from the historical record. Of all the barbarian kings and barbarian nations, Attila and his Huns are the most famous, yet aside from their fame as cruel marauders they have left little perceivable trace upon the modern world.

Genghis Khan, on the other hand, knew exactly what he wanted for his Mongols—he wanted to build nations, he wanted his people to acquire the technological and artistic skills the Chinese possessed. At his death, his empire extended from China to eastern Europe, from Beijing to Moscow, and at each city Genghis conquered, he sorted out the engineers, the builders, the men of science, the craftsmen, and the artists, and sent them to Mongolia to teach their secrets to his people.

Commerce was also part of Genghis' plan for lifting the Mongols to greatness. He reopened and made secure the Silk Road that linked the markets of India and China with those in Asia Minor, North Africa, and Europe.

It is often said that Greece, Rome, Judaism, and Christianity are the four pillars of western civilization—and that is true. They gave us our ideas about government, architecture, philosophy, literature, music, morals, what is true, and what is beautiful. But our world was also shaped by much

AT CHALONS IN FRANCE THE ROMAN COMMANDER ACTIUS WITH HIS GOTH ALLIES DEFEATED ATTILA THE HUN, BRINGING TO A HALT THE HUN'S CONQUEST OF WESTERN EUROPE.

Attila nach dem entscheidenden Angriffe der Westgothen.   Zeichnung von Hermann Vogel.

more violent, much less noble forces—the Goths, the Franks, the Angles, the Saxons, the Vikings, and the Mongols. This book searches through ancient sources and modern studies to disclose how the barbarians shaped our world.

"THE BRIGHTEST LIGHT OF THE WHOLE WORLD IS EXTINGUISHED": THE GOTHS SACK ROME

THE WORLD HAS NEVER A KNOWN AN EMPIRE AS GREAT AS Rome's; certainly, in terms of long-lasting influence, the Roman Empire has few or no peers.

From the Romans we received our alphabet, our calendar, and our ideas about law, justice, and representational government. The Romans invented the arch and the dome and the sports arena, but they also gave us such mundane but useful things as concrete, sewers, indoor plumbing, and paved roads.

To this day, more than 1,500 years after the city fell to the Goths, the influence of Roman government, technology, architecture, and literature can be found from the Americas to Australia, to the farthest reaches of Africa and Asia, and of course, across Europe. Not until the British Empire of the nineteenth and early twentieth centuries would the world see another such power. And it goes without saying that British civilization was rooted in Roman civilization, too.

A VAST—AND PAVED—EMPIRE

In its glory days during the second and third centuries after Christ, the Roman Empire covered 2.2 million square miles and ruled more than 120 million people—approximately two-fifths of the world's population at that time.

But perhaps this is the most impressive statistic: to link all its provinces and all its people, the Romans built 50,000 miles of stone-paved roads through everything from the deserts of North Africa to the forests of Romania to the marshlands of Britain. This international network of roads made it easy for the legions to march wherever they were needed, and opened new territories to commerce. Furthermore, the roads were so extensive and so well-maintained that a courier riding a fast horse could get a message from the emperor in Rome to a governor or a general in Gaul in a matter of days.

Of course, roads were just one of the impressive technological achievements of the Romans. All across the empire they built aqueducts to carry an unfailing supply of fresh water from mountain lakes into towns and cities. To keep the water moving, the Romans used the simplest principle on the planet: gravity. By building the aqueducts on a slight downward grade, they could make the water go exactly where they wanted it—to public fountains, public baths, and city sewer systems. It was simple, ingenious, and convenient.

A SEVENTEENTH-CENTURY MAP OF THE MEDITERRANEAN WORLD USES THE OLD ROMAN NAMES FOR THE LANDS OF EUROPE—HISPANIA, BRITAINIA, AND DACIA.

TIMELINE

150: THE ROMAN EMPIRE COVERS THE ENTIRE MEDITERRANEAN, PLUS ENGLAND AND SOUTHERN GERMANY.

263: FIRST GOTH RAIDS ON THE ROMAN EMPIRE STRIKE THE PROVINCE OF PANNONIA (AUSTRIA, HUNGARY, CROATIA, AND SERBIA).

312: ROMAN EMPEROR CONSTANTINE I ENDS PERSECUTION OF THE CHRISTIANS AND EMBRACES CHRISTIANITY; GOTHS BEGIN TO CONVERT TO THE ARIAN SECT OF CHRISTIANITY.

c. 370: ALARIC, FUTURE KING OF THE VISIGOTHS, IS BORN NEAR THE BLACK SEA IN MODERN-DAY ROMANIA.

378: GOTHS DEFEAT THE ROMAN LEGIONS AT BATTLE OF ADRIANOPLE. ROMAN EMPEROR VALENS DIES IN THE FIGHTING.

c. 387: ALARIC ENLISTS IN THE ROMAN ARMY AS A MERCENARY.

THE TEMPTATION OF ROMAN GOLD

The fatal blow came in 330 when Emperor Constantine I relocated the imperial capital to Byzantium (the site of modern-day Istanbul in Turkey) on the Bosphorus, the strait that separates Europe and Asia. As Rome declined, the eastern provinces of the Roman Empire flourished. They were the new center of prosperity, of learning, and of art and culture. It was a kind of renaissance, and Constantine moved his capital east so he and his court could enjoy it. The emperor renamed the town Constantinople and, with the exception of the Roman Senate, moved the entire imperial government there. Once the emperor was gone, Rome became almost a backwater.

Rome's weakness was the barbarian nations' opportunity. Some raided the frontiers of the empire. Others, particularly the Goths, couldn't resist the temptation of Roman gold and served as mercenaries in the Roman army. In many cases these Gothic mercenaries settled their families in Roman territory, and it was not unusual for their children to become "Romanized" by marrying Romans and converting to Christianity.

Of all the barbarian nations, the Goths had perhaps the best chance of eventually assimilating into Roman society. The Goths had a king. They lived in settled towns. Some of the Goths were farmers and others were merchants. They had a written language. They were deeply attached to their warrior culture. And most of the Goths had been baptized; granted, they belonged to the heretical

TIMELINE

394: FIGHTING ON THE SIDE OF ROME, ALARIC LEADS THOUSANDS OF GOTH MERCENARIES AT THE BATTLE OF THE FRIGIDUS RIVER. AFTER THE VICTORY, IN SPITE OF THE GOTHS' COURAGE AND THEIR HEAVY LOSSES, THE GOTHS RECEIVE NO ACKNOWLEDGMENT FROM THE EMPEROR.

408: ROMANS ATTACK THE WIVES AND CHILDREN OF GOTH MERCENARIES, KILLING THOUSANDS. IN RETALIATION, ALARIC LEADS A GOTH ARMY AGAINST ROME.

AUGUST 24, 410: THE GOTHS BREACH THE CITY'S DEFENSES AND RAMPAGE THROUGH THE STREETS OF ROME.

SEPTEMBER 410: ALARIC DIES OF A FEVER IN SOUTHERN ITALY. AFTER ALARIC'S DEATH, OTHER BARBARIAN NATIONS INVADE ROMAN TERRITORY. TO MEET THE THREAT, ROMAN LEGIONS FROM THE OUTLYING PROVINCES ARE CALLED HOME.

Arian sect rather than to the doctrinally orthodox Catholic Church, but at least they were Christians. And physically the Goths were attractive: both men and women tended to be tall and well-built, with fair skin, blonde hair, and blue eyes. In their social structure, in their high regard for martial valor, in their religion, the Goths were not very different from the Romans.

Given a few more generations and the Goths and Romans would have intermarried, much as Gauls and Britons and North Africans had married with Romans and adopted a Roman way of life. Tragically, the Goths and the Romans never got a chance to assimilate peacefully.

BARBARIANS AT THE GATE

On August 24, 410, the Goths poured through the Porta Salaria on the northeast side of Rome. They did not have to scale the walls or batter down the massive Salarian doors because someone inside the city opened the gates for them.

No one knows the identity of the traitor, but there are two different stories that try to solve the mystery. One story says a Roman noblewoman named Proba, moved by pity for her starving neighbors whom the famine of the siege had reduced to cannibalism, commanded her slaves to open the gates. The second story claims that Alaric, the king of the Goths, had sent 300 young male slaves as gifts to various important senators. In fact these slaves were Goth saboteurs, instructed to wait until the Romans were weak from hunger and disease,

CINDASUINTUS REX   RECESUINTUS REX   EGICA REX

URRACA REGINA   SANCIO REX   RANIMIRUS REX

BELASCO SCRIBA   SISEBUTUS EPS   SISEBUTUS NOTARIUS

NO MORE WORLDS TO CONQUER

The fall of the city of Rome to the Goths in 410 was the cataclysmic event in the history of the empire. The Roman Empire in western Europe limped along for another 66 years, until Odoacer, a Germanic chieftain who had seized power in Italy, forced the last emperor, a boy named Romulus Augustus, to abdicate. Nonetheless the Romans dated the beginning of the end of their empire to that day in 410 when the Goths sacked the city the Romans had always believed to be invulnerable.

In fact the Roman Empire had been in decline for almost two hundred years, and it had begun just when the empire appeared to be most stable. During the time of the Emperor Commodus (reigned 180–192) Rome's expansion into new territory came to an end. The nations that had given the Romans the most trouble—the Gauls, the Germans, and the Parthians—had all been pacified, however, the empire was now so vast and so complicated that it was becoming hard for one man to rule the entire thing.

Ironically, peace was bad for the Roman military and the Roman economy.

With no new enemies to fight or new lands to conquer, the Roman legions were recast in the unexciting roles of border guards and the local police force. The famous military discipline and training of the legions grew lax. For the robust young men of Rome, a soldier's life lost its appeal. Nonetheless, the state still needed a standing army, and since Romans were reluctant to enlist, the government hired barbarian mercenaries to fill the gap.

Just as foreign wars had kept the Roman legionnaires sharp, loot from those wars had kept Rome rich. To fuel its economy, the Roman imperial administration had come to rely on that steady stream of plunder from conquered nations, as well as profits from the sale of captives and prisoners of war as slaves.

Once the conquests stopped, the flow of treasure and slaves dried up, but the expense of operating the empire did not decrease, and the underemployed people of Rome still expected the regular government handouts of food that they had been receiving at least since the days of Julius Caesar.

A PAGE FROM A TENTH-CENTURY SPANISH MANUSCRIPT FEATURES STYLIZED PORTRAITS OF NINE GOTH KINGS AND QUEENS.

and then open the gates to their brother Goths. Both stories are hard to take seriously; the only thing that is certain is that someone let the barbarians in.

It is one of the oddities of history that no detailed eyewitness account of the fall of Rome has come down to us. There are bits and pieces of stories from a variety of sources, but nothing survives that gives us an in-depth, on-the-ground report of one of the central events in the story of the Western world.

We do know that for three days the Goths ransacked the city, carrying off everything of value from temples, palaces, and private houses. They looted, then burned, the villas on the Aventine Hill, a fashionable part of town where many wealthy families lived. They broke into the Mausoleum of Augustus, dumped the ashes of the caesars on the floor, and ran off with the precious burial urns and other tomb ornaments. The magnificent house and gardens of Sallust near the Salarian Gate, as well as the Basilica Aemelia in the Roman Forum, were consumed in a great fire, but by and large the city survived. In the meantime the Goths rounded up survivors; the wealthy and well-born the Goths were held for ransom, the rest were sold as slaves.

The churches were the only place where Romans were safe from the marauding Goths. Although the churches were Catholic and Alaric was an Arian, he decreed that out of respect for the apostle St. Peter, the first bishop of Rome, no church could be looted, and anyone—Catholic, Arian, or pagan—who sought shelter in a church should be left unmolested.

Finally, after three days of looting, the Goths marched out of Rome, loaded down with plunder and carrying away among their captives and slaves an especially valuable hostage, Galla Placidia, the 16-year-old sister of Emperor Honorius.

THE FIRST ENCOUNTER

The Goths first swept down on the Roman world in 263, when they launched a four-year-long spree, sacking the rich cities and towns of the Roman province of Pannonia, a region that includes parts of present-day Austria, Hungary, Croatia, and Serbia.

Such assaults were irksome, but the Romans had been attacked by barbarians before, and Emperor Gallienus responded as every emperor since Augustus had done: he assembled his legions and marched out against the Goths.

MARCELLA'S STORY

Alaric's men had imagined that once they were inside Rome, gold and silver would be lying about in every house and villa. It was an unreasonable assumption, and in some cases, when Goth looters did not find as much treasure as they had expected, they tortured Roman men and even women to force them to reveal where they had hidden their valuables.

One of those victims was Marcella, a widow, once very wealthy, who lived in her fine house as a nun. It was the splendor of the house that led the Goths to believe Marcella still had chests full of gold and silver stashed away somewhere, so they whipped her to make her talk. And as they beat her, they made a young nun named Principia watch. But all Marcella did was beg the Goths not to harm Principia, and all Principia did was plead with the Goths to spare old Marcella because there really was no gold.

The officer in charge of the beating did not believe her. True, the old woman and the girl were dressed in rough sackcloth; they wore no jewelry, no cosmetics, no elaborately coiffed wigs like other well-born Roman women. Nonetheless, the old lady's house was magnificent: frescoes and a fountain in the atrium, marble sculptures in the garden. This was the home of a Roman patrician, and patricians always had gold.

Yet as the beating went on and neither woman changed their story, it occurred to the Goth officer that perhaps his prisoners really were nuns who had given away their wealth years ago. He stopped the torture, and ordered some of his men to escort Marcella and Principia to sanctuary in the Basilica of St. Paul Outside the Walls. For Marcella, this act of mercy came too late; in the church, amid a crowd of terrified refugees, she died of her wounds.

The two armies met at Naissus, modern-day Nis in Serbia. Although outnumbered by the Goths, the Romans, in a classic cavalry maneuver, swung around in a wide arc and attacked the Goths' rear, while the Roman infantry charged head-on into the Goths. Hemmed in on two fronts, the Goths panicked and ran back to their fortified camp. The Romans followed, stormed

TWO TYPES OF GOTHS

For simplicity's sake, this book refers to "the Goths." Technically there were two branches of this barbarian nation that originated in southern Sweden in the area known as Götaland. The Western Goths, also known as the Visigoths, was the branch that Alaric led against Rome. They would eventually carve out a kingdom for themselves that extended from central France to the southern coast of Spain.

The Eastern Goths, or Ostrogoths, took power in Italy in the sixth century, but since their impact on the Roman Empire was minimal, particularly when compared to their cousins the Visigoths, the Ostrogoths' story is beyond the scope of this book.

---

into the camp, slaughtered perhaps as many as 30,000 Goths, and took thousands of prisoners. The Goths who escaped the massacre fled back to their home territory on the northern side of the Danube River.

Over the next century, Gothic interaction with the Romans moved in a decidedly different direction. The Goths abandoned looting Roman towns in favor of trading with Roman merchants. Rather than attempt to conquer Roman territory, they entered into a military alliance with the Roman governors in the empire's eastern provinces.

After 312, when Emperor Constantine put an end to the persecution of the Christians, the Goths began to convert, although heretical Arian bishops and priests got to them before the Catholics could. The Goths even volunteered for the Roman army, and in many cases these barbarian legions were led by Goth officers. Though thousands of Goth mercenaries brought their families to live within the borders of the Roman Empire, the majority still lived in their home territory on the north side of the Danube.

Then, about the year 370, a new barbarian horde appeared in eastern Europe. Thundering out of central Asia came the Huns, a nomadic, warlike people so fierce and, so merciless that even the Goths were afraid of them.

EMPEROR CONSTANTINE I WEAKENED ROME WHEN HE MOVED THE IMPERIAL CAPITAL TO BYZANTIUM, WHICH HE RENAMED CONSTANTINOPLE.

THE PRICE OF A CHILD

In 376 the Goths' King Fritigern petitioned Emperor Valens to permit him to lead his people across the Danube. Fritigern believed that because the river was so wide, the Huns, who were cavalrymen, would not be able to cross easily, or at least not before the Goths could mount a defense. Valens gave his consent and even promised to send boats to ease the Goths' passage into Roman territory.

The emperor imagined that by letting the Goths into Roman territory he was getting the better part of the bargain. New Goth settlers in Roman territory meant new recruits for his army and new taxpayers contributing to the imperial treasury. Furthermore, if the Huns did manage to cross the Danube, they would fall on the Goths first, giving the Romans time to assemble the legions.

Once Valens learned, however, that as many as 200,000 Goths were waiting to cross the river, he adopted a new strategy. He insisted that only the young, the healthy, and the strong would be permitted into Roman territory—the old, the infirm, and the weak must take their chances with the Huns on

BARBARIAN TRIBES ARE
DEPICTED PROMISING
ALLEGIANCE TO ROME.

the Danube's north shore. Furthermore, once the Goths arrived on the south side of the river, they were commanded to surrender their weapons—an order intended to humiliate them.

Then, adding treachery to humiliation, the emperor reneged on his promise to send supplies and food to the Goth refugees. Since the countryside could not support the local population, the Roman garrison, and tens of thousands of hungry Goths, the Romans herded the Goths into a kind of concentration camp where they posted guards around the clock so none of the detainees could leave.

With food in short supply inside the camp and regulations forbidding anyone to go outside to buy provisions, the Goths faced almost certain starvation. As the Goths grew weak and their situation more desperate, the Romans made them a cruel offer: the Goths could trade their children for dog meat, the rate of exchange being one child per dog. The children would be sold as slaves, but at least the parents would live.

FRESH TREACHERY

With no one else to whom he could appeal, Fritigern begged Valens to show mercy. The emperor, perhaps believing that he had all but crushed the Goths, ordered their release from the internment camp so they could travel to the city of Marcianople to trade for food and other necessities. It was a distance of 100 miles; countless Goths, sick and weakened by malnutrition, died along the way.

Yet when the Goths at last arrived at Marcianople they found the city gates shut against them. City officials and the officers of the garrison refused to sell the Goths any food. This prompted the Goths' rage to boil over. They fanned out across the neighboring countryside, plundering farms and small towns, then rampaged across the Roman provinces of eastern Europe just as their ancestors had done a century earlier.

The cruelty and treachery of Valens and his representatives had transformed the Goths from friends and allies into implacable enemies.

THE DEATH OF VALENS

It took Emperor Valens six years to summon the courage and resolve to face the Goths. When at last he did so, he led 60,000 legionnaires to the fields outside Adrianople (modern Ediren in Turkey) to meet his nemesis, Fritigern. It was August 9, 378, a scorcher of a day with temperatures hovering near 100 degrees.

As the Romans stood in battle formation beneath the hot sun, sweating and miserable in their heavy armor, Fritigern ordered his men to set fire to the dry grass near the Roman lines. As the Roman infantry fell back from the flames and the intense heat, the Goth cavalry surrounded the Roman cavalry, while Goth foot soldiers hemmed in the Roman infantry. What followed was a massacre that lasted until dark.

Desperate to save themselves, Valens' own bodyguards deserted him. The abandoned emperor tried to escape, too. One account says he was cut down somewhere on the battlefield by a Goth who didn't know he had killed a caesar. Another says he hid in a nearby farm house where the Goths burned him alive. Perhaps as many as 40,000 Roman troops were killed, wounded, or taken prisoner that day. Encouraged by the victory at Adrianople, over the next three decades the Goths raided and harassed Roman settlements near the Danube and the Rhine rivers.

Yet contrary to all expectations, the Romans and the Goths formed an alliance. The reasons for this, as is often the case with ancient history, are not entirely clear. It's likely that by this time the Romans needed Goths in their army, and the Goths had become attached to Roman gold and Roman comforts. However, this pragmatic relationship would not last forever.

STILICHO AND ALARIC

After Emperor Valens' death on the battlefield, the future of Roman-Goth relations was shaped by two men: a Roman commander, Flavius Stilicho (c. 359–408), and a Goth mercenary named Alaric (c. 370–410).

As the son of a Roman mother and a Vandal father, Stilicho was a "semi-barbarian" in the eyes of some Romans. Yet nothing could have been further from the truth. Stilicho was steeped in Roman culture and understood virtually nothing about the Vandals or any other barbarian nation that threatened the empire at this time. He rose to power through the military, and proved himself to be so loyal that Emperor Theodosius the Great married his beloved adopted daughter Serena to Stilicho.

After the wedding, Theodosius heaped one honor after another upon his new son-in-law; he named Stilicho Count of the Sacred Stables, which gave him authority to reorganize the Roman cavalry, and appointed him Count of the Domestics, which made him the chief officer of the emperor's bodyguard. Furthermore, Theodosius encouraged more intermarriage between the imperial family and the house of Stilicho. The emperor chose Stilicho's daughter Maria as the future bride for his son and heir Honorius, and Stilicho's son Eucherius as the future husband for Theodosius' daughter, Galla Placidia. Stilicho was rapidly becoming one of the most powerful men in the Roman Empire.

While Stilicho grew in the emperor's favor, the Goths elected a new king. Alaric, about 25 years old, belonged to the Balthings, one of the most prominent clans among the Goths, but he was also at ease among the Romans—while still in his teens he had enlisted as a mercenary in the Roman army. In the interest of reviving the old alliance between Romans and Goths, Alaric was willing to forget the crimes Emperor Valens had committed against his people. In 394 that renewed alliance was put to the test.

AN ILL WIND

For nearly a century, the Roman Empire had experimented with the concept of rule by co-emperors, one of whom governed the European provinces, while the other governed the provinces in Asia and North Africa. Theodosius was emperor in the east, while Valentinian was emperor in the west.

Then, in 392, Valentinian was murdered by one of his generals, Arbogast, a pagan who was active in the movement to bring back the cult of the old gods, or perhaps by agents working for the general. With Valentinian out of the way, Arbogast set up a pagan rhetorician named Eugenius as his puppet emperor. Arbogast and Eugenius planned to eliminate Theodosius, unite the two halves of the empire under one caesar again, restore paganism, drive out the Christians from political and public life, and perhaps unleash a new wave of anti-Christian persecution.

On September 5, 394, an army led by Arbogast and Eugenius met an army led by Theodosius, Stilicho, and Alaric at the Frigidus River in present-day Slovenia. The antagonists were evenly matched—each army had about 100,000 men.

ALARIC WAITED FOR THEODOSIUS TO RECOGNIZE HIS ROLE IN THE BATTLE AND THE SACRIFICE THE GOTHS HAD MADE BY GRANTING HIM A HIGH RANK IN THE ROMAN ARMY. THE APPOINTMENT NEVER CAME, AND ALARIC NEVER FORGAVE THE SLIGHT.

THE TWO EMPERORS

By the beginning of the fourth century, the Roman emperors had come to the conclusion that the empire had become too vast and too complicated to be ruled by one man. A new system was introduced that installed an emperor of the western provinces and an emperor of the eastern provinces. Valentinian II was emperor of the western provinces from 375–392.

At this time, Valentinian's colleague was Theodosius I, who had become emperor of the eastern provinces in 378. As an ambitious man, Theodosius was dissatisfied with the two-emperor system. At the death of Valentinian II in 392, Theodosius reunited the entire Roman Empire under his own rule. Nonetheless, he was the last emperor of the east and the west. At Theodosius's death in 395, his successors split up the empire again.

As the battle began, Alaric and his 20,000 Goth warriors took up their position on the front line and made a valiant, headlong charge against the enemy. Arbogast's men, who were well-entrenched along the river, had little trouble driving back the Goths. After repeated assaults on Arbogast's defenses—assaults that had cost the lives of 10,000 Goths—Alaric ordered his men to fall back. That night Arbogast and Eugenius celebrated, while Theodosius, Stilicho, and Alaric prepared gloomily for what they believed would be certain defeat.

When the two armies met again the next day, both sides fought with such ferocity that it was uncertain who would win. Then nature intervened. The battlefield lay near the Alps, close to a pass where violent north winds known as the Bora sometimes sweep down from the mountains into the plains; these winds are known to reach 60 miles per hour and sometimes even 125 miles per hour. Precisely how strong the winds were that day is unknown, but they were strong enough to unnerve Arbogast's army.

Theodosius's men, on the other hand, interpreted the windstorm as a gift from God and roused themselves for a fresh assault on the enemy lines. Unwilling to face the wrath of God, the emperor, and the Goths, Arbogast's

ALTHOUGH HALF-VANDAL, GENERAL STILICHO REGARDED HIMSELF AS THOROUGHLY ROMAN.

men ran from the field. Eugenius was captured, paraded before Theodosius, and then beheaded. As for Arbogast, he fled into the Alps, where he killed himself.

THE FORGOTTEN HERO

In the celebrations that followed the victory, everyone associated with the battle of the Frigidus River was hailed as a hero—with one exception. Alaric waited for Theodosius to recognize his role in the battle and the sacrifice the Goths had made by granting him a high rank in the Roman army. The appointment never came, and Alaric never forgave the slight.

Within months of the battle, Alaric repudiated his alliance with Rome and led his army into the Roman province of Thrace, in present-day Bulgaria, to loot rich men's villas and sack poorly defended Roman towns.

In the meantime, members of the imperial court who envied Stilicho's close ties to the imperial family and powerful influence over the eleven-year-old boy-emperor Honorius (he had inherited the throne after the death of Theodosius in 395) watched for an opportunity to get rid of the general. By 408, Stilicho's enemies had cobbled together a list of his "crimes": He was an Arian heretic, he was plotting with Alaric to seize the throne for his son Eucherius, and he had sought to undermine the power of Rome by permitting barbarians to settle in Gaul.

A full-blown coup d'etat against Stilicho erupted in August 408 while he was in the northern Italian town of Ravenna. As his enemies came for him, the general took sanctuary in a church.

Early the next morning, the soldiers sent to seize Stilicho swore to the bishop of Ravenna that they were instructed by Emperor Honorius only to place the general under arrest, so that no harm would come to him. Perhaps the bishop was gullible, or perhaps he was fearful of opposing Honorius; whatever his reasons, he let the soldiers take Stilicho from the protection of the church.

Once out in the street, Stilicho was informed that he had already been condemned to death. Without putting up any struggle, he submitted to execution, dying on August 22, 408. A few days later in Rome, the conspirators caught up with his son, Eucherius, and murdered him, too.

After the death of Stilicho, Romans who believed that he had been in league with Alaric attacked and killed the wives and children of Goth warriors who were serving in the Roman army. When news of the massacre reached the Goth soldiers, they deserted en masse and went over to Alaric, demanding that he lead them against the Romans so they could avenge their murdered families. It is said that as many as 30,000 Goth fighting men joined Alaric. Within days of the massacre, Alaric and his Goths were marching on Rome.

THE SIEGE OF ROME

Alaric turned Roman technology against the Romans. Using the Flaminian Way, one of the famous Roman roads, Alaric and his army moved swiftly through Italy.

They paused along the way to sack the cities of Aquileia and Cremona, and they ravaged the lands along the Adriatic Sea, but with their hearts fixed on Rome, they left many more cities and towns along their route undisturbed. Once they arrived outside Rome, the Goths surrounded the city and blockaded the Tiber River so no provisions could reach the citizens.

The Romans, though they were not prepared for a siege, did not despair yet. In fact, their pride was wounded by the idea that barbarians would even attempt to conquer their city. After all, it had been nearly 700 years since a foreign army had tried to breach the walls of Rome. Nonetheless, in their indignation, they looked for a scapegoat—and they found one.

Stilicho's widow, Serena, was in Rome at the time, and gossips spread the rumor that letters passed between her and Alaric, that she was plotting with the barbarian king to betray the city. Rome's senators became caught up in the panic and, without a shred of evidence of Serena's guilt, sentenced her to be strangled.

Meanwhile, the city's supply of food dwindled daily. The government handout of free bread fell from three pounds per person per day to one and a half pounds, then to half a pound, until the storehouses were completely empty. Merchants who still had stores of food could ask any price—and they did. Some wealthy Romans, such as Laeta, the widow of the Emperor Gratian, gave their gold and silver to the poorest inhabitants of the city so they could buy something to eat, but no amount of charity could prevent the inevitable: Rome was running out of food.

Famine struck first, followed by an epidemic. As the corpses piled up inside the houses and out in the streets, Romans of every class became desperate.

REVERTING TO THE OLD GODS

The pagans in the city blamed the empire's troubles on the Christians. As long as Romans worshipped the old gods, the pagans argued, the city had been inviolate.

They told how at the town of Narni in Umbria the citizens had made a traditional public sacrifice to the gods, and immediately thunder crashed overhead, fire fell from heaven, and the army of Alaric abandoned its siege of the town and fled. The pagans of Rome insisted that the cult of the gods should be restored, and sacrifices should be offered on the Capitol and in the Forum, with the entire Senate attending—including Christian senators—as had been customary in the days before Emperor Constantine abandoned the gods of Rome for Christ.

It was the notion of a public sacrifice that unsettled the senators. For nearly a century the emperors had banned pagan rites; if some Romans wanted to make a sacrifice in private, the senators were willing to turn a blind eye, but a public ceremony with all the senators in attendance was impossible. Even in their current dire predicament they still were afraid to antagonize the emperor.

THE RANSOM FOR ROME

Rather than rely on the old gods, the senators hoped to touch the Christian compassion of Alaric. They selected two ambassadors to plead the city's case—Basilius, a senator, and John, a tribune who knew Alaric. So, under a flag of truce, the ambassadors entered the camp of the Goths.

Basilius and John started the negotiation on the wrong foot. They adopted a haughty tone, claiming that if Alaric attacked the city he would find tens of thousands of angry, well-armed citizens ready to resist him. Alaric laughed at such an obvious lie. "The thicker the hay," he said, "the easier it is to mow."

Then, before the ambassadors could make bigger fools of themselves, Alaric presented them with his demands. The Goths would leave Rome in peace in return for the liberation of all slaves from any barbarian nation, plus 5,000 pounds of gold, 30,000 pounds of silver, 4,000 silk tunics, 3,000 leather hides dyed scarlet, and 3,000 pounds of pepper. (In ancient times pepper had to be imported from India's Malabar Coast, which made it tremendously expensive. The Romans and the Goths valued pepper in the same way that we value Périgord black truffles.)

After hearing the king's ransom demand, John asked, "But what, then, will you leave us?"

Alaric replied, "Your lives."

With no other option, the senate agreed to Alaric's terms. When the carts bearing the treasure rolled out of the city gates, all of Rome's barbarian slaves went with them. It is said the 40,000 slaves entered Alaric's camp that day. True to his word, Alaric broke the siege and led his army north to Tuscany, where he planned to spend the winter.

In the meantime, he asked Emperor Honorius once again to grant him a military title, specifically, commander of Rome's army in the western provinces of the empire. After dithering for a time, Honorius sent his answer, but in an indirect manner. He wrote to the chief of the Praetorians, the emperor's personal bodyguards, instructing him never to grant high rank to a barbarian. Such an action, Honorius wrote, would prostitute the honor of Rome's proud legions. At the same time that he dispatched the letter, Honorius arranged for the contents of it to be leaked to Alaric. Enraged by this flagrant insult, the king of the Goths collected his army and marched on Rome again.

The Goths took up their old positions around the city. Then in the middle of the night of August 24, 410, someone inside Rome flung open the Salarian Gates, and the people of the city awoke to the terrible sound of Gothic war trumpets and war cries echoing through the streets of Rome. The city that had had been mistress of a great empire was now in the hands of barbarians.

THE PLIGHT OF THE REFUGEES

News of the fall of Rome stunned the world. From his hermitage in Bethlehem, St. Jerome lamented, "The brightest light of the whole world is extinguished!" Panic spread throughout Italy as tens of thousands fled to the far corners of the empire. Some even ran as far as the Holy Land, where they took refuge in the pilgrims' hospice St. Jerome and his friends, Ss. Paula and Eustochium, had built in Bethlehem. We have a letter written by Jerome at the time in which he says that so many refugees have poured into the little town that he has taken a break from translating and explaining biblical texts in order to feed the hungry, nurse the sick, and comfort the grief-stricken.

"I have set aside my commentary on Ezekiel," he wrote, "and almost all study. For today we must translate the words of the Scriptures into deeds."

About five years after the fall of the city, an anonymous Christian poet in Gaul, wishing to summon up a scene of perfect human misery, drew upon what he had seen and heard from refugees who had survived the sack of Rome:

> This man groans for his lost silver and gold,
> Another is racked by the thought of his stolen goods
> And of his jewelry now divided amongst Gothic brides.
> This man mourns for his stolen flock, burnt houses, and drunk wine,
> And for his wretched children and ill-omened servants.

THE BIBLICAL SCHOLAR ST. JEROME PUT ASIDE HIS STUDIES TO CARE FOR REFUGEES FROM THE SACK OF ROME.

SALVAGING A CIVILIZATION

The fall of Rome in 410 marked the beginning of what would be the utter collapse of the Roman Empire in Europe.

In the centuries that followed, virtually the entire imperial infrastructure fell apart. As the barbarians conquered one Roman province after another, the old Roman administration broke down; the bureaucrats who had maintained the roads, the aqueducts, and the public baths were dead or had run away.

The villas, libraries, and academies were looted and destroyed. Roman law barely existed outside the city of Rome itself. The literacy rate plummeted. Even Latin, the language that had united the Mediterranean world, morphed into local dialects that became Italian, Spanish, French, Portuguese, and Romanian. And the provinces that had once been ruled by the emperor were carved up by the barbarians into new territories that eventually became the nations of modern Europe.

PRESERVING THE PAST

One organization was determined, however, to salvage something from the chaos. The Catholic Church became the guardian of classical civilization.

In the absence of the emperor, beginning in the fifth century, the popes took up the job as the chief administrators of Rome. Following this example, bishops assumed the role once filled by Roman governors and magistrates. By the sixth century, monks were actively collecting and copying Roman and Greek books—what they managed to save was only a fraction of what had once existed, but it was better than nothing.

About the same time, small schools opened in monasteries and convents; from these schools evolved the first universities. And of course Latin survived as the language of the Church, the schools, and the two most prestigious professions at the time, law and medicine. Thanks to the Church, then, some part of the legacy of Rome was preserved, and endures to this day.

"THEY FILLED THE WHOLE EARTH WITH SLAUGHTER AND PANIC": THE ARRIVAL OF THE HUNS

THE ONLY PERMANENT LEGACY OF THE HUNS IS THEIR NAME, which has become a synonym for barbarism. During World War I and World War II, the Allies routinely referred to their German enemies as "Huns," despite the fact that the Huns were not a Germanic tribe but rather Asian, probably related to the Mongols. Ethnic inaccuracy aside, the Huns truly were barbarians par excellence—so fearsome, so murderous, so destructive, that even other barbarian nations were afraid of them.

Unlike their barbarian neighbors, however, when it came to advancing the course of civilization, the Huns' contribution was almost nil. They did not establish kingdoms, found cities, or open new trade routes. They produced no technology, no works of art. They never even settled down to farm. Instead, the Huns remained violent, unpredictable wanderers upon the earth who filled the settled people of the known world with terror at their coming and left only destruction in their wake.

CAMPING BY THE SEA

In 395, the Huns stampeded out of the passes of the Caucasus Mountains—the dividing line between Asia and Europe—and into some of the richest provinces in the eastern half of Rome's Empire. They overran Cappadocia in Turkey, conquered the mighty Christian kingdom of Armenia, and ravaged large parts of Syria. Those inhabitants that the Huns didn't murder, they led off in large gangs back through the Caucasus to be sold as slaves. Then word spread that the Huns were riding toward the Holy Land to plunder the gold-rich churches of Jerusalem.

Hysterical rumors circulated among the Romans that the Huns killed the old and infirm, and then ate the corpses. Another rumor claimed that when a

AFTER SACKING AND BURNING A VILLAGE, TWO HUN CHIEFTAINS DISCUSS WHERE TO STRIKE NEXT.

TIMELINE

C. 358: THE HUNS, A NOMADIC PEOPLE FROM CENTRAL ASIA, BEGIN RAIDING THE EASTERN FRINGE OF THE ROMAN EMPIRE.

C. 370: THE ALANS, WARLIKE NOMADS LIVING IN WHAT IS NOW IRAN, ARE OVERWHELMED BY THE HUNS. MANY OF THE SURVIVING ALANS ALLY THEMSELVES WITH THEIR CONQUERORS.

376: ERMANARICH, KING OF THE OSTROGOTHS, COMMITS SUICIDE RATHER THAN FACE THE HUNS IN BATTLE.

Hun wanted to take an especially solemn oath, he killed his mother and father and swore on their bodies. Wilder still was the claim that the Huns were descended from Scythian witches who had copulated with the demons who inhabited the deserts of Bactria in what is now Afghanistan.

From his monastery in Bethlehem, St. Jerome captured the terror he and countless thousands of others felt when word reached them that the Huns were coming. "They filled the whole earth with slaughter and panic alike as they flitted hither and thither on their swift horses…. [B]y their speed they outstripped rumor, and they took pity neither upon religion nor rank nor age nor wailing childhood." A friend from Rome, a wealthy Christian widow named Fabiola, was visiting Jerome at the time. When she heard that the Huns were on their way, she packed her bags, bid her friend a hasty goodbye, and boarded the first ship back to Italy.

The inhabitants of the Holy Land could not decide what to do: If they stayed, they risked being massacred or sold into slavery; if they ran away, they might never be able to return to their homes again. So Jerome and hundreds of others like him chose a half-way measure. With their trunks and bags they fled to the seaports of Palestine, loaded their luggage aboard ship, and then camped out on the beach and waited. Jerome wrote that at night it became bitterly cold along the sea, yet fear kept everyone from leaving their impromptu camp and returning to their warm houses.

As it happened, the Huns never did get as far as Jerusalem or Bethlehem. After a few anxious days, Jerome and his fellow refugees collected their baggage and went home. But this corner of the empire was not out of danger yet. There were no Roman legions to defend the eastern provinces because Emperor

395: THE HUNS OVERRUN CAPPADOCIA IN TURKEY, IN ADDITION TO ARMENIA AND SYRIA.

WINTER 395–396: LED BY THEIR CHIEF ULDIN, THE HUNS DEVASTATE THE ROMAN PROVINCE OF THRACE (ROMANIA).

400: THE HUNS OCCUPY MOST OF WHAT IS NOW HUNGARY.

C. 406: THE GERMANIC BARBARIAN TRIBES, PANICKED BY THE COMING OF THE HUNS, MOVE WESTWARD INTO ROMAN TERRITORY.

Theodosius the Great had taken virtually the entire army to the West. Nonetheless, a eunuch named Eutropius found enough Goth warriors and Roman soldiers in the East to put up at least a token resistance until he managed to broker a truce with the Huns in 398.

BARELY HUMAN

What made the Huns an object of universal dread? A variety of things, not the least of which was their physical appearance. The Huns practiced scarification, slashing the faces of their male infants with swords. Many societies practice scarification as a sign of passage from childhood to adulthood, or as a permanent token of mourning. Why the Huns scarred the faces of their babies is a mystery.

Hun adults tended to be short, swarthy, and bow-legged from spending so much time on horseback. To Romans, accustomed to classical notions of beauty, the Huns with their squat physique, mutilated faces, broad noses, squinting eyes, and coarse black hair looked grotesque. The Gothic historian Jordanes wrote that the Huns concealed "under a barely human form the ferocity of a wild beast."

For their clothing, the Huns sewed together the skins of marmots, rodents that lived in burrows all across northern Asia. The Huns never washed these clothes and did not change into new ones until the tattered skins fell off their bodies.

The Huns' horses had a scrawny, underfed appearance. Since the Huns had no settled towns or farms, they had no hay or grain to feed their horses, so the animals survived by grazing. Nonetheless, these horses were very fast, and the Huns rode them so skillfully it appeared that man and beast were a single creature.

TO THE ROMANS, THE HUNS MUST HAVE LOOKED LIKE AN ARMY OF CORPSES CHARGING DOWN ON THEM.

Unlike the Roman legions who made a splendid appearance outfitted in their armor and uniforms and standing in precise formation for battle, the Huns thundered across the plains howling their battle cry, their faces hideous, their ratty clothes flapping in the wind, their gaunt, bony horses moving with astonishing speed. To the Romans, the Huns must have looked like an army of corpses charging down on them.

Typically, as the Huns drew close to their enemy, their massive frontal charge broke up into many small bands of riders who attacked from every direction. Some rode right into the ranks of the enemy, slashing with their swords or entangling men with their lassos. Then just as suddenly they would ride off as if they were retreating. Once they reached a safe distance, the Huns would turn suddenly, releasing a deadly volley of arrows. Romans, Armenians, and Syrians who had faced the Huns on the battlefield never forgot the terrible experience.

LETHAL WEAPONRY AND SKILL

Notwithstanding the psychological impact of the Huns' fearsome appearance and unorthodox tactics on the battlefield, ultimately it was their superior horsemanship and skill with a bow that gave them an advantage in warfare.

The Huns' war bow (they used a different type of bow for hunting) had a wooden core reinforced with animal horn, bone, and dried sinew. It was a reflex bow—a bow that even when unstrung preserved its distinctive curve—and on average measured about six feet long. A trained Hun bowman was almost 100 percent certain of hitting his target at distances of up to 180 feet, but even from 525 feet away he could still be lethal.

Virtually every warrior society had archers, but generally these archers fought on foot. The Huns were an army—or perhaps a better term is swarm—of archers on horseback. Even riding at full speed across rough terrain, they could shoot and kill foes, with appalling accuracy. And the Huns did not just shoot straight ahead, they could also shoot from side to side. Even as they rode away, Hun archers would turn in the saddle and keep firing arrow after arrow at their enemies.

The Huns did have saddles, as archaeological excavations of Hun graves have proven. They were made of wood and had a bow that rose straight up in the front, and a second, longer inclined bow at the rear. What's unclear is whether the Huns

WRITING OF THE HUNS FROM HIS MONASTERY IN BETHLEHEM, ST. JEROME SAID, "THEY FILLED THE WHOLE EARTH WITH SLAUGHTER AND PANIC."

THIS SECOND-CENTURY
CARVING DEPICTS A
ROMAN LEGIONNAIRE
LOCKED IN HAND-TO-
HAND COMBAT WITH
A BARBARIAN.

had stirrups. On the one hand it would appear impossible that the Huns could have been so nimble on horseback without stirrups, yet none have been found in any Hun graves. It's possible that the Huns made stirrups from leather or bits of wood, perishable material that would decompose quickly. Given the Huns' extraordinary horsemanship, most historians these days believe that the Huns had stirrups and even introduced them to Western Europe.

THE DEATH OF TWO KINGS

The king of the Goths at this time was an old man named Ermanarich. The Roman historian Ammianus Marcellinus described him as "a very warlike prince" who had a lifetime of victories to his credit, particularly against the Slavic tribes in what is now northwestern Russia.

As the conqueror of thirteen different nations, Ermanarich was hailed by his own people as a Gothic version of Alexander the Great. Nothing in the old king's career, however, had prepared him for the Huns. He had heard horror stories of what the Huns had done to the Alans, and then couriers straggled in to report that in a string of skirmishes the Goths had been crushed by the Huns. Afraid to lead out his warriors and take his chances against such an enemy and unwilling to see the empire he had built fall into the hands of the Huns, King Ermanarich despaired and killed himself.

After Ermanarich's suicide the Goths could not agree what to do. One splinter group collected around the old king's son, Hunimund, who made the best of a bad situation by imitating the Alans and submitting to the Huns. This band of Goths was absorbed into Hun society, just as the vanquished Alans had been.

The majority of the Goths were too proud to surrender but too frightened to fight. Instead, they sent a frantic petition to Emperor Valens, begging his permission to cross the wide Danube River where they would be under the protection of Rome.

The river did keep the Huns at bay—until the brutal winter of 395, when the Danube froze. Lured on by the promise of easy plunder in the Roman province of Thrace—part of present-day Romania—the Huns stormed across the ice, massacring rich and poor alike, and burning peasant villages as cheerfully as they burned patricians' villas.

The historian Claudian described the destruction the Huns left behind: "They cut down fruit trees, they stopped wells; their chiefs boasted that where their horses had once trod no harvests ever grew. Their invasions were like the descent of devouring and disgusting locusts. The land was as the Garden of Eden before them; behind them it was a desolate wilderness."

The man leading the invasion was Uldin, whom the historians of the period refer to as "the king of the Huns." The title is unusual, since typically

> "THEIR INVASIONS WERE LIKE THE DESCENT OF DEVOURING AND DISGUSTING LOCUSTS. THE LAND WAS AS THE GARDEN OF EDEN BEFORE THEM; BEHIND THEM IT, WAS A DESOLATE WILDERNESS."
> The Greek historian and poet Claudian

each band of the Huns had its own chief. Nonetheless, surviving accounts from the time make it clear that Uldin, somehow, became recognized by the Huns occupying Romania and Hungary as their principal leader.

In the hope of putting an end to the Huns' rampage across Thrace, the prefect of the Roman troops in the province asked for an audience with Uldin. As the prefect began to speak of the advantages of peace, Uldin scoffed and cut him off. Pointing to the sun, he said, "All that he shines upon I can conquer if I will." Then he declared that if the emperor wanted peace with the Huns, he had to pay an annual tribute in gold to Uldin.

Since he was getting nowhere with the Huns' king, the prefect initiated a series of clandestine meetings with various leading men among the Huns. He played up the comforts of Roman life and the rich gifts and generous pay that

IN THEIR BATTLES
AGAINST THE ALANS,
THE HUNS USED BOWS
AND LASSOS TO BRING
DOWN THEIR ENEMIES.

THE FLIGHT OF THE ALANS

As one wave of Huns attacked the Middle East, a second wave struck eastern Europe. Inconveniently situated directly in the Huns' path were the Alans, a nation of warrior nomads who lived in a vast territory that covered parts of southern Russia, modern-day Iran, and the lands east of the Caspian Sea.

The ancient sources describe the Alans as a handsome people—tall and muscular, with blonde hair and fair complexions. They lived in wagons with pitched hide roofs, a kind of tent on wheels. Their diet was almost exclusively meat and milk. They were devoted to their horses, considered it beneath their dignity to walk, and adorned their favorite mounts with the scalps of their enemies. And when they prayed, they first stuck a sword in the ground, an emblem of their favorite deity, the god of war.

Aside from periodic raids on the easternmost frontier of the Roman Empire, the Alans tended to stay on their own turf, where they enjoyed a reputation for being swift cavalrymen and fearless fighters. But as tough as the Alans were,

they met their match when the Huns swarmed down on them, slaughtering thousands without pity. Of course the Alans fought back, but the short, stocky Huns on their wiry little ponies moved like lightning through and around the mass of tall, heavy Alans mounted on their big warhorses.

Fearful that the Huns would exterminate them completely, large bands of Alans did the unthinkable— they ran away. They headed west, toward the Roman provinces. In the years that followed the Huns' first attack, large populations of Alans settled in France, Spain, and North Africa—lands where they prayed the Huns would never find them.

Those Alans who were not so fortunate as to escape did the next best thing: They submitted to their new overlords. To the Alans' relief, the Huns accepted their surrender, granted the survivors their lives, and drafted the remaining Alan warriors into the Hunnic army. When the Huns attacked their next target, the Goths, the Alans rode with them.

PERPETUAL NOMADS

While virtually every other barbarian nation that invaded the Roman Empire lived in established communities with farms and villages and markets for trade, life for the Huns was decidedly unsettled.

They did not farm. They did not live in permanent communities. They probably had separate encampments for winter and summer in and around the Crimea region of the Black Sea, or they may have kept almost continuously on the move. This is another of the mysteries of Hun life: As the Huns had no written language, they left us no account of their migrations.

In addition to their horses, the Huns had flocks of sheep and herds of cattle. The sheep provided milk and cheese, and from sheepskins the Huns made their tents as well as some of their clothing. They also used linen, but scholars disagree about whether they traded for it or produced it themselves. Since linen is made from flax and the Huns did not farm, it seems more likely that they acquired the yarn or the finished cloth from other peoples.

Aside from a few trinkets, the Huns did not produce metalwork for war, cooking, or other day-to-day necessities. They did make their own bows and arrows, which were tipped with bone, but all other weapons and armor—swords, spears, shields, breastplates, chain mail, and helmets—the Huns acquired through trade, looting, or by stripping them from the dead bodies of their enemies.

Typically, Hunnic settlements were arranged in groups of about 500 tents, or households, led by a chief. If one such group made a military treaty or a trade deal with one of their neighbors, none of the other groups were under any obligation to honor it. Among the Huns this system preserved their independence; their neighbors, however, saw it a different way, concluding that the Huns did not honor their promises.

Whether the Huns had kings is another topic that is open to debate. Certainly Uldin acted like a king, and the Romans treated him as such. In the years after Uldin's death, other Huns took on kinglike status, Attila being the prime example. It's possible the Huns regarded Uldin and Attila as commanders in chief of the warriors rather than as monarchs with authority over every aspect of Hun society, but 1,600 years after the fact it is impossible to determine precisely how the Huns looked upon these men.

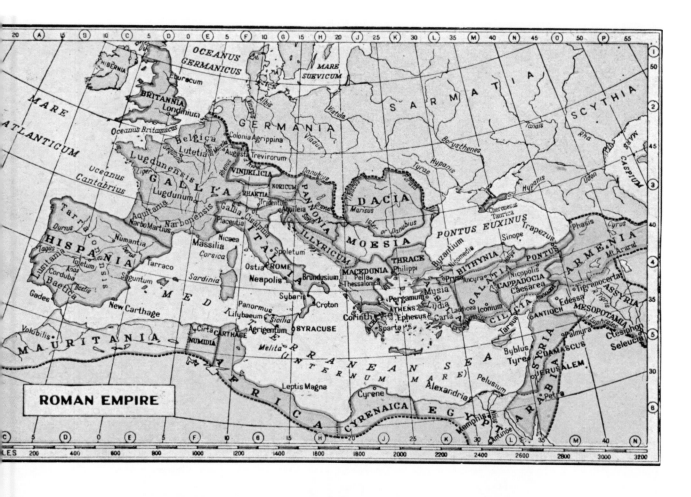

the emperor lavished on the men who fought for him. The trick worked; alone, or in twos and threes, Uldin's subordinate officers deserted to the Roman camp, often taking groups of Hun warriors with them.

Encouraged and reinforced by the deserters, the Roman prefect attacked Uldin's depleted army and crushed them. Almost all the Huns in Uldin's camp were killed or captured. Their king escaped into the mountains, where soon thereafter he died—of illness, or wounds, or at the hands of his own outraged people. In any case, Uldin was never heard from again.

MYSTERIES OF THE HUNS

The size of Hunnic nations has remained a mystery. Chinese accounts from the pre-Christian era mention Hun armies ranging between 100,000 and 400,000 men. Later, Roman sources say that Attila led between 600,000 and

THE ROMAN EMPIRE
AS IT APPEARED IN
THE FOURTH CENTURY,
AT THE TIME OF THE
HUN INVASION.

700,000 Huns—men, women, and children—into the territory of the Roman Empire. Those numbers must be inflated.

In spite of their herds and flocks, the Huns never had enough to eat; they had to hunt wild game and gather roots almost on a daily basis to survive. It is very hard to believe that an entire nation numbering well over half a million and all traveling together could have survived by foraging. It is much more likely that it was a few thousand Hun warriors who scattered the Alans and the Goths and terrorized the cities of the Middle East.

The Huns, then, lived in poverty, barely at the subsistence level. For such people, the luxuries to be found in such abundance in the Roman Empire—the soft clothes, fine weapons, useful tools, and storehouses stuffed with food—must have been an irresistible temptation.

The Huns did not resist one temptation of settled society: At a time when slavery was ubiquitous throughout the world, the Huns had almost no slaves at all. Their reasons were practical, not moral. First of all, the nomadic Huns didn't have a lot of work for slaves to do; and second, in a society constantly on the move, it would be easy for the slaves to run away.

Nonetheless, the Huns, realizing there was an enormous market for new slaves, had no scruples about profiting from their captives. The Huns held captives of high rank for ransom. Professional soldiers or warriors might be pressed into joining the Hun army (although these men could buy their freedom with the loot they took in battle). However, the Huns sold most of their prisoners to slave dealers. It was essential to the Huns that they unload their captives quickly because, for an army with places to go and cities to loot, crowds of wailing captives just slowed things down. Besides, they were just hundreds of more mouths that had to be fed.

The Huns' intentions in the Roman Empire remain a mystery. Around the year 400, a contingent of the Huns was encamped in what is now Hungary, but it was still a nomadic nation showing no inclination to set up villages and start plowing fields. Did they plan to remain in Hungary, striking out from time to time on pillaging expeditions? Or would they sweep across western Europe, destroy everything in their path, and then return to their homeland in central Asia laden with all their spoils? It was a question that troubled an empire, from the emperor in his gilded palace in Constantinople to the mother of a family in her wattle hut on the Seine. For a definitive answer, they all would have to wait for the coming of the Huns' greatest king, Attila.

THE SCOURGE OF GOD: ATTILA THE HUN

O VER THE COURSE OF FIVE OR SIX HUNDRED YEARS, dozens of barbarian kings and chiefs ravaged the old Roman Empire, but the only one whose name everyone knows is Attila, generally called Attila the Hun.

He has another title—"the Scourge of God." It means that God used Attila as his unwitting instrument to punish sinners, make them mindful of their wickedness, and cause them to repent. The idea comes from the biblical Book of Isaiah, in which God promises to punish the faithless people of Israel by sending the Assyrians to make war on them. The Assyrians, God says, will be "the rod of my anger, the staff of my fury! Against a godless nation I send [them] to take spoil and seize plunder." (Isaiah 10:5–6) Exactly who was the first to refer to Attila as the Scourge of God is not known, but the name seemed so apt that it passed into common usage quickly and is still used in our own day.

The Huns were rapacious and destructive; unlike other barbarian nations, they had no interest in settling down in Roman territory—they loved their nomadic life and never did give it up. Consequently, it is difficult to identify any long-lasting impact the Huns had on the world. Attila, however, did leave behind two positive contributions: as he swept across northern Italy, the region's

A NINETEENTH-CENTURY ENGRAVING SHOWS THE HUNS IN A SWIFT CAVALRY CHARGE, TRAMPLING OVER A CAPTIVE WOMAN AND A DEAD INFANT.

TIMELINE

c. 406: ATTILA IS BORN. HIS BIRTHPLACE IS UNKNOWN.

432: MOST BANDS OF THE HUNS RECOGNIZE RUGILA, ATTILA'S UNCLE, AS THEIR KING.

434: RUGILA DIES. THE CROWN PASSES TO HIS NEPHEWS ATTILA AND BLEDA.

441–443: THE HUNS RAID ROMAN TERRITORY IN EASTERN EUROPE AND ASIA MINOR.

445: BLEDA DIES. ATTILA BECOMES SOLE RULER OF THE HUNS.

---

inhabitants fled into a vast swamp at the northern edge of the Adriatic Sea. Their settlement became the city of Venice—so Attila, inadvertently, inspired the founding of what would become one of the most glorious cities in Europe.

Attila's second contribution is more prosaic but practical—the introduction of the stirrup. Riders in Asia developed the stirrup about 800 B.C., but it was not widely used in Europe until the years after Attila's invasion in the fifth century. The stirrup made the Huns the masters of fighting on horseback; it made it easy for the rider to control his horse and also gave him stability when he fought on horseback. The Romans experienced firsthand the advantages the stirrup gave the Hun cavalry. After the wars with Attila came to an end, the stirrup became standard equipment in every stable in the Roman world.

Attila was great—in the eyes of his own people—because he unified them and made them strong and rich. Although all the Huns came from Central Asia, probably from the region in or around Mongolia, before Attila the many bands or tribes of the Huns acted independently of each other. It was Attila who realized that if the Huns acted as a united people, they would be virtually unstoppable, and to a great extent his assessment was correct.

Led by Attila, the Huns pillaged their way from Persia to the gates of Paris. Atilla lifted the Huns from their wretched life of barely scraping by and made them incredibly wealthy: The carts that had once held nothing more glamorous than battered cooking pots were laden now with tribute from the Roman emperor, loot from countless cities and towns, and bags and chests brimming with gold and silver coins acquired by the sale of thousands of captives to slave traders. By 448, Attila had become the most powerful barbarian king in the history of Europe.

TIMELINE

450: ROMAN EMPEROR VALENTINIAN III'S SISTER HONORIA WRITES TO ATTILA OFFERING TO MARRY HIM AND MAKE HIM LORD OVER A LARGE PORTION OF THE ROMAN EMPIRE.

451: VALENTINIAN REFUSES TO PERMIT ATTILA TO MARRY HONORIA; ATTILA LEADS THE HUNS INTO GERMANY AND FRANCE.

JUNE 20, 451: AN ARMY OF ROMANS, VISIGOTHS, AND OTHER BARBARIAN ALLIES DEFEAT ATTILA AT CHALONS, FRANCE.

452: POPE ST. LEO THE GREAT PERSUADES ATTILA NOT TO SACK ROME AND TO WITHDRAW FROM ITALY.

453: ATTILA DIES IN HIS SLEEP ON HIS WEDDING NIGHT. WITH NO ONE CAPABLE OF TAKING ATTILA'S PLACE, THE HUNS RETREAT TO CENTRAL ASIA AND DISAPPEAR FROM HISTORY.

MURDERS AND BLOODLETTINGS

For centuries the Huns had lived in small, independent bands with no king, no central authority. By the beginning of the fifth century, however, the Huns were beginning to accept the idea that, given their successful conquests in Asia Minor and eastern Europe, it was more efficient to fight under a single commander.

In 432, most of the Huns recognized Rugila as their chief or king. At his death in 434, authority over the Huns passed to Rugila's two nephews, Bleda and his brother Attila.

Attila would have been about 28 years old at this time; Bleda was about 44. The historical record for Bleda is especially thin. The only story about him found in period documents tells of his fondness for one of his slaves, a Moorish dwarf named Zerco who acted as a kind of court jester. About 445, Bleda died and Attila became the supreme ruler of the Huns. Some Roman sources say Attila murdered his brother, but there is no evidence to support the charge.

Attila and Bleda began their careers as joint rulers by hammering out a new, audacious treaty with the Romans. Realizing that the Romans were deathly afraid of the Huns, the brothers demanded 700 pounds in gold—double the annual tribute the Roman emperor had paid to Rugila. They wanted all Hun deserters who had sought safety in Roman territory to be handed over. Roman prisoners of war who had escaped from the Hun camp were to be returned or ransomed. The Romans were to swear never to ally

THE PROPOSAL

Emperor Valentinian III was a weak, indecisive, mistrustful creature who stood by and watched as the western provinces of the Roman Empire were ravaged by barbarians. During his reign, Attila devastated Germany, France, and northern Italy; the Vandals seized north Africa and plundered Sicily; other barbarian nations carved out as their own large pieces of Spain and France; and the last Roman legions were withdrawn permanently from Britain, leaving the population defenseless against the marauding Angles, Saxons, and Jutes. In the face of all these disasters, Valentinian did nothing.

The one member of the imperial family who had the courage and the drive to take on these troubles was the emperor's sister, Honoria. Unhappily for the Roman Empire in the West, even if her brother died, or if she arranged to have him killed, Honoria could not inherit the throne.

Had Honoria been a gentle, pious girl, she might have found happiness pursuing a quiet routine of regular periods of daily prayer followed by works of charity, while she waited to be married off to some wealthy Roman patrician. But Honoria's temperament was defiant and resentful. In addition, she had a healthy libido.

In 434, when Honoria was sixteen, she began an affair with one of her servants, a man named Eugenius. The affair may have been just a teenage girl's sexual fling, but some historians have suggested that there was more to the Honoria-Eugenius liaison, specifically that they were plotting to assassinate Valentinian. Then Eugenius would seize the throne and marry Honoria, and she would rule through him. It's plausible, but the details of the conspiracy—if there was one—have not come down to us.

Once Valentinian and his mother Galla Placidia learned of the affair they acted swiftly: They had Eugenius killed and locked up Honoria. The princess's confinement has led to another bit of speculation—that she was pregnant with Eugenius's child and was kept out of the public eye until she had given birth. As for the baby, it certainly would have been killed.

The next time the historical record mentions Honoria is the year 450. She is about thirty years old and, though she is still unmarried, Valentinian has arranged for her to marry Flavius Bassus Herculanus, a senator and a quiet, respectable man who was not at all ambitious—in other words, a perfectly safe choice as the emperor's brother-in-law. Honoria, predictably, hated the idea of marriage to Herculanus, but if Valentinian thought his sister was powerless to oppose the match, he should have thought again.

As the emperor's sister, Honoria enjoyed privilege, wealth, and status, but virtually no political influence in her own right. If she were to become a player in imperial politics, she would have to marry a powerful man—and the man the princess chose was her brother's nemesis. Summoning one of her most trusted servants, a eunuch named Hyacinthus, Honoria gave him her signet ring and a letter and instructed him to deliver both into the hands of Attila. In her letter, Honoria promised to marry the king of the Huns and present him with a substantial portion of the Roman Empire as her dowry if he would rescue her from her brother the emperor.

The sudden disappearance and then reappearance of Hyacinthus made Valentinian suspicious. He had the eunuch tortured, and after the poor man had revealed all the secrets of his mission to Attila, ordered him beheaded. Valentinian was ready to execute his sister, too, but his mother, Galla Placidia, would not permit it—and the emperor was still under his mother's thumb. Rather than kill Honoria, he kept her under strict house arrest.

When news of what had befallen Hyacinthus and Honoria reached Attila, he sent an embassy to Valentinian to protest. The emperor had been unjust to torture and kill a faithful servant of Attila's fiancée. He demanded that Valentinian liberate Honoria and issue guarantees that after Honoria became Attila's wife she would receive her fair share of imperial lands and power. Valentinian ignored Attila's demands. A year later, Attila sent a second embassy to the emperor, this time enclosing Honoria's ring as a certain sign that she and Attila were truly engaged to be married. If Valentinian did not release Honoria, Attila promised to invade Italy and free her by force. And Attila had one final demand—he wanted half of the western empire as Honoria's dowry.

EMPEROR VALENTINIAN III HAD THIS COIN STRUCK TO COMMEMORATE ROME'S VICTORY OVER ATTILA AT CHALONS IN 451.

Sketch showing
THE LOCALITIES & GRADUAL ADVANCE
of the
BARBARIAN NATIONS.

Scale of English Miles

themselves with any barbarian nation at war with the Huns. And there would be no restrictions on trade between Huns and Romans.

These were humiliating terms, yet the emperor, Theodosius II, agreed to them all. He paid the exorbitant tribute, ransomed the escaped prisoners of war, and even handed over two adolescent Hun princes, the sons of a Hun tribe that would not submit to Attila and Bleda's authority; these boys Attila and Bleda had crucified.

A RICH YET UNSETTLED KINGDOM

By alternating between hard bargaining and acts of frightful cruelty, such as crucifying the two Hun princes, all the while occupying an immense area in central Europe, Attila and Bleda made the Romans feel anxious and insecure. As the Romans fretted over what the Huns might do next, Attila and Bleda collected their tribute and waited patiently for an excuse to start a new war against the empire.

The peace between Huns and Romans lasted until 441, when Attila complained that the tribute money was not arriving in a timely fashion and

A NINETEENTH-CENTURY MAP IDENTIFIES THE BARBARIAN NATIONS THAT CARVED UP THE ROMAN EMPIRE.

the Romans were still giving sanctuary to Hun deserters. When the imperial government ignored his protests, Attila besieged the city of Ratiaria (Archar) in Bulgaria.

From his camp outside the doomed city, he lodged another complaint: The bishop of Margus in Serbia had ransacked the graves of the Huns' chiefs, and Attila wanted the stolen grave goods returned. By this point, the emperor had sent ambassadors to negotiate a new treaty with the Huns, but they considered the charge against the bishop ludicrous. The discussions came to an abrupt end, and the Huns began a systematic campaign against all the cities and towns along the Danube.

A chronicler named Callinicus tells us, "There were so many murders and blood-lettings that the dead could not be numbered. [The Huns] took captive the churches and monasteries and slew the monks and virgins in great numbers."

After two years of such destruction, the Romans had had enough. Theodosius agreed to pay an annual tribute of 1,050 pounds in gold, plus an immediate penalty payment of 6,000 pounds of gold. The Huns were becoming immensely rich. They were already immensely powerful—Attila's "kingdom" extended over present-day Austria, Hungary, Romania, and southern Russia.

Yet, in spite of their wealth and power, the Huns remained a nomadic people. They founded no towns, and never moved into the towns and cities they conquered. They never became farmers. They never did anything that suggested they were beginning to make the transition to a stable life. The centuries-old tradition of nomadic life was so ingrained in the Huns that they could not imagine giving it up.

AS THE ROMANS FRETTED OVER WHAT THE HUNS MIGHT DO NEXT, ATTILA AND BLEDA COLLECTED THEIR TRIBUTE AND WAITED PATIENTLY FOR AN EXCUSE TO START A NEW WAR AGAINST THE EMPIRE.

CHOSEN BY THE GODS

Over the centuries, artists have depicted Attila as a tall, regal character with European features. Thanks to two firsthand descriptions of Attila, though, we know that he was none of those things.

The Goth historian Jordanes described Attila as a short man with a broad chest and a large head. His eyes were small and dark, his nose was flat, and his face had a dark, weather-beaten appearance. He swaggered when he walked. And although Attila was, as Jordanes puts it, "unrestrained in war," the historian adds that the king of the Huns could be "gracious to suppliants."

"AFFECTING ONLY TO BE CLEAN"

In 448, Emperor Theodosius II sent Priscus, a Greek historian, on a diplomatic mission to Attila. By this time, Attila's wars had made the Huns rich, as Priscus saw when he joined Attila and his court for dinner. Priscus speaks of the gold and silver plates on which the meal was served and the gold and silver goblets that were set out for each guest.

Attila, however, drank his wine from a wooden cup and ate his food from a wooden platter. Even his clothes were simple, "affecting only to be clean," as Priscus put it. It was an act, of course, this feigned indifference to luxury items. Attila had unified the Hun tribes precisely so he and his people could acquire gold and silver and jewels and silk. But by pretending not to care at all about them, Attila created an impression that he was just a simple chief.

Priscus was lucky to see Attila at all. Unknown to him and his friend and fellow ambassador Maximin, a nobleman and a senior officer in the household of Emperor Theodosius II, their embassy to Attila was a front. The most influential powerbroker at the imperial court, a eunuch named Chrysaphus, had planted several assassins among Maximin and Priscus' party who were to watch for an opportunity to murder Attila. They would be helped by a Hun named Edeco, a man whom Attila had employed several times to carry messages between him and Theodosius, and whom Chrysaphus had bribed to play a leading role in the plot.

Once they reached Attila's camp, Edeco went to his king and revealed the conspiracy. To everyone's surprise, Attila did not order the execution of the ambassadors; instead, he treated them with every courtesy and sent them safely home. Perhaps he intended to use this failed plot against his life to further humiliate Theodosius and squeeze even more tribute money out of the emperor.

A GIFT FROM THE WAR GOD

AS ST. GENEVIEVE PRAYS FOR THE DELIVERANCE OF THE CITY OF PARIS, THE HUN ARMY ON THE RIGHT FALLS BACK IN TERROR.

Around the time of Priscus's visit, Attila acquired something he would use to inspire his Huns to even more ambitious conquests. It began when a heifer wandered away from her herd. When she wandered back again, she was limping. The cowherd lifted the leg that was giving the heifer trouble and saw a cut on the pad of her foot. Curious to find the source of the injury, the herdsman left his cattle and followed the trail of blood through the tall grass.

It led to a bit of sharp metal protruding an inch or two out of the ground. The man began to dig, and soon he unearthed an old rusty sword.

At the end of the day, when he returned with his cows to camp, the herdsman presented the sword to Attila. Another man might have discarded the useless weapon as junk, but Attila turned the discovery into a major event. He displayed the sword to his people, declaring that it was the sword of the god of war.

For generations, Attila said, it had been handed down among the chief warriors of the Huns and it had always brought them victory. Then, long ago, under mysterious circumstances, the sword had been lost. The fact that it had been rediscovered now was a clear sign that he, Attila, had been chosen by the gods to rule over all the Huns and conquer the world.

With a sacred talisman to rally his people and Valentinian's refusal to let him marry Honoria as an excuse, Attila marched west into Germany and France in 451. This was the campaign that made his reputation as a ruthless conqueror. He left in smoking ruins the German cities of Strasbourg, Worms, Mainz, Cologne, and Trier, and the French cities of Rheims, Tournai, Cambrai, Beauvais, and Amiens.

For a time it appeared that he would march on Paris, too. The terrified Parisians were ready to abandon their city when a much-respected holy woman, St. Genevieve, persuaded her neighbors to put their trust in God and pray for deliverance. Most of the citizens of Paris stayed, hunkered down behind the walls, praying earnestly for a miracle. And their prayers were answered: Attila did not attack Paris. Instead, Orleans was Attila's next target. The Huns laid siege to the city, but before they could capture it, an army of Romans and their barbarian allies came to Orleans's rescue. Their commander was the Romans' finest military strategist, Flavius Aetius.

GROWING UP AMONG THE HUNS

Fifty-five years old, the son of a Roman mother named Aurelia and a Scythian father named Flavius Gaudentius, Aetius became acquainted with the Huns at an early age. When he was about thirteen years old, the Romans made a treaty with the Huns. As a token of good will, each side exchanged hostages from their most influential families. Because Gaudentius was the emperor's master of the cavalry, his son Aetius was among the hostages handed over to the Huns.

COMMANDER AETIUS
(IN THE UPPER HALF OF
THE SCENE) PRESIDES
OVER A WILD ANIMAL
HUNT IN A ROMAN ARENA.

THE POPE AND THE BARBARIAN

Rather than retreat back to the Huns' lands in central and eastern Europe, Attila formulated a bold new strategy: invade Italy and kill or capture Emperor Valentinian.

From the moment Attila and his Huns spilled over the Alps and into the plains of northern Italy, they were unstoppable. City after city, town after town fell to them. They burned Aquileia to the ground, then Padua, Verona, Vicenza, Bergamo, and Brescia, and sold the surviving inhabitants to slave dealers.

Attila captured Milan, too, but for unknown reasons did not burn the city or slaughter its people. There is a story that in one of the looted palaces Attila saw a mural of a Roman emperor seated on his throne with the bodies of dead barbarians under his feet. Attila called for a local artist and commanded him to paint a new mural. This painting depicted Attila seated on a throne while at his feet the two Roman emperors of the East and the West poured out sacks of gold, the tribute they paid to keep him happy.

Everyone in Italy expected that Attila would turn south and march on Rome— certainly the Romans thought so, because they sent a distinguished embassy to persuade Attila to leave

Rome unharmed. Pope Leo I, also known as St. Leo the Great, rode into the Huns' camp on the Mincio River accompanied by two of Rome's senior government officials. Attila received the ambassadors privately in his tent. No record of the conference has survived, but when the pope and his associates emerged, they had Attila's promise to leave Rome in peace and to withdraw from Italy.

Why, when he had such a rich country at his feet, did Attila agree to pull back beyond the Alps? He was not a Christian, so it is unlikely that he would have been moved by respect for Pope Leo's spiritual authority.

Legend says that as Leo presented his case, Attila saw an apparition: behind the pope stood the figures of St. Peter and St. Paul, the patron saints of Rome. Each of the apostles held a sword—a clear sign that God would strike down Attila if he was so wicked as to scorn Leo's appeal for peace and tried to carry his scorched earth campaign to Rome and beyond. It is a wonderful story, and throughout the centuries artists have delighted in depicting the scene—the serene Vicar of Christ in his papal robes bravely yet gently admonishing a shaggy barbarian chief while in the background two saints brandish their swords.

POPE LEO I APPEALS TO ATTILA TO SPARE ROME, AS A VISION OF ST. PETER AND ST. PAUL, BEARING SWORDS, SUGGESTS WHAT WOULD HAPPEN IF THE KING OF THE HUNS REFUSED.

Attila may have seen an ominous vision of irate saints during his conference with the pope, but it is more probable that Attila decided to play the gracious conqueror and grant Pope Leo's request because he knew something the ambassadors did not—that he had every intention of withdrawing from the country. The year before, virtually all the crops in Italy had failed. In 452 there were still food shortages, and the devastation the Huns had wrought in the north did nothing to ameliorate an already desperate situation.

If Attila and his army moved deeper into Italy, they risked starvation and the epidemics that accompanied a famine. For the health and safety of his men, Attila marched his army back across the Alps.

At this time, hostage-taking was commonplace in Europe and Asia, and it endured for centuries to come. In most cases hostages were treated as honored guests, not as prisoners. Young Aetius, for example, became part of the household of the Rugila, king of the Huns.

In many cases, hostages spent years among their captor-hosts, often forming bonds of friendship and even deep affection. Nonetheless, there was always the chance that such friendships could end violently. If the Romans broke the treaty, the Huns were free to slaughter all their Roman hostages. If the Huns broke the peace, the Romans would do the same with their Hun hostages.

As it happened, no one broke the peace, and Aetius grew to young manhood among the Huns. They taught him their battle tactics, as well as how to shoot a bow while riding at a full gallop. By the time he returned to the Roman world, Aetius had made many friends among the Huns, including Rugila's nephew, a boy named Attila.

THE BATTLE FOR AN EMPIRE

With Aetius bearing down on him, Attila broke camp and retreated to the Marne River. Meanwhile he sent word to two reconnaissance forces near Arras and Besancon, ordering them to rejoin the main Hun army on the plains of Chalons-sur-Marne. The plains here were vast and the ground flat, ideal for the Huns' favorite type of warfare, fighting on horseback. Aetius knew this, so he frustrated Attila's plan by occupying the summit of a steep sloping hill and refusing to come down onto the plain to fight.

Attila had no choice but to command his men to charge the hill. As the Huns scrambled up the hillside, the Romans' Goth cavalry suddenly charged into the Huns' left flank. As this wing of Attila's army collapsed, he ordered his center to retreat from the hillside back to the camp. The Goth cavalry pursued them, but once the Huns were safe behind the earthworks that surrounded their camp, they rallied, firing volley after volley of deadly arrows into the charging Goth warriors who, after heavy losses, fled back to the Roman camp.

All night, Attila waited for Aetius to attack, but the final Roman onslaught never came. At dawn, Aetius made no move to storm the Huns' camp, or even to surround it to starve them out. He left the field clear so Attila and the remnant of his army could get away. No one understands why. Nor can anyone say how many men died at Chalons—the ancient historians make implausible claims of casualties that numbered between 165,000 and 300,000. The actual number was probably in the neighborhood of 10,000.

Although Aetius did not press his advantage, the Battle of Chalons was a tremendous victory for the Romans. They had thwarted Attila's plan of an empire that stretched from Russia to the Atlantic, they had forced him to retreat, and they inflicted serious casualties on the Hun army. In the great scheme of history, Aetius and his Roman army had saved western Europe and Western civilization from utter devastation at the hands of the Huns.

COFFINS OF GOLD, SILVER, AND IRON

In 453, about a year after the Hun army had returned to their home encampment on the Danube, Attila took a new wife, a beautiful young Goth named Ildico. While the Huns celebrated, Attila and Ildico retired to his bedchamber. Exhausted from a strenuous night of lovemaking, or passed out from a day of heavy drinking, Attila fell into a deep sleep. As he slept he suffered a massive nosebleed and choked to death on his own blood.

Legend says the grief-stricken Huns encased their king's body in three coffins—one of gold, one of silver, and one of iron. Then they diverted the Tisza River and dug a grave in the riverbed. After Attila was buried, the Huns returned the Tisza to its usual course, obliterating all trace of the grave of Attila the Hun.

At his death, Attila left behind many sons, the offspring of his several wives and concubines, but none of them inherited his genius for command. The Huns, unified under Attila, now split up into factions. They were still nomads, and as such they drifted away from the lands they had occupied in eastern Europe. Most likely they went back to their original homelands in central Asia where they may have been absorbed by other tribes. No one knows what became of the Huns. This barbarian nation that almost destroyed the western Roman Empire, that almost conquered Europe, simply vanished from the historical record.

KING OF THE LAND AND THE SEA: GAISERIC AND THE GLORY DAYS OF THE VANDALS

VANDALISM IS THE TERM WE USE TO CHARACTERIZE AN act of wanton destruction or defacement. Tagging and other forms of graffiti are vandalism. Knocking over tombstones is vandalism. Damaging or destroying a public monument is vandalism.

So it may come as a surprise to learn that the term dates back only to 1794, when Henri Grégoire, a bishop who supported the French Revolution, complained to the revolutionary government that the army was injuring or destroying works of art and cultural monuments. To convey his point that the soldiers were acting like barbarians rather than enlightened citizens of the new French republic, Bishop Grégoire coined a new word: He accused the troops of "*vandalisme*," or vandalism.

But the bishop misspoke. In terms of wanton destruction of cultural treasures, the Vandals were no worse than any other barbarian nation. If anything, they ought to get some credit for exercising heroic restraint during their sack of Rome in 455, when they looted the city but did not destroy so much as a plebeian's hovel.

The significance of the Vandals is not what they added to the French and English vocabulary but how they hastened the end of the Roman Empire in the West. Theirs is the most astonishing success story in the entire history of the barbarian invasions.

Alone among all the barbarians who created such havoc during the fourth and fifth centuries, the Vandals evolved from a weak, frightened tribe of refugees to a mighty nation with dreams of an empire. They were the only barbarian people to learn how to build ships and form a navy. They were the only barbarian people to carve out of the Roman Empire an empire of their own. They were the only barbarian nation to significantly improve the lives of all their people by seizing some of the richest, most fertile lands in the Mediterranean.

In a period when the Romans were militarily weak and psychologically unsure of themselves, the encroachment of the warlike, self-assured, enterprising Vandals moved the city of Rome, the imperial family, and the West itself closer and closer to ruin.

THE ICE BRIDGE

On New Year's Eve 406, as the temperature plummeted, the Rhine River froze solid. On one side lay the Germanic tribes; on the other, the rich cities and fertile farms of the Roman province of Gaul. That night, the Vandals walked en masse across the ice and into history. Famine and the Huns had been driving the Vandals westward for several years, pinning them down at last along the eastern banks of the Rhine, where the Vandals feared they would be completely annihilated by the Huns. They saw the ice bridge across the river, then, as a gift from God (almost all the Vandals were Christians by this time, members of the Arian sect rather than the orthodox Catholic Church).

The Roman historian Tacitus (c. 56–c. 117) wrote that in his day the Vandals were an aggressive nation famous for their skill as night fighters. To slip among their enemies undetected, they blackened their faces and hands, as well as their shields and weapons. At some point, either in the region of central Poland that was their homeland, or in Germany where they scrambled to escape the Huns, the Vandals fell on hard times. Three hundred years after Tacitus wrote admiringly of them, the Christian historian Salvian (c. 400–?) characterized the Vandals as the weakest of all the Germanic tribes. That wondrous ice bridge across the Rhine was the Vandals' last chance to restore their fortunes and reinvigorate their people.

THE SIGNIFICANCE OF THE VANDALS IS HOW THEY HASTENED THE END OF THE ROMAN EMPIRE IN THE WEST. THEIRS IS THE MOST ASTONISHING SUCCESS STORY IN THE ENTIRE HISTORY OF THE BARBARIAN INVASIONS.

TIMELINE

C.100: THE ROMAN HISTORIAN TACITUS PRAISES THE VANDALS AS ONE OF THE MOST FEARSOME TRIBES IN GERMANY.

C. 400: THE CHRISTIAN HISTORIAN SALVIAN ASSERTS THAT THE VANDALS ARE THE WEAKEST OF THE BARBARIAN NATIONS.

NEW YEAR'S EVE 406: THE RHINE RIVER FREEZES AND THE VANDALS WALK ACROSS THE ICE INTO GAUL.

407: GODGISEL, KING OF THE VANDALS, DIES IN BATTLE IN GAUL AGAINST THE FRANKS.

408: THE VANDALS, LED BY GODGIEL'S SON GUNDERIC, INVADE SPAIN.

422: GUNDERIC DIES SUDDENLY WHILE PLUNDERING THE CITY OF SEVILLE. HIS HALF-BROTHER, GAISERIC, BECOMES KING.

If the Vandals had tried to cross the Rhine 200 years earlier, they never would have gotten beyond the western bank. It had been Roman policy to station garrisons along all the borders of the empire; there would be skirmishes between legionnaires guarding the frontiers and barbarian marauders trying to breach the border, but inland the inhabitants of the empire would enjoy peace and tranquility. The German historian Alexander Demandt described this golden age of Roman Empire this way:

> Flourishing cities, an orderly administration, an economy with highly divided labor, lively traffic in the entire region between the North Sea and the Red Sea: Never before had the ancient world seen anything of the kind. Cities stood in the countryside unfortified; barely 1 percent of the empire's population was under arms. The army was stationed along the Rhine, the Danube, and the Euphrates, and protected the *Pax Romana*.

By the year 400, however, Rome could no longer afford the expense, or the men, to defend all its borders. This vulnerability was laid bare by the Pictish raid in 367 on Hadrian's Wall, the fortification on the Scottish/English border that marked the limit of Roman rule in Britain. The Roman troops who survived the Picts' attack were withdrawn from the wall; no new garrison was sent to replace them. That retreat from Hadrian's Wall became a sign of the times as, throughout the western provinces, the Romans pulled back from

THE ROMAN HISTORIAN TACITUS (C.56–C.117) DESCRIBED THE VANDALS AS FEARSOME WARRIORS. BY THE FOURTH CENTURY THE VANDALS WERE WEAK AND STARVING.

TIMELINE

428–429: GAISERIC CONSTRUCTS A FLEET OF SHIPS TO CARRY ALL 80,000 VANDALS TO NORTH AFRICA.

430: GAISERIC LEADS THE VANDALS IN THE CONQUEST OF NORTH AFRICA. THE CITY OF HIPPO REGIUS, IN MODERN DAY ALGERIA, FALLS FIRST.

435: GAISERIC MAKES PEACE WITH ROMAN EMPEROR VALENTINIAN III.

439: IN VIOLATION OF THE PEACE TREATY, GAISERIC CAPTURES CARTHAGE IN A SURPRISE ATTACK.

C. 440: GAISERIC LAUNCHES A PERSECUTION OF CATHOLICS IN NORTH AFRICA.

1794: HENRI GRÉGOIRE, A FRENCH BISHOP, COINS THE WORD "VANDALISM."

WILD NIGHTS

The Romans had been familiar with the Germanic tribes for centuries, and to some degree they even admired them. The Germans tended to be a head or so taller than the Romans, fair-skinned and fair-haired, the women shapely, the men muscular. They were fearless in battle, and unswervingly loyal to their chieftains.

But the Romans also believed that the Germanic tribes had other qualities that were not so attractive. The Romans claimed that the Germans styled their hair with rancid butter, that they never bathed, that they wore their furs even in summer, making the stench of a German village even more rank than usual. Furthermore, the Romans believed the Germans were oversexed beasts who spent their long winter nights copulating wildly. The end product of all these nights of barbaric passion, of course, was the barbarian horde—an immense swarm of shaggy, smelly, fur-draped banshees poised to spill over the borders of the empire and destroy everything in their path. The barbarian horde was Rome's boogeyman, yet close study of the demographics of the Germanic tribes has found that the concept of the horde is a myth.

Most of the Germanic tribes numbered about 100,000, of which only 10,000–15,000 were fighting men. Living conditions in the barbarous north did not permit overpopulation. Tribes such as the Vandals depended for survival on their harvests, supplemented by whatever they could get by hunting and foraging. In a good year there would be enough grain to get the tribe through the winter, but unlike the Romans, the Germanic tribes did not have huge granaries where they stored excess grain for an emergency such as famine, drought, or the destruction of the crops in war.

And for many of these tribes warfare was a full-time occupation as they battled with enemies in the next valley or rivals in the neighboring village. Such a situation elevated the warrior to the upper strata of barbarian society, but it made life miserable and anarchic for the non-warrior members of the tribe who at any moment might have to flee into the forest as their huts and fields burned—sacrifices to their tribe's warrior cult.

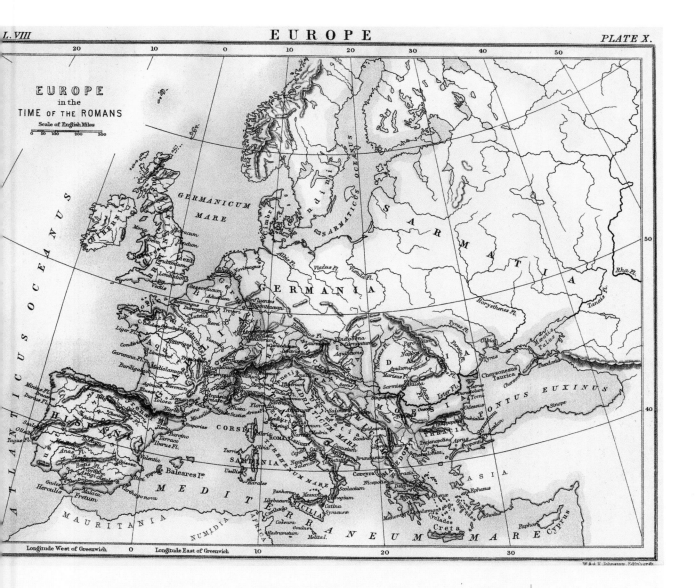

EUROPE
in the
TIME OF THE ROMANS

the frontiers of their empire, essentially leaving the empire's back door wide open to whole armies of barbarian invaders.

Instead of policing the frontier, the Romans placed large armed detachments, known as field armies, in fortified camps, castles, or walled towns located deep within the provinces. These field armies could be very effective; they were the troops Aetius had called up at Chalons, where they defeated Attila. The trouble with this arrangement was distance—a barbarian army could ravage a considerable part of the province and still skirt around the field army holed up in its encampment or castle. People who lived in the immediate vicinity of the

A NINETEENTH-CENTURY MAP SHOWS THE ROMAN EMPIRE IN EUROPE AT THE HEIGHT OF ITS GLORY IN THE LATE SECOND/EARLY THIRD CENTURIES.

field army were safe, but farms, estates, and towns outside the perimeter were essentially undefended. However well-intentioned the field army tactic may have been, Rome's last-ditch effort to maintain some control over its territory was failing as, one by one, the provinces of the empire were overrun by barbarians.

THE FIRST BARBARIAN NAVY

The path of the Vandal raids through Gaul is unknown, but we do know that the Franks, a Germanic tribe allied with the Romans who had permitted them to settle in Gaul, put up a stiff resistance to the invasion.

In about 407, Godgisel, the king who had led the Vandals across the frozen Rhine, died in battle against the Franks. He was succeeded by his son,

THE ROMANS AND THE REST
OF THE WORLD

From the Roman point of view, the world was divided into two types of people: There were the Romans, who were socially, culturally, and intellectually advanced, and the guardians of civilization, and there was everybody else, irrational subhuman creatures who had to be kept in carefully controlled situations such as slavery, in which they were subject to a rational Roman master or mistress.

Precisely because they were less than human, these barbarians could perform tasks a Roman could not. For example, they could be gladiators and actors, entertainments the Romans loved but nonetheless regarded as degrading (for the gladiators and the actors, not for the spectators).

But slavery and fighting in the arena were not the worst things that could happen to a non-Roman—a barbarian who violated Roman law could be executed in public in the most gruesome manner imaginable. On the other hand, if a Roman (or an individual from a subject nation to whom Roman citizenship had been given) broke the law, he would be granted a swift, painless death. A classic example of this double standard is the martyrdom of the apostles St. Peter and St. Paul, both of whom died about the year 67, during Nero's persecution of the Christians. St. Paul was a Roman citizen, so he was beheaded; St. Peter was not a Roman citizen, so he was crucified. (At his execution, Peter said he was unworthy to die as Christ had died; he asked to be crucified upside down. His executioners granted his request).

Gunderic, who urged the Vandals to move south into Spain. Within weeks of Godgisel's death, the Vandals attempted to cross the Pyrenees, but in the mountains they were met by Didymus and Veranianus, two Roman brothers who were distantly related to the emperors Theodosius and Honorius. With their private army the brothers stopped the Vandals' advance, driving them back into Gaul.

A year later, Constantius, an ambitious Roman general who was scheming to wipe out the imperial family and become emperor himself, captured Didymus and Veranianus, along with their wives, and had them all executed.

With the brothers dead and no other Roman force prepared to stop them, the Vandals surged through the passes of the Pyrenees and into Spain.

St. Isidore of Seville (c. 560–636), a historian and polymath, tells us that in Spain the Vandals "did much killing and ravaging in their bloody raids, set cities on fire, and exhausted the property which they plundered." Between 408 and 411, four waves of epidemics as well as famine swept across Spain. There were rumors of cannibalism among the starving population, and of wild animals devouring the corpses of the unburied dead. But once the entire Iberian Peninsula was firmly under their control, the Vandals settled down to enjoy life in a fertile, fat country blessed with a warm climate.

From time to time, however, they still went out on the occasional raid. In 422, Gunderic and his army were plundering the city of Seville when the king suddenly died. Isidore says the Arian king was struck down by God when he attempted to steal gold and silver votive offerings from the tomb of the martyr St. Vincentius. At Gunderic's death, the succession passed to his half-brother, 33-year-old Gaiseric, the illegitimate son of old King Godgisel.

Resistance among the native inhabitants of Spain and the Roman colonists had virtually collapsed by the time Gaiseric became king, but the Vandals were not the only Germanic tribe in the country. The much more numerous Visigoths also wanted the Iberian Peninsula as their own.

After repeated, costly battles with the Visigoths, around the year 428 Gaiseric ordered the construction of a fleet of ships to carry his people to North Africa. This in itself is remarkable, as the Vandals were not a seafaring people: Like all the other barbarian nations, they traveled on horse or foot. But during the dozen years or so that they had occupied southern Spain they learned from the local people around the port of Cartagena how to build and sail ships. The Vandals, thus, became the first barbarians to have a navy.

The exodus began in 429 with approximately 80,000 Vandals making the crossing. Only twenty-one years earlier they had been cold, hungry tribesmen who couldn't even build a rowboat to get them across the Rhine; now they were a mighty nation on the move, with a fleet of their own construction. They crossed at the Straits of Gibraltar, where scarcely seven miles of water separates Europe from Africa, landing at modern-day Ceuta, on the Moroccan coast.

De sanct yssodoze avecues que dispalensect de ses
estozpe

ce mesmee tempe ysidore dispa
leuse fu ennobli ce espaignee

KING OF THE LAND AND THE SEA

Gaiseric's mother was a Roman and had been captured and enslaved by the Vandals. She gave birth to Gaiseric around the year 390. The historian Jordanes described Gaiseric as "a man of moderate height and lame in consequence of a fall from his horse. He was a man of deep thought and few words, holding luxury in disdain, furious in his anger, greedy for gain, shrewd in winning over the barbarians, and skilled in sowing the seeds of dissension to arouse enmity."

Gaiseric enjoyed two advantages that all the other barbarian kings of the period lacked: He was a creative thinker, and he was blessed with a very long life, dying at about 87 years of age on January 25, 477. In the 40-year reign that fate granted to him, Gaiseric accomplished what no other barbarian king ever had—he established a barbarian empire that rivaled Rome. The fact that the Vandal empire was centered in the Mediterranean must have been especially galling to the Romans, who for 400 years had regarded it as their private lake. In Latin the Romans called the Mediterranean "Mare Nostrum," or "Our Sea." The Vandals' Mediterranean-based empire was not some petty act of barbarian bravado—it was an affront to Rome.

Some historians of the period assert that the Vandals did not migrate to North Africa to escape the Visigoths but rather came at the invitation of Bonifacius, governor of the province, who planned to use them as mercenaries in a war against his nemesis, Galla Placidia, the mother of Emperor Valentinian III. Galla Placidia had charged the African governor with treason and planned to drag him to Rome for execution. With thousands of Vandal warriors in his army, Bonifacius was confident that he could repel any force the empress-mother sent against him.

It was a 1,250-mile march from Ceuta to the governor's palace in Carthage. By the time Gaiseric and his 80,000 Vandals arrived outside the great city, Bonifacius had patched up his relationship with the imperial family; the empress mother had even made her old enemy a patrician, so that he was now referred to as Count Bonifacius. The arrival of a true barbarian horde at the gates of Carthage must have terrified the Roman citizens, yet Count Bonifacius assumed a serene demeanor, thanked Gaiseric for his trouble, and informed him that his services were no longer necessary. If

ST. ISIDORE, BISHOP OF SEVILLE, REPORTED THAT IN SPAIN THE VANDALS "DID MUCH KILLING AND RAVAGING IN THEIR BLOODY RAIDS [AND] SET CITIES ON FIRE."

THE ROMANIZING OF THE VANDALS

The Vandals were barbarians, but they were not heathens. In Germany the entire Vandal nation had converted to Christianity, but to an unorthodox permutation of the faith. They were Arians, followers of an Egyptian priest and theologian named Arius (c. 250–336), who taught that Christ was not the Son of God, the Second Person of the Holy Trinity, but a kind of semi-divine superman created by God.

This was flagrantly contrary to what the Christian Church had always believed, and caused such discord in the empire that Emperor Constantine urged Pope Sylvester I and other influential churchmen to call for a council at which the bishops of the Roman world could sort out the controversy.

In 325, in the town of Nicaea, in what is now Turkey, more than 300 bishops as well as many priests and deacons assembled to debate the question. The discussion concluded with a public declaration of what the Church believed regarding the nature of Christ and the Holy Trinity. This statement, known as the Nicene Creed, was inserted into the Catholic Mass and is still recited every Sunday in Catholic churches around the world. After asserting what they believed, the members of the council published a second document condemning Arius's teachings.

AT THE FAR RIGHT IN A DARK ROBE AND NO HALO STANDS ARIUS THE HERETIC AS ST. NICHOLAS OF MYRA, ONE OF THE BISHOPS AT THE COUNCIL OF NICAEA, SLAPS HIM ACROSS THE FACE.

Bonifacius believed that the Vandals would make an about-face and march back to Ceuta for a quick return voyage to Spain, he had badly misjudged Gaiseric. North Africa was the garden of the empire, shipping boatload after boatload of grain, wine, olive oil, and fruit to her sister provinces. In terms of wealth and comforts, Carthage was a second Rome, full of rich men's villas, opulent public baths, splendid arenas and theaters, and markets stuffed with the luxuries of the East. The Vandals had just spent a year strolling through this paradise, and were not about to leave without realizing a profit. Rather than go back to Spain, Gaiseric set about to conquer North Africa.

He began at Hippo Regius, a port city in modern-day Algeria, famous at the time and ever since as the cathedral city of the great theologian and philosopher, St. Augustine of Hippo. As the Vandals surrounded the city,

St. Augustine slipped into his final illness, dying on August 28, 430, in the third month of the Vandal siege. Eleven months later, after many lives had been lost on both sides, Gaiseric came to an understanding with the people of Hippo Regius: He would hold back his army while the citizens, with all their valuables (including the body of St. Augustine), abandoned their town. Only then would Gaiseric and the Vandals move in.

Gaiseric launched his African war from Hippo Regius. Because the emperors had considered North Africa safe from invasion, the province was only lightly garrisoned. Though this worked in Gaiseric's favor, the Romans put up a fight nonetheless. Five years later, the Vandals were masters of a large stretch of central North Africa, but they had not managed to conquer Carthage. In 435, Gaiseric, as realistic as he was patient, signed a treaty with Valentinian's representatives. The text of the treaty has not survived, but we know that the emperor handed over to the Vandals all the territory they had already seized in North Africa. The area covered most of northeastern Algeria—not exactly a Vandal empire, but still infinitely better than what they had known in Germany. Furthermore, this was a land of many ports and harbors, which the Vandals, as a seafaring people, could use to their advantage.

Gaiseric kept the peace for four years but then in 439, he made a surprise attack on Carthage, taking the city easily. Over the next three years, the Vandals expanded their conquest until Valentinian had no choice but to make yet another treaty with Gaiseric, recognizing his authority over a realm that extended from Numidia to Tunisia. The Vandals, proud of their lord who had brought them so many victories and such great wealth and prestige, began to hail Gaiseric as "King of the Land and the Sea."

INTENSIFYING ANTAGONISM

In spite of the verdict at Nicaea, Arius refused to go quietly. In defiance of the pope, the bishops, and the council, he continued to teach his heterodox ideas, made converts, and soon pockets of Arian Christians were found in many corners of the eastern provinces of the empire. In 341, a Goth Arian bishop named Ulfilas began a mission to the Germanic tribes. He invented an alphabet for them, translated the Bible into the Goths' language, and by the time of his death in 381 had converted almost all the Goths, as well as the Vandals, to the Arian form of Christianity.

By the time the Vandals conquered Carthage and North Africa, the antagonism between Arians and Catholics had intensified. Although there was a significant Arian population in Egypt, Arius's homeland, the rest of North Africa had remained staunchly Catholic.

Regarding these Catholic Romans and Africans as his enemies, Gaiseric began a full-scale persecution. He banned all forms of Catholic worship; seized Catholic churches and gave them to Arian clergy; and especially targeted Catholic bishops, priests, and deacons: Some he murdered outright, and others he tortured. Catholic churchmen who were only exiled considered themselves fortunate. The laity did not escape, either, as Vandals massacred an entire congregation of Catholics as they attended Mass one Easter.

A CONVERSION OF ANOTHER KIND

Catholicism aside, the Vandals adopted every other facet of Roman life in North Africa. In imitation of the life of the Roman patricians, they spent long hours at the public baths, attended games and other spectacles in the arena, and applauded Greek tragedies and Roman farces at the theater.

Contrary to their reputation, Gaiseric's people did not commit gross acts of vandalism in Carthage or elsewhere in Roman Africa; rather, once they had driven the rightful Roman owners from their opulent villas and estates, the Vandals moved in. They adopted Roman dress, savored Roman cuisine, and even gave up their Germanic language for Latin. In fact, the Vandal language died out so quickly that, aside from personal names, not a single word of it has survived.

The Goths were the first barbarian nation to sack Rome. The Huns nearly reduced the empire in the West to a smoking ruin. But the Vandals were the only barbarian people to build something, to have more to show for their raids than a huge pile of plunder amid a field full of dead bodies. They became a naval power that threatened Rome's dominance in the Mediterranean, and by creating an empire of their own they placed an additional strain on Rome's already overextended military resources. That their own remarkable achievements took place at the moment when Rome was stumbling from one act of folly to the next accelerated the Vandals' successes and Rome's final collapse.

AN EMPIRE OF THEIR OWN: THE VANDALS AND THE SECOND SACK OF ROME

THE FALL OF ROME TO ALARIC AND THE GOTHS IN 410 GETS all the attention, yet it was the capitulation of Rome to Gaiseric and the Vandals in 455 that was the true death knell of the empire in the west.

In 410, the Romans had at least summoned sufficient courage to put up a token resistance to the Goths. Only forty-five years later, the city was so dispirited that throngs of Roman citizens clogged the roads leading from the city, desperate to get away before the Vandals arrived at the gates. Even the emperor tried to escape, scurrying incognito through the crowd.

In 410, Rome fell through treachery: Someone—no one has ever discovered who—threw open the Salerian Gate and let in the Goths. In 455, the Romans, by a prior arrangement, opened all the gates, then kept out of the way as the Vandals ransacked the Eternal City—but left the buildings and the Romans unharmed. It was the best deal that Pope St. Leo the Great could wring out of Gaiseric.

Nonetheless, centuries would pass before the city of Rome recovered from its submission to the Vandals. Very few of the citizens who ran away ever came back. Rome, once a metropolis with a population of more than 1 million, slipped to the status of a backwater whose population plummeted with each passing year. By the year 500, barely 50,000 souls still lived within the city walls.

For decades the Roman Empire in the West had been fading away, but it was Gaiseric and the Vandals who gave it the final shove into oblivion.

THE ASSASSINS

March 16, 455, dawned warmer and sunnier than Romans expected so early in spring. Eager to make the most of such a fine day, the 35-year-old emperor Valentinian III put aside all the administrative tasks that usually occupied him and rode out to the Field of Mars, a 600-acre open space along the River Tiber that for centuries had been the training ground for Rome's legionnaires.

Valentinian rode there intending to practice his archery and watch his soldiers exercise. He had been on the field a short time, just long enough to take a few practice shots with his bow, when two barbarians, swords in hand, sprang out of a clump of laurel bushes nearby and hacked the emperor to death. None of the soldiers present on the field that day, not even Valentinian's bodyguard, rushed to defend their lord, which suggests that the emperor was the victim of a wide-ranging conspiracy.

The two barbarian assassins had belonged to the army of Flavius Aetius, a brilliant, charismatic Roman general who had defeated Attila at the Battle of Chalons in 451, turned back the Hun invasion that was devastating Western Europe, and saved Western civilization from ruin. To his troops, both Romans and barbarian allies, Aetius was a hero; in the mind of the ever-suspicious and resentful Valentinian, General Aetius was at the very least an annoyance, reproach, and at worst a threat.

On September 21, 454, Aetius met with Valentinian to make a report on the finances of the army. When the general looked away for a moment, Valentinian pulled out a dagger and stabbed Aetius to death. It is said that after the murder, a bishop, Sidonius Apollonaris, was the only man at the imperial court with the courage to confront the emperor.

"I am ignorant, sir, of your motives or provocations," Apollonaris said. "I only know that you have acted like a man who has cut off his right hand with his left."

FOR DECADES THE ROMAN EMPIRE IN THE WEST HAD BEEN FADING AWAY, BUT IT WAS GAISERIC AND THE VANDALS WHO GAVE IT THE FINAL SHOVE INTO OBLIVION.

A SHORT-LIVED REIGN

Valentinian died without a son, so the legions around Rome selected a successor—Petronius Maximus, a senator, about 55 years old, who in his thirties had been an able and dynamic administrator. Whatever he had been 20 years earlier, Maximus in 451 was not up to running a crumbling empire beset on all sides by barbarian invasions, economic instability, and a military so undependable that some of Rome's finest fighting men had stood by quietly and watched as their emperor was murdered before their eyes.

Maximus' lack of sound judgment became apparent when he refused to punish the two barbarians who had assassinated Valentinian; instead, he made them part of his entourage. When he tried to force Valentinian's widow, the Empress Eudoxia, to marry him, she gave him a stinging reply that sent him scurrying out of her private apartments.

Meanwhile, in North Africa, Gaiseric listened with interest to the reports, first of the murder of Aetius, Rome's most able general; then of the assassination of Valentinian, Rome's legitimate if sniveling caesar; followed by the elevation of the inept Maximus as emperor.

After a reign full of successes, it seemed to the Vandal king that the ultimate prize, Rome itself, was ready to fall into his lap. Barely three months after Maximus had become emperor, Gaiseric assembled his navy, marched his men on board, and sailed for Ostia, the port of Rome. Word that the Vandals were coming plunged the city into panic. Emperor Maximus's only thought was to abandon the city. As the street corner newsreaders delivered the emperor's proclamation urging the Romans to run for their lives, droves of Romans citizens were already abandoning the city.

Petronius Maximus decided to take his own advice and leave, too. Two accounts of what happened to him have come down to us. One version says that he slipped out of the imperial palace disguised as an ordinary Roman citizen. He had just gotten outside the city walls when he was recognized and attacked by a mob that beat him to death with clubs and stones. The second version says that the emperor's own bodyguard killed him, dismembered his corpse, and tossed the pieces into the Tiber.

CONQUERING FERTILE GROUND

Gaiseric must have been a remarkable man. The Goths had conquered Rome, and the Huns had nearly destroyed the empire in Europe, but neither of these barbarian nations attempted to set up its own empire. The Vandals, on the other hand, did just that.

Personal information about Gaiseric is virtually nonexistent, but it is clear from the historical record that he was an innovative leader, a man who responded to difficult situations in unexpected (and almost always successful) ways, who recognized a great opportunity when it appeared, and did not go to war if he believed he could get what he wanted by negotiation, political pressure, or thinly veiled threats. The Vandal empire fell apart after Gaiseric's death because his son and successor, Hunneric, lacked theose inventive qualities that Gaiseric possessed in such abundance.

THIS PRINT SHOWS
GAISERIC AND
THE VANDALS IN A
CELEBRATORY MOOD
AS THEY INVADE ITALY.

After establishing himself firmly in North Africa with the magnificent city of Carthage as his capital, Gaiseric sent his Vandal navy into the Mediterranean, seized the islands of Sardinia and Corsica, as well as the Balearics, turning all of them into naval bases.

If the Romans ever attempted a naval assault on his realm in North Africa, the Vandal fleet in the Mediterranean could intercept the Roman ships before they came anywhere near Carthage. In the meantime, Gaiseric sought to expand his Mediterranean empire. The Greek historian Procopius (c. 500–565) tells us, "Every year at the beginning of spring, Gaiseric invaded Sicily and Italy, enslaving some of the cities and razing others to the ground, and plundering everything."

Gaiseric was especially keen to acquire Sicily, the largest, wealthiest, most fertile island in the Mediterranean. Since Sicily was situated between Carthage and the toe of the Italian peninsula, almost dead center in the Mediterranean, any fleet that used the island as a base could control almost all the shipping lanes of the Mediterranean. In 440, the Vandals acquired their first seaport in Sicily.

FEELING THE PINCH

The Vandals never ruled all of North Africa; in fact, Gaiseric probably did not want to. Any attempt to control the entire northern stretch of the continent would have stretched Gaiseric's Vandal army too thin. He was satisfied to encourage a half dozen Berber princes in the western provinces to follow his example, drive out the Roman administrators, and set up their own little kingdoms.

The territory the Vandals did control was more than enough to keep the pressure on Rome, and even to an extent annoy the Byzantine emperor in Constantinople, because the Vandals ruled over the North African "grain belt," a vast agricultural area that stretched east and west from Carthage and produced approximately 10 million bushels of grain per year.

The 1 million or so inhabitants of Rome relied upon regular shipments of grain from this area, not just for sale in the city's markets, but to feed an enormous number of Roman citizens who expected daily handouts of free grain from the government. In 455, city officials distributed, every day, free rations of grain to 120,000 of the city's poor, plus thousands of civil servants, Catholic clergy, and retired soldiers for whom free grain was a coveted perk—one of the benefits of their position in Rome. Furthermore, the administrators in

Constantinople expected Rome to send a daily donation of grain sufficient to feed the 80,000 poor citizens in of their city.

North Africa was not Rome's only source of grain—about 5 million bushels of grain came annually from Egypt, and approximately the same amount from Sicily (yet another reason why Gaiseric wanted Sicily under Vandal control). Without North African grain, Rome would not starve, but it would feel pinched. Gaiseric believed he could use that uncomfortable feeling as a tool, or better yet as a weapon, to win almost any concession he wanted from the empire.

A DEATHLESS SIEGE

It had worked before. Three years earlier Pope St. Leo the Great had ridden to northern Italy to persuade Attila to leave Rome in peace. The king of the Huns had agreed to turn back, but his was a calculated strategic retreat—his men were weary, their numbers were depleted after their defeat at Chalons, and there was famine and plague in Italy.

With Rome's fate once again in the balance, Pope Leo rode out to face another barbarian king, Gaiseric. The king of the Vandals was an Arian, but Alaric had been an Arian, too; when he sacked Rome in 410 he had spared the churches and all Romans who took refuge in them. Leo prayed that if he could not turn the Vandals away from the city altogether, perhaps he could save the Romans from a full-scale massacre.

Unlike Attila, Gaiseric was an in an excellent position to seize Rome. His men were strong, no famine or plague raged across the land, the emperor was dead and the city depopulated. Gaiseric refused to call off the attack, but as a Christian he did grant the pope several concessions: There would be no slaughter of the citizens, no torturing of patricians to make them reveal where they had hidden their treasure, no burning of the city. On the question of looting Gaiseric would not give way—Rome was full of riches, and he and his men wanted them. It was as good a deal as Pope Leo could get from the Vandals, so he returned to tell the Romans that while the Vandals plundered the city it would be best if they remained quietly in their homes.

On June 2, 455, Gaiseric and his army entered Rome. Over the next two weeks they fanned out across the city, stripping everything of value from every pagan temple, Christian church, government building, and private home.

THE VANDALS IMPOVERISHED AND DEMORALIZED THE ROMANS, BUT IN EVERY OTHER RESPECT THEY KEPT THEIR WORD: NOTHING WAS DEFACED OR MARRED OR DESTROYED— IN OTHER WORDS, IN THE 455 SACK OF ROME, THERE WERE NO ACTS OF VANDALISM.

They tore up the gilded copper plates that covered the roof of the Temple of Jupiter Capitolinus. They pried gold and silver ornaments off the tombs of the martyrs and even from the altars. Rare bronze sculptures, exquisite jewelry, furs, silk, wine, and anything else of value was loaded into heavy oxcarts and hauled off to the Vandal ships at Ostia.

It is said that among the treasures the Vandals carried away were the golden menorah and other sacred vessels that Titus had looted from the Temple in Jerusalem in the year 70. Yet it seems hard to believe that nearly 400 years after the Temple treasure had been brought to Rome it was still intact. If some caesar had not melted it down, certainly Alaric's Goths would have taken it in 410.

Once everything precious was stowed aboard his ships, Gaiseric claimed one final prize—the Empress Eudoxia and her two daughters, 15-year-old Eudocia and her younger sister Placidia. Kidnapping the imperial family had not been part of the bargain Gaiseric had made with the pope, but his conquest of Rome led him to dream of even grander things, such as new dynasty of Vandal-Roman emperors born of a union between Eudocia and Gaiseric's son, Hunneric. (Indeed, once back in Carthage, Gaiseric did force Eudocia to become Hunneric's wife).

Along with the empress and her daughters the Vandals also carried off thousands of Romans from wealthy, distinguished families, including many members of the Roman Senate. Since these captives could be ransomed for large sums, he regarded them as portable property, just as valuable as the gold and silver he had looted from their villas.

Back in Rome Pope Leo looked out over an impoverished, depopulated city. No one knows how many thousands fled before the Vandals arrived; thousands more deserted Rome after Gaiseric and his army were gone. Hard numbers are difficult to come by for this period, but it is possible that after the Vandal sack of Rome in 455, approximately 100,000 still remained in the city.

OBSERVED BY ODOACER AND HIS ADVISORS, ROMULUS AUGUSTUS ANNOUNCES HIS ABDICATION TO THE ROMAN SENATE, BRINGING THE LINE OF CAESARS TO AN END.

By the year 500, the city population fell to about 50,000. The Vandals robbed and demoralized the Romans, but in every other respect they kept their word: nothing was defaced or marred or destroyed—in other words, in the 455 Sack of Rome, there were no acts of vandalism.

AN EMPIRE OF GRAIN

In 468, Gaiseric completed the conquest of Sicily. Now he dominated the Mediterranean and controlled three-quarters of the grain supply Rome depended upon. Granted, in the city's current reduced conditions it did not need the millions of bushels once necessary to keep the Romans fed and happy; nonetheless, for the first time since Julius Caesar had united the entire Mediterranean region under his rule, the overwhelming majority of the western empire's grain producing regions were in foreign and hostile hands.

As the French historian Christian Courtois put it, the Vandals were now lords over an "empire of grain." Gaiseric was prepared to use his new power to gain by pressure what he could not take by conquest—and what he wanted was the authority to appoint the prefect, or ruler, for all of Italy.

About this time, the Byzantine emperor Leo I in Constantinople felt that Gaiseric had caused enough disruption in the western empire. In the summer of 468, the same year Sicily fell to the Vandals, Emperor Leo assembled an armada of 1,100 ships under a general named Basiliskos and sent the fleet to attack the Vandals at Carthage. At a cape known today as Ras Addar in Tunisia, Basiliskos dropped anchor. Although he was only a few miles from Carthage, the general did not land his troops or prepare to attack or besiege the city—no one knows why.

During this brief breathing space Gaiseric sent an embassy to Basiliskos to ask for his terms and then to beg for a five-day truce during which he would consult with his advisors. Basiliskos, confident that he had the upper hand over the Vandals, believed he could afford to be generous. As for Gaiseric, he was gambling that within five days the winds, which had been blowing from an easterly direction, would change. His gamble paid off. When the winds did change the Vandals were ready: They sent fire ships into the closely massed Byzantine fleet. As the Byzantine ships burst into flame, thousands of Basiliskos's troops died in the fire or drowned in the sea.

POPE ST. LEO THE GREAT

No record survives to tell us when or where Leo was born or anything about his early life. We know that about the year 425 he was ordained a deacon and was serving as an advisor to Pope Celestine I (reigned 422–432).

In the papal household he developed a reputation as an energetic young man who could be relied upon to accomplish any task assigned to him. Finding that Leo had a genius for negotiations, Pope Celestine and his successor, Pope Sixtus III, sent him on diplomatic missions.

In 440, a quarrel between the commander of the Roman legions in Gaul and the governor of the province threatened to undermine the stability of the province. Pope Sixtus sent Leo to arbitrate the dispute before the barbarian nations got wind of it and seized the opportunity to launch another invasion of Gaul. Leo was still trying to reconcile the general and the governor when messengers arrived with the news that Sixtus had died and he, Leo, had been elected pope.

Pope Leo is most famous for using his powers of persuasion to convince Attila to leave Italy in peace, and Gaiseric not to destroy the city of Rome.

After Gaiseric returned to North Africa with many Roman captives, Leo sent priests after him, with chests full of silver and gold and instructions to ransom as many captives as possible.

Leo's office was primarily religious, and he did work hard to instruct the people of Rome in sound doctrine; more than 100 of his sermons have survived, and they are remarkable for their clear, concise explanations of the Christian faith. At the same time, the Roman Empire in the west was crumbling, and more and more of the administration of cities and provinces was falling to bishops.

In Rome, Pope Leo took over much of the upkeep of the city's infrastructure, and also become responsible for responding to crises such as famine and epidemics in the surrounding countryside. After his death on November 10, 461, Pope Leo was so beloved and respected by the citizens of the Rome that they venerated him as a saint and gave him the title "the Great."

POPE ST. LEO THE GREAT PERSUADED GAISERIC NOT TO MASSACRE THE ROMANS OR BURN THE CITY.

In retaliation for Emperor Leo's attack Gaiseric sent an invasion force of his own to Greece. At Kenipolis in the Peloponnese, the local Greek militia met the Vandals and inflicted on the barbarians one of the worst defeats they had endured in decades. As they retreated home to Carthage, the Vandal fleet made a detour to raid the Aegean island of Zakynthos, where it carried off 500 hostages.

Once they were at sea, the Vandals massacred their captives, mutilating the bodies and then tossing the pieces overboard.

The situation in the Mediterranean remained the same until 474, when Emperor Leo's successor, Zeno, sent a diplomatic mission to Gaiseric to begin negotiating a treaty. In the final document Zeno gained more than Gaiseric. In exchange for the Byzantine emperor's formal recognition of the Vandal kingdom, Gaiseric agreed to release his Roman prisoners of war, permit the

THE LAST EMPEROR

Since 455, the year Valentinian III was assassinated, Romans had seen the Vandals sack their beloved city and a huge percentage of the population desert the Eternal City. The city was spiraling downward ever more swiftly.

In twenty-one years, the city had seen eight men who called themselves "emperor" come and go—some in a matter of weeks. The last contender for the throne of the caesars was a thirteen-year-old boy name Romulus Augustus. The first Romulus was the legendary founder of Rome; Augustus, of course, was the first emperor; that the last emperor should bear both of these distinguished names struck everyone as a cruel irony.

Worse, there was not much of an empire in the west for the boy to rule. Aside from Italy, bits of Slovenia, Croatia, Serbia, and Bosnia, a sliver of Morocco, and the region around Paris, everything was in barbarian hands. Even Italy was not

really the emperor's since King Odoacer was the real strongman in the country.

On September 4, 476, Odoacer summoned the Emperor Romulus Augustus to appear at his court. Given the current political situation, Odoacer could see no reason why the West should keep up this charade that Rome had a real emperor. Once Romulus was shown into the audience hall, Odoacer informed the boy that he was deposed. The next step would have been to order his guards to escort Romulus to a place of execution, but Odoacer felt pity for the boy. Rather than kill the ex-emperor, he sent him to Campagna in southern Italy, near the city of Salerno.

No one knows what became of Romulus Augustus. After that final audience with King Odoacer, he vanishes from the historical record.

THE EASTERN PROVINCES OF THE ROMAN EMPIRE, SHOWN IN THIS MAP, NEVER SUFFERED FROM THE BARBARIAN INVASIONS THAT DESTROYED WESTERN EUROPE.

Romans he kept as slaves to be ransomed, and grant freedom of worship to all Catholics in his realm.

Furthermore, Gaiseric agreed to turn over control of Sicily to Odoacer, a barbarian chieftain of Germanic origin who had declared himself king of Italy and become the country's primary powerbroker. Determined to have the island under Italian control, Odoacer had already invaded Sicily, scoring several victories over the Vandals. In exchange for the island, Odoacer agreed to pay tribute to Gaiseric. The treaty was signed in 476, a momentous year that saw the dismissal of Rome's last emperor.

THE TRANSFORMATION OF A STARVELING RACE

Almost five months after the exile of Rome's last emperor, on January 25, 477, Gaiseric died in Carthage. He was about 87 years old, an extraordinary age for the time. In his lifetime he saw his people evolve from a starveling band in the German forests to a great power on land and sea, with an empire that extended over some of the best lands in the Mediterranean. He had personally seized great Carthage and made it his capital, and then looted Rome.

It is true that Rome had been in decline for decades, but Gaiseric and his Vandals hastened it toward its end. Before he died, Gaiseric witnessed the end of the imperial line in Rome and secured recognition of the Vandal kingdom from the Byzantine emperor (the only true imperial power left in the old Roman world).

Gaiseric's kingdom could not last long. The Vandals never evolved beyond a warrior society; they never created a kingdom in which Roman Africans and Vandals merged into a single cohesive people. In North Africa, the Vandals adopted the trappings of Roman life—the Latin language, the public baths, the luxurious pleasures of the villas—But they were no good at nation-building. They exploited the territories they conquered and continued to harass African Catholics.

Gaiseric's son and heir, Hunneric, disregarded the freedom of worship clause in the treaty his father had signed with Zeno and began a fresh round of anti-Catholic persecution. He drove 5,000 Catholic churchmen into the desert to die and sent hundreds more into forced labor on the island of Corsica. In 533, when the Emperor Justinian sent an army to Carthage, the Vandals' African subjects rushed to the aid of the Byzantines. Within six months, the

THE RUINS OF CARTHAGE, WHERE GAISERIC ESTABLISHED THE CAPITAL OF THE SHORT-LIVED VANDAL EMPIRE.

Vandal kingdom collapsed, most of the Vandals were dead or in hiding, and the last Vandal king, Gelimer (Gaiseric's great-nephew) was captured and banished to a remote corner of Asia. No one knows what became of him.

Though Gelimer's legacy is shame, failure, and oblivion, the Vandals as a whole handed down something truly substantial to subsequent generations: the modern Mediterranean world. They rang the death knell of Rome's emperors, of Rome's prestige among the world's cities, of Rome's sovereignty in the Mediterranean. By setting up a rival empire, by keeping Rome's grain supply in a stranglehold, by stripping the city itself of everything of value, the Vandals accelerated the twilight of the western empire. After 455, Rome and the West were not in a gentle, decorous decline—they were in freefall.

THE GROANS OF THE BRITONS: THE ANGLE, SAXON, AND JUTE INVASION OF BRITAIN

E NGLAND IS A SMALL PLACE—APPROXIMATELY 50,350 square miles, about the same size as Greece and Nicaragua. Yet it is the mother country of the United States, Australia, and (along with France) of Canada.

Until fifty years ago, England had an empire that circled the globe. The empire is almost entirely gone, but English ideas about law, justice, representational government, and individual liberties endure, in one form or another, on every continent where Queen Victoria once ruled. English civilization continues to flourish throughout the world: Schoolchildren in New Delhi study Shakespeare, regional theater troupes in Kansas perform operas by Gilbert and Sullivan, and Maori congregations in New Zealand worship in Gothic-style churches that would fit perfectly in Sussex or Kent.

As for the English language, it is the international language of commerce; it has surpassed French as the language of diplomacy, and it is spoken by approximately 340 million native speakers and more than 300 million non-native speakers.

THE LAST ROMAN LEGIONS SAILED AWAY FROM BRITAIN IN 407. BECAUSE OF UPHEAVALS ELSEWHERE IN THE EMPIRE, THEY WERE NEVER REPLACED.

TIMELINE

55 B.C.: JULIUS CAESAR INVADES BRITAIN BUT DOES NOT OCCUPY THE ISLAND.

43 A.D.: ROMAN GENERAL AULUS PLAUTIUS CONQUERS THE BRITONS.

200: 50,000 ROMAN TROOPS ARE STATIONED IN BRITAIN.

360: PICTS FROM SOUTHERN SCOTLAND SWARM OVER HADRIAN'S WALL AND RAID ROMAN TOWNS AND ESTATES.

400: THE NUMBER OF ROMAN TROOPS IN BRITAIN DROPS TO 6,000.

401: ROMAN EMPEROR THEODOSIUS I WITHDRAWS 1,000 TROOPS FROM BRITAIN TO HELP IN A WAR AGAINST THE GOTHS.

407: THE LAST ROMAN LEGIONS IN BRITAIN SAIL FOR THE CONTINENT.

c. 449: BRITISH WARLORD VORTIGERN INVITES THE JUTISH CHIEFTAIN HENGEST TO BRITAIN TO HELP IN A WAR AGAINST THE PICTS.

A PROVIDENTIAL INVASION

All these achievements can be traced back to the fifth century, when three ships of Germanic warriors came ashore on the eastern coast of England.

The warriors represented three tribes—the Angles and Saxons from the area of northern Germany known as Schleswig, and the Jutes from southern Denmark. There may have been Frisians, a Germanic tribe from Holland, among them, too. The Britons referred to all these tribes simply as "the Saxons," and for convenience we will, too. Yet Roman Britain did not become known as "Saxland," but "England"—after the Angles. No one knows why. And the Germanic language that warriors spoke became known as English.

For the Britons, who lived in the territory that would become known as England, and the Romans, who had come as colonists beginning in the first century A.D., the Germanic invasion was an unmitigated disaster that destroyed their civilization, took countless lives, and compelled the survivors to look for safety in the most remote corners of the island. But for the future of Europe and the larger world, the coming of the Angles, Saxons, and Jutes, and Frisians was providential.

C. 455: ROME'S COMMANDER-IN-CHIEF, FLAVIUS AETIUS, RECEIVES A LETTER KNOWN AS "THE GROANS OF THE BRITONS," PLEADING WITH HIM TO SEND ROMAN TROOPS TO DRIVE OUT THE SAXONS.

488: HENGIST DIES, BUT HIS SON AESC COMPLETES THE CONQUEST OF BRITAIN.

C. 493: BRITONS, UNDER THEIR ROMAN-TRAINED COMMANDER, AMBROSIUS AURELIANUS, INFLICT A CRUSHING DEFEAT ON THE SAXONS AT MOUNT BADON. THE BRITISH ASCENDANCY IS SHORT-LIVED; THE ANGLES, SAXONS, AND JUTES RALLY AND DRIVE THE BRITISH INTO THE WESTERN PART OF THE ISLAND.

597: ST. AUGUSTINE LEADS THE FIRST CHRISTIAN MISSION TO ANGLO-SAXON ENGLAND.

C. 600: SAXONS REFOUND LONDON.

A CONQUERED COUNTRY

The weather was typical for late winter in Britain: a cold drizzle, a stiff, icy wind off the sea, and heavy clouds obscuring the sun in a steel-gray sky. Drawn up in orderly ranks on the seashore were a few thousand Roman troops, patiently waiting their turn to board the ships that would carry them across the English Channel to Gaul. They were keen to get to the Continent and begin their march to Rome to see their commander, Constantine, crowned emperor. They had already proclaimed him so in their camp, and he now called himself Constantine III. For the men in ranks, this gray, dank day in the year 407 was the most thrilling moment of their lives.

The small crowd that watched the soldiers board the ships did not cheer and did not share the soldiers' excitement. The civilians—a mix of men who worked on the waterfront, shopkeepers, a few wealthy gentlemen, and quite a few slaves—must have felt uneasy, even frightened. The soldiers climbing into the boats were the last Roman legionnaires in all of Britain; once they were gone, there would be no professional troops on the island to protect the inhabitants from the Picts (a Celtic tribe related to the Irish and the Britons, whose territory extended across southern Scotland), the Irish, the Saxons, and the other barbarians who had been burning villas, looting seaside towns, and carrying off honest citizens to sell as slaves. Now the question was, would the legions come back?

IN THE YEAR 200 THERE WERE 50,000 ROMAN TROOPS STATIONED IN BRITAIN. BY THE STANDARDS OF MEDIEVAL ENGLISH KINGS WHO NEVER COULD AFFORD TO HAVE A STANDING ARMY OF MORE THAN 5,000 MEN, THIS WAS AN ASTONISHING INVESTMENT OF MANPOWER. FOR ROME IT WAS STANDARD PROCEDURE.

The Romans had left once before. In 55 B.C., Julius Caesar invaded the island, established a client king, took some hostages, and then sailed back to Gaul after spending barely a year in Britain. He took all his troops with him. Rome did not conquer the island for another century, until 43 A.D., when Emperor Claudius's general Aulus Plautius subdued the Britons. For the next 300 years, Britain was the westernmost province of Rome's great empire.

To keep the Britons under control, the Romans erected forts throughout the country, and to keep the Picts at bay, they built Hadrian's Wall along the length of the British/Scottish border. They built roads, dug canals, and founded many cities, including present-day London, Manchester, York, Lincoln, Winchester, Canterbury, Dover, and Bath. They exploited the island's gold, silver, lead, and iron mines, and taught the British how to make glass and mass produce fine pottery.

In the year 200, there were 50,000 Roman troops stationed in Britain. By the standards of medieval English kings who never could afford to have a standing army of more than 5,000 men, this was an astonishing investment of manpower. For Rome it was standard procedure—the best way to keep a conquered province quiet, protect Roman citizens who settled there, and drive off barbarian raiders. By the year 400, though, the Roman garrison in Britain was down to about 6,000 men.

"A RACE HATEFUL BOTH TO GOD AND MEN"

The handful of sentries posted along the coast of Kent watched as three Saxon ships, their sails swollen by the wind, made for the shore. As the hulls scraped across the gravel and sand, the first band of Saxon warriors leapt over the gunwales and waded up the beach.

They wore woolen tunics that fell just above their knees; their only armor was sleeveless leather jerkins. All carried round wooden shields; some held long spears, while others came ashore with their swords drawn. The coast guard did not attack the foreigners, however—these were not Saxon pirates, but mercenaries hired by an ambitious British warlord named Vortigern to march north and subdue the Picts.

Months earlier, at an assembly of British nobles and warriors, as well as a handful of the surviving patricians of Roman Britain, Vortigern had proposed

A LONG DECLINE

It is traditional to point to 360 as the year when we can chart the beginning of the end of Roman Britain. In that year the Picts swarmed over Hadrian's Wall and raided Yorkshire, while Irish pirates attacked the towns and villas along Britain's western coast, carrying off hundreds of civilians to sell into slavery.

Though it is true that 360 is a watershed moment in the history of Britain, it is also true that the province had been in decline for years. Archaeologists have found that after the year 300, buildings that burned down in the Roman town of Viroconium (Wroxeter) in Shropshire were not rebuilt. About the same time, in Verulamium (St. Albans) in Hertfordshire, the pavement in the streets and forum was no longer repaired with freshly cut stone but patched up with clay.

Wealthy families that had never given a thought to security began to feel nervous and unprotected in their country estates; they abandoned their villas and moved into walled cities and towns. The suburbs of London became so depopulated that when a construction crew was ordered to shore up the city's defensive walls, it did not bother to requisition building materials—it just dismantled all the derelict houses. And as the fourth century rolled on, matters in Britain only grew worse.

In 383, a commander named Magnus Maximus convinced most of the legions in Britain that it was foolhardy to keep faith with Rome's twelve-year-old emperor, Valentinian II. The soldiers proclaimed Maximus emperor and then crossed the English Channel with him to march on Milan, the imperial capital at that time. The legions Maximus took with him were never replaced.

In 401, when Emperor Theodosius I needed more troops to fight the Goths, he withdrew another 1,000 soldiers from Britain. Six years later, another usurper, the officer who styled himself Constantine III, took all of Britain's remaining troops and sailed away to the Continent to press his claim to the throne. No Roman legions ever returned to Britain.

that they follow the example of Rome and hire barbarian mercenaries to fight the Picts. The council approved the motion and sent emissaries to the land of the Jutes in what is now southern Denmark to invite the chieftain Hengest to do battle for the Britons. This was about the year 449.

A century later, a British monk, St. Gildas, wrote an account of the pact the British had made with the barbarians and the disasters it brought upon the British. Railing against the "dullness of mind" and "darkness of soul" of Vortigern and his kind, Gildas damned the short-sighted councilors.

"They sealed [Britain's] doom," he said, "by inviting in among them (like wolves into the sheep-fold), the fierce and impious Saxons, a race hateful both to God and men."

Initially, to Vortigern and the council, their decision appeared to be a stroke of genius. Hengest led his warriors to northern Britain, where they met the Picts in battle, defeating them so completely that the barbarians scurried back across Hadrian's Wall and into their own country.

THE GROANS OF THE BRITONS

The details of Vortigern and Hengest's arrangement are unknown, but a certain sum in silver must have been promised. When it came time to pay the Saxons, however, Vortigern found that he did not have enough silver coins on hand. This was understandable—Britain had replied on regular shipments of coins from Rome. Now that the legions were gone, the trunks full of freshly minted coins stopped coming, too.

To make up the difference, Vortigern offered cattle, weapons, and other goods; Hengest accepted them. But when the payment in kind arrived at the Saxon camp, Hengest disputed the valuation. Vortigern sent word insisting that the goods he had sent were equal in value to the promised silver. With neither chief willing to back down, negotiations collapsed. In retaliation, Hengest led his men against the British.

Gildas paints a grim picture of what followed: the ruination of whole towns, defensive walls battered down, high towers overthrown, houses fallen in upon themselves, and everywhere the wholesale murder of "the inhabitants, along with the bishops of the church, both priests and people, whilst swords gleamed on every side and flames crackled."

ACCORDING TO LEGEND, VORTIGERN SEALED HIS ALLIANCE WITH THE ANGLES, SAXONS, AND JUTES BY MARRYING HENGIST'S DAUGHTER, ROWENA.

Meanwhile, more Saxons came over to Britain to get their own share of adventure and plunder. It was at this time that the Roman commander Flavius Aetius received a letter that has come to be known as "The Groans of the Britons," pleading with him to send Roman troops to defend the people from the Saxons. "The barbarians drive us to the sea," the letter read, "the sea drives us back to the barbarians; by one or other of these two modes of death we are either killed or drowned." It was an eloquent, heart-rending appeal for help; sadly, we do not know who wrote it.

Aetius was more concerned about Attila and the Huns who were rampaging west across the Roman Empire; he had no legions to spare for Britain, so the Roman Britons were left to fend for themselves. They did not do very well.

In 457, Hengest and his son Aesc led the Saxons against the Britons at a place called Crecganford, where 4,000 Britons were killed. In 465, at a place called Wippedesfleot, the British suffered another crushing defeat at the hands of this father-and-son team, including the loss of a dozen British chieftains. A battle in 473 ended with the British running from the field "as if they were fleeing a fire." In 488, Hengest died, but Aesc had consolidated his gains in the east country well enough to proclaim himself king of Kent, where he reigned for the next 24 years.

AMBROSIUS AND ARTHUR

In 493, from the summit of Mount Badon, the British warlord Arthur watched as the Saxon host assembled its shield wall, ready to repel the British charge. Arthur had a small band of cavalry with him, but it was enough to splinter the shield wall—assuming the Saxons did not bring down too many of the horses with their spears. It was a risk. In eleven battles against the Saxons he had driven them from the field every time. Would he be victorious again? Arthur touched the large cross he had pinned to his cloak and gave his horsemen the order to charge.

Gildas tells us that a man of Roman blood named Ambrosius Aurelianus won the victory over the Saxons at Mount Badon. Three hundred years after Gildas, a Welsh monk named Nennius compiled ancient sources into a history of Britain. In this composite account, Nennius says that the warlord who led the British to victory at Mount Badon was named Arthur. Eleven

ONE PLACE THE BRITISH DID NOT TRY TO KEEP WAS LONDON. BETWEEN 450 AND 500, THE ENTIRE POPULATION WALKED AWAY FROM THE CITY. NO ONE KNOWS WHY THE LONDONERS DESERTED.

times Arthur and his men had triumphed over the Saxons, but at Mount Badon, Nennius says, "nine hundred and forty [Saxons] fell by his hand alone, no one but the Lord affording him assistance."

Were Gildas's Ambrosius and Nennius's Arthur the same man? It's possible. It is even likely that Ambrosius/Arthur was the inspiration for the vast body of

MAGNUS ARTURUS REX POTENTISSIMUS ANGLIAE

DOMINUS LAUNCELOT DU LAC EQUES INVICTUS

legends about Camelot, the Knights of the Round Table, Lancelot and Guinevere, and Sir Galahad's quest for the Holy Grail. They are wonderful stories, but they have no basis in history—especially not the history of the final conflict between the natives of the island of Britain and the Angle, Saxon, and Jute invaders.

In spite of the destruction of so much of the Roman civilization they had loved, the Britons clung to the remnants. From inscriptions dating to this period we know the Britons still understood Latin. They remained Catholic and did not drift back into paganism. And many parents gave their children Roman names, although these were often mangled into a British form: Tacitus became Tegid, Constantine became Custennin, Paternus became Padarn. Aurelianus could have become Arthur.

After the first wave of the Saxon conquest in the mid- to late fifth century, many Britons sought safety in the mountains of Wales, or in Cornwall, the most remote corner of the island, or sailed to Gaul, settling in the province that became known as Brittany—Little Britain. Yet even in this extremity some of the Britons recovered their courage thanks to the emergence of a leader who was named Ambrosius Aurelianus, or Arthur.

Information about this man is scant, but Gildas supplies more details than Nennius. He describes Ambrosius Aurelianus as "a man of unassuming character, who, alone of the Roman race chanced to survive in the shock of such a storm." Ambrosius Aurelianus was a war leader among the Britons, a Christian, and of Roman ancestry.

Gildas tells us that his parents were killed by the Saxons and that his ancestors "had worn the purple." Purple was the color of the Roman emperors, but it is not likely that Ambrosius belonged to the imperial family. Senators and tribunes wore togas and cloaks trimmed with a band of purple, and this is probably what Gildas wanted to convey, that the savior of the Britons was a member of the upper tier of Roman society.

The decisive battle against the Saxons at Mount Badon took place about the year 493. We are less certain of the battle's location, although Mynydd Baedan in South Wales or Badbury Hillfort in Dorset are both likely candidates.

At Mount Badon, Ambrosius probably faced Aelle, king of the South Saxons. Gildas does not mention him, but the Venerable Bede, writing in 731, places Aelle first in a list of England's Anglo-Saxon kings. The Anglo-Saxon Chronicle that was assembled from earlier documents about the year 890 has three entries for Aelle: 477, when he and his three sons raided Wales; 485, when the family fought another battle against the Welsh; and 491, when Aelle

A STAINED GLASS WINDOW DEPICTS KING ARTHUR ON THE LEFT AND HIS GREATEST KNIGHT, SIR LANCELOT, ON THE RIGHT.

THE CASUALTIES OF THE SAXON CONQUEST

With the collapse of Roman influence in Britain, the look of the land changed dramatically. It would no longer be known as Britain, or Britannia in Latin, but as the land of the Angles and the Saxons—England for short. And the inhabitants were no longer called British or Britons, but English. Among the other casualties were the villas, temples, baths, and other Roman structures been built of stone that now stood empty and forsaken—the Saxons did not move into them because they did not know how to build in stone or how to maintain and repair existing stone structures.

The pinnacle of comfort and civilized living for a high-ranking Saxon was not a villa but a high-gabled timber hall where a large fire burned on a stone hearth in the center of the room and his family, household, and warriors sat at long trestle tables down the whole length of the chamber. Some vivid descriptions of such a hall can be found in the eighth-century epic poem, *Beowulf*.

The Saxon lord sat at the far end of the hall on a large wooden throne, often elaborately carved with intertwined serpents and mythical beasts. This was the high seat from which the lord presided over banquets in the evenings and dispensed justice during the day. On the walls hung the household's weapons, as well as woven or embroidered tapestries of wool or painted leather wall hangings.

Outside the hall, arranged around the entrance courtyard, were a host of smaller buildings—stables, a dairy barn, a kitchen, a pantry where food was stored, a brewery, perhaps a smithy, and small houses for the women, children, and favored servants. There might also be a wooden palisade around the compound to shield it from enemy attack. Among the Saxons the hall was the pinnacle of luxury, a source of pride and envy. Men of the next rank in Saxon society lived in log houses that tried to mimic the lord's great hall on a smaller scale.

Like stone buildings, garments of silk and fine cotton vanished from Britain with the Romans. The Saxons wore linen and wool, with fur outer garments during winter. They loved gold and silver, but especially gold, and large, brilliantly colored jewels. Both men and women wore gold chains or collars around their necks, and pinned large brooches to their chests. Men wore arm rings, usually the gift of their lord for performing some service or displaying skill or valor in battle.

From their belts women wore a leather pouch that held their little

AFTER THE ANGLES, SAXONS, AND JUTES COMPLETED THEIR CONQUEST OF BRITAIN, MOST OF THE SURVIVING BRITISH AND ROMAN POPULATION RETREATED TO WALES.

workboxes, usually made of bronze, generally embellished with gold or silver filigree. Inside they kept needles, tweezers, small knives, and threads—the things a woman would use every day.

Learning and literacy were also casualties of the Saxon conquest. The Saxons loved poetry and music but had no interest in philosophy or abstract thought.

For the Saxon warrior caste, reputation was everything. They strove to build a reputation for courage, skill, and dependability in battle; they wanted to win the respect of their comrades and the respect (tempered by fear) of their enemies. They longed for fame. And though no Saxon warrior would have admitted ever to having experienced fear, there were things about which they were apprehensive. As their lives tended to be violent and therefore rather brief, they had a morbid fascination with death.

The Romans tamed and civilized the wilderness, but the Saxons, outside of their relatively small farmsteads, left the wilderness alone. Consequently they had a deep attachment to the community within the hall. Inside was light, warmth, food, ale, music, women, and camaraderie; outside the hall the world was a dark and cold place where enemies and wild beasts prowled in the forests.

and his son Cissa attacked "Andredes Cester" (Andred's Castle) "and killed all who lived in there; there was not even one Briton left there." Andred's Castle was an old Roman fort that stood outside Pevensey in East Sussex along Britain's southern shore. If the date given in the Anglo-Saxon Chronicle is accurate, the massacre at the castle may have been the event that motivated the surviving Britons to rally around Ambrosius.

As the Battle of Mount Badon suggests, the Saxons suffered some reversals in their conquest of Britain. Reading Gildas, one imagines the Saxons swept ashore and took over the whole country in record time.

In fact, it was a slow process because the Britons did not give up easily. Around the year 500, Kent, the Isle of Wight, Norfolk, Suffolk, Lincolnshire, and the coastal areas of Northumbria and Yorkshire were under Saxon control, but that left half of Britain still in British hands. It was the violence of the attacks and the rapid destruction of the Roman infrastructure, as we can see in Glidas' account, that created the impression that the Saxons had rolled over the Britons unhindered.

One place the British did not try to keep was London. Between 450 and 500, the entire population walked away from the city. The Roman city covered 330 acres, extending roughly from such well-known landmarks as St. Paul's Cathedral to the Tower of London and from the Thames River to Bishopsgate. In its heyday Roman London was home to 30,000 people. No one knows why the Londoners deserted their city—perhaps its location on the Thames exposed them to too many Saxon raids. About the year 600, when the Saxons decided to found a new settlement along the Thames, they did not try to revitalize the ruined Roman city but chose instead to make a fresh start farther west, in the area near Covent Garden.

INTO THE EUROPEAN MAINSTREAM

In 597, forty Italian monks led by an abbot named Augustine entered the city of Canterbury, the capital of Aethelbert, King of Kent, hoping to convert the king and his people to Christianity.

Back in Rome, the monks had heard hair-raising tales of what the barbarian Saxons had done to the Christians of Britain when they had first invaded the island. Now, as they made their way through the dirty streets to

Aethelbert's great hall, the missionaries expected a howling band of Saxon warriors to ambush them at any moment, making martyrs of them all.

To the monks' surprise, however, the Saxons adopted Christianity rather quickly. A merciful God surrounded by a host of helpful, sympathetic saints was more appealing to the Saxons than their own world view in which every man, woman, and child was predestined to some grim, inescapable fate. Even the priests of the old Saxon gods found Christianity attractive.

In 627, the first Christian missionaries from Rome arrived at the court of King Edwin in York. As the king and his retainers debated the merits of Christianity, Coifi, one of Edwin's chief warriers, made this comparison:

> The present life of man upon earth, O king, seems to me, in comparison with that time which is unknown to us, like to the swift flight of a sparrow through the house wherein you sit at supper in winter, with your ealdormen and thegns, while the fire blazes in the midst, and the hall is warmed, but the wintry storms of rain or snow are raging abroad. The sparrow, flying in at one door and immediately out at another, whilst he is within, is safe from the wintry tempest; but after a short space of fair weather, he immediately vanishes out of your sight, passing from winter into winter again. So this life of man appears for a little while, but of what is to follow or what went before we know nothing at all. If, therefore, this new doctrine tells us something more certain, it seems justly to deserve to be followed.

By conquering Britain, the Saxons had destroyed Roman civilization on the island. Then, by adopting Christianity, the Saxons welcomed Roman civilization back to Britain and took England, an outpost of Germanic society, into the European mainstream.

THE LONG-HAIRED KINGS: THE FRANKS

O F ALL THE BARBARIAN NATIONS THAT CARVED UP THE Roman Empire, the Franks were the most Roman and least barbarous. For generations dating back at least to the third century and perhaps as early as the time of Julius Caesar, Franks served in the Roman army. By the year 350, three Franks held very influential positions in the Roman military: Magnentius was commander of the imperial guard; Silvanus was a tribune and *Magister militum*, meaning a senior military officer, the equivalent of a commander of a particular theater of war; and Arbitio was commander of the Roman cavalry in Gaul.

It is common to identify Roman Gaul with modern France, but in fact Gaul covered a much more extensive territory. In addition to France, Gaul embraced Belgium, the southern half of the Netherlands, the western half of Switzerland, Germany west of the Rhine River, and even a bit of northwestern Italy—a region the Romans called Cisapline Gaul ("Cisalpine" comes from the Latin term for "this side of the Alps").

The Franks were so steeped in the Roman military tradition that even a century after the last Roman legion had left Gaul, the "barbarian" Franks

A MAP OF GAUL AS
THE ROMANS AND
THE FRANKS WOULD
HAVE KNOWN IT.

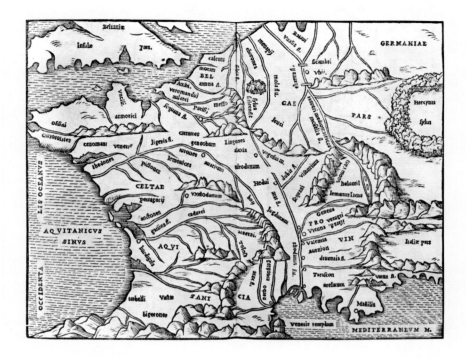

drilled in the Roman fashion and carried into battle the old standards and insignia of the legions under which their ancestors had fought. In the Roman province of Pannonia (modern-day Hungary and Serbia) archaeologists discovered a third-century gravestone of a Frankish recruit who served in the legions. The inscription reads *Francus ego cives, miles romanus in armis*, meaning, "I am a Frank by nationality, but a Roman soldier under arms."

As a nation that over the years had benefited from its ties to Rome, the Franks were not nearly as destructive to Roman society in Gaul as the Huns, Goths, or Vandals would be in other parts of the empire. And whereas the Goths and Vandals converted to the Arian form of Christianity, which did not recognize the spiritual authority of the pope, when the Franks embraced Christianity they became Catholics, which could be seen as another manifestation of their affinityfidelity to and partiality for things Roman.

The Franks did not even impose their language on the people of Gaul. Granted, the Latin-speaking Gallo-Roman population vastly outnumbered the Franks, who ruled the country, but a more important factor was the Franks' familiarity with Latin. Members of the Frankish upper class and

TIMELINE

275: FRANKS INVADE ROMAN GAUL, PLUNDERING SEVENTY CITIES AND TOWNS.

276: ROMAN EMPEROR PROBUS DEFEATS THE FRANKS; OFFERS CLEMENCY TO FRANKS, WHO WILL ENLIST IN THE ROMAN LEGIONS.

487: THE FRANKS, LED BY CLOVIS, CONQUER SOISSONS, THE LAST ROMAN OUTPOST IN GAUL.

493: CLOVIS MARRIES A BURGUNDIAN CATHOLIC PRINCESS, CLOTHILDE.

Franks who had served in the Roman army spoke Latin, and the language probably spread through the rest of Frankish society, too. Consequently, the Franks in Gaul gave up their Germanic dialect and adopted Latin, which over time mutated into French.

THE STANDARD BEARER

It was Christmas Day, 496, yet in spite of the bitter cold outdoors and the damp chill inside the stone church, the king of the Franks stood nearly naked in a deep pool of water. Standing outside the pool, the bishop of Rheims, St. Remy, warm and comfortable in layer upon layer of heavy vestments, took his time reading the baptismal rite; when he anointed the thirty-year-old king's back and chest with holy oil, he could feel the goosebumps on the royal flesh. At the climactic moment, the bishop bent double to fill a golden scallop shell with holy water from the pool and then raised it above the king's head.

"Bow your head, Sicamber," the bishop commanded. "Adore what you have burned. Burn what you once adored." Then he poured the water over the king's head and made him a Christian.

The king's name was Clovis; Sicamber was the Frankish tribe to which he and his family belonged. That neatly turned phrase about burning and adoring was a bit of poetic license on Bishop Remy's part: Clovis had not persecuted the Church, although when he sacked a town he did loot churches. But Remy was doing more than tossing off a *bon mot*—in a subtle way he was encouraging Clovis to destroy the sanctuaries of the Frankish gods.

TIMELINE

496: AT THE BATTLE OF TOLBIAC, CLOVIS VOWS TO CONVERT TO CHRISTIANITY IF CHRIST WILL GRANT HIM VICTORY OVER HIS ENEMIES. CLOVIS WINS THE BATTLE.

CHRISTMAS DAY, 496: CLOVIS IS BAPTIZED IN RHEIMS CATHEDRAL.

507: THE EMPEROR IN CONSTANTINOPLE RECOGNIZES CLOVIS AS THE RULER OF ALL GAUL.

511: CLOVIS DIES AFTER HAVING KILLED ALL OF HIS RIVALS—INCLUDING MEMBERS OF HIS OWN FAMILY. HIS THREE SONS UNDO HIS WORK BY SPLITTING THE KINGDOM INTO THREE PARTS.

The effect of Clovis's conversion to Catholicism, and the subsequent conversion of his senior officers and most of his army, cannot be overestimated. In the first place, it made the Frankish rulers one with their Gallo-Roman subjects, all of whom were Catholic. In North Africa and Spain, Arian Vandals and Goths were often in conflict with their Catholic subjects, but in Gaul Gallo-Roman farmers, craftsmen, and aristocrats shared the same point of view as their Frankish rulers. The situation not only encouraged cooperation between Gallo-Romans and Franks, it also made blending of the two ethnic groups easy, even inevitable. Clovis had begun the unification of Gaul militarily, now he had confirmed that unification religiously.

Clovis created a unique society by "marrying" the Germanic tribal culture of the Franks to the proven administrative system of the Romans. He acted like a German warlord who possessed the administrative genius of a Roman bureaucrat. When he dispensed justice, his decisions were guided by Roman law (or at least Frankish law that had been recast in the Roman style). The economics of his kingdom were based on taxation, and he followed the Roman method of assessing and collecting taxes.

The pope in Rome and the emperor in Constantinople looked on other barbarian kings with suspicion, but they treated the Catholic, Romanized king of the Franks as a friend and ally. Clovis had chosen the side that would bring him the greatest degree of prestige while also elevating his kingdom to the status of standard bearer of classical Roman and orthodox Christian civilization. Because the Frankish takeover of Gaul was less disruptive than the Anglo-Saxon invasion of Britain or the Vandals' conquest of North Africa, the country we know as France flourished virtually from the moment it began.

ST. REMY,
BISHOP OF RHEIMS,
BAPTIZED CLOVIS,
KING OF THE FRANKS,
ON CHRISTMAS DAY 496.

BEASTLY ENTERTAINMENT

It was midday about the year 276 in Trier, a Roman colonial town in what is now Germany. The morning's entertainment of battles between armed men and wild beasts had concluded, and the combat between gladiators would not start until late afternoon. But during the interim there would still be spectacles to see in the arena—from noon until four, criminals were brought out for execution.

Many in the audience went home at this time to eat their midday meal and take a siesta, but there were plenty of spectators in the stands, curious to see who would be brought out to die and how they would be executed.

On this day, the doors that led down to the prison under the arena swung open as teams of slaves rolled twenty-four crude chariots into the stadium. Mounted on each chariot was a rough wooden post; tied to each post was a naked Frank. These barbarians had been captured after raiding Roman towns and villas along the Mediterranean coast;

too dangerous to be sold as slaves and too valuable to be executed on the spot, they had been taken to Trier, a Roman city near the Franks' own country, where they were condemned to be mauled by the beasts in the area.

After arranging the chariots around the arena so everyone in the stands would have a good view, the slaves scurried back the way they had come, locking the big doors behind them. Moments later, many smaller doors and grills swung open and a roaring pack of lions, leopards, and bears rushed into the arena. In the wild, a man was not their typical meal, but in captivity, in preparation for this day's sport, their keepers had fed the beasts human flesh so they would develop a taste for it. And then the animals had been starved. As the helpless Franks shrieked and wept and struggled to break free of their bonds, the hungry beasts leapt upon the first of their victims.

CHARLEMAGNE, RENAISSANCE RULER

His name is French for "Charles the Great," and great he was. He expanded the kingdom of the Franks into a vast empire that included the lands we know as France, Germany, Belgium, the Netherlands, Luxemburg, Switzerland, western Austria, the Czech Republic, northern Italy, and even the northeast corner of Spain. Charlemagne's dream was to revive the Roman Empire in western Europe, and his dream was realized on Christmas Day, 800, when in St. Peter's Basilica in Rome the pope crowned him Holy Roman Emperor.

Most of his empire Charlemagne (c.747–814) acquired by conquest, and he kept his borders secure by crushing his enemies—the Slavs, the Danes, the Moors in Spain, and the Avars, an Asiatic people who had invaded Hungary. But Charlemagne was much more than a warlord.

In an effort to revive classical education and classical culture in his empire, he coaxed the finest scholars in Europe to come teach at his newly opened schools. He gave lavishly to scribes who copied books, commissioned fine works of art, and sponsored the construction of at least 600 new cathedrals, monasteries, and churches throughout his empire, plus two new palaces at Aachen and Paderborn. In this way Charlemagne initiated the first renaissance Europe had known since the collapse of the Roman Empire.

By founding an empire, Charlemagne consolidated a multitude of tiny, fragmented kingdoms and principalities into a political, military, and cultural powerhouse that brought stability to western Europe and served as a counterbalance to the Byzantine Empire in eastern Europe. Since his death Charlemagne has been hailed as a model of chivalry, a saint, and even "the Father of Europe." The founders of the European Union may have taken the old emperor as their inspiration—certainly the Union has given Europe a degree of political and economic clout it has enjoyed only rarely since the days of Charlemagne.

AN INDEPENDENT STREAK

As illustrated above, not all the Franks served Rome. Around the year 275, Franks invaded Gaul and ravaged seventy Roman cities and towns, including Trier on the Moselle River.

In 276, Probus, who had just become emperor, led an army against the Franks, driving them out of Gaul. He offered his prisoners a chance to regain their freedom by serving in the Roman legions. Those who accepted Probus split up into small units that were sent to outposts all across the empire.

If the new Frankish recruits were not concentrated in any one area, the emperor reasoned, they would not become a source of trouble later. In general, he was correct. One of the rare exceptions occurred in 280 in Pontus on the southern shore of the Black Sea, where Probus had sent one of the bands of Franks.

It was about as far from their homeland as Rome could send them, and the Franks did not like it. They rebelled against their officers, seized some ships, and sailed to the Mediterranean, where they harried the coastlands of Greece, Sicily, and Spain. Then they passed through the Strait of Gibraltar and, following the coast of France, sailed north, coming ashore in Belgium or Holland, and from there made their way back to their own people. It was an epic voyage, made all the more impressive as the Franks had no tradition of seafaring.

This independent streak among some groups of Franks survived for centuries. As late as the time of Charlemagne, in the late eighth/early ninth centuries, there were still Franks who still lived as hunter-warriors, who had refused to convert to Christianity, and who refused to recognize Charlemagne's authority.

ROME'S LAST OUTPOST

The Ardennes Forest is a dense, dark, gloomy place, but Clovis, the twenty-one-year-old king of the Franks, did not let the rough, disagreeable landscape impede him. Urging on his army of 6,000 men, he covered the distance of about 120 miles in a few days.

When the Franks surged out of the woods, the Roman garrison of Soissons was taken completely by surprise. Syagrius, "the King of the Romans," as some called him, tried to put his troops into battle formation, but the fright and disorder among the legionnaires was too pervasive—only a few Roman soldiers took up their positions and prepared to repulse the barbarians. In a short time, perhaps less than an hour, the Romans threw down their weapons and ran.

As the Franks cut his army to pieces, Syagrius spurred his horse and galloped away toward Toulouse, the court of Alaric II, the king of the Goths. Clovis sent a messenger after him informing Alaric that if he did not surrender Syagrius at once, Clovis would make war on the Goths. Alaric complied with Clovis's demand immediately; in his defense, the king was only ten years old. The Franks took Syagrius to a prison in Soissons where Clovis had him executed in secret.

The Kingdom of Soissons, as it was called, was unique in western Europe. The "realm" extended from Burgundy in eastern France up to the English Channel, covering the land between the Seine and Somme rivers. It included such important cities as Orleans, Rheims, and Paris. By the year 450, this area was the last bit of Roman territory in Gaul—everything else had been seized by various barbarian nations. As the last Roman outpost, the kingdom preserved Roman culture, the Roman administrative system, and Catholic Christianity.

At this time the ruler was Aegidius, a Gallo-Roman patrician whom Aetius (the Roman commander who defeated Attila at the Battle of Chalons) appointed *Magister militum*, Master of the Soldiers, for what remained of Roman Gaul. By 457, Aegidius's authority did not extend beyond the Kingdom of Soissons. To strengthen his own position, Aegidius allied himself with Childeric I, the king of the Franks who lived in and around the cities of Tournai in Belgium and Cambrai in France. With the help of the Franks, Aegidius succeeded in repelling an invasion of Goths. Aegidius died in 464 and was succeeded by his son, Syagrius. Childeric died in 481 and was succeeded by his son, sixteen-year-old Clovis.

A YOUNG AND AMBITIOUS RULER

By this time, all the Roman provinces of western Europe were in barbarian hands: the Angles and Saxons held Britain, the Goths held Spain, and various Gothic and Frankish war-bands had divvied up Gaul among themselves. Only Soissons still regarded itself as part of the Roman Empire.

Though only a teenager, Clovis had higher ambitions than ruling over a slice of southern Belgium and northern France—he wanted to be king over every bit of Gaul. His surprise attack on Soissons and his execution of Syagrius was the first step in his plan to become sole king of the territory we know as France, Belgium, and Rhineland Germany.

Physically, the Franks were indistinguishable from the other Germanic tribes. They tended to be taller than the Romans and, they liked to believe, more muscular. Frankish young men and women were encouraged to refrain from any sexual contact until they were married; by not wasting their vitality in random sexual encounters, the Franks believed, the women would grow more robust and the men would grow stronger.

Blond and red were the two dominant hair colors among the Franks. The men wore their hair very long, in two thick braids. They also groomed their moustaches to drop well below the jaw line. When a Frankish warrior prepared for battle, he wore chain mail over which he slipped a short, sleeveless fur tunic. From his belt dangled a battle axe, a dagger, and a double-edged sword. In one hand he carried a lance, and on his other arm he bore a shield that usually had a sharp-pointed boss in the center. With 6,000 such men, Clovis intended to conquer a kingdom.

CLOTHILDE'S GOD

The Frankish lines were wavering. In spite of an early advantage in the battle, the Alamanni had launched an aggressive counterassault. As Clovis watched, his army began to give way. At this critical moment the king raised his eyes to heaven and invoked the help of Christ, although he did not believe in the Chistian God.

"I have called upon my gods," he said, "but they are far from helping me. If you will grant me victory over my foes … then I will believe in you, and will be baptized in your name." As Clovis prayed, the Franks rallied against the Alamanni, made their own counterassault, and sent the enemy running from the battlefield. The place of the battle was Tolbiac—probably Zuelpich on the German/Belgian border—and the date was 496.

Three years earlier, Clovis had married a Burgundian princess named Clothilde, eighteen years old. Clovis did nothing to prevent his devoutly Catholic queen from practicing her faith. Clothilde, on the other hand, looked

IN RECOGNITION OF HER PROFOUND FAITH AND THE ROLE SHE PLAYED IN BRINGING ABOUT THE CONVERSION OF HER HUSBAND, THE CATHOLIC CHURCH HONORS CLOVIS' QUEEN CLOTHILDE AS A SAINT.

for any opportunity to try to persuade Clovis to convert. When she became pregnant, she pleaded with her husband to let her have their son baptized. Clovis agreed, but to the grief of both parents the boy died almost immediately after the baptismal rite.

"If the boy had been dedicated in the name of my gods," a bitter Clovis said, "he would certainly have lived; but as it is, since he was baptized in the name of your God, he could not live at all."

In 495, Clothilde gave birth again, to another son, and once again she prevailed upon Clovis to let the boy be baptized. He gave in, but then the infant fell ill soon after the ceremony. Angry and afraid that he was about to lose another child, Clovis lashed out at his wife. Just as anxious and grief-stricken as her husband, Clothilde prayed for a miracle, and her son was cured.

Clovis did not understand the god Clothilde worshipped, but he respected power, and the sudden restoration of his infant son proved to him that Christ had power and sometimes exercised it. That may be the reason Clovis turned to Christ for help on the battlefield at Tolbiac. Inspired by their king, or perhaps commanded by him to do so, 3,000 of Clovis's most important officers and warriors converted to Christianity, too. In the years that followed, virtually the entire Frankish nation in Gaul embraced the Catholic faith.

By accepting Catholicism, Clovis broke down a significant barrier that had kept the Franks and the Gallo-Romans in separate camps. Now the ruling Frankish party shared the same religious point of view as the Gallo-Roman population, which encouraged a closer cooperation between the two ethnic groups, and more important, intermarriage. It can be said that after Clovis and his war band stepped out of the baptismal font, the French nation was born.

A KING IN THE ROMAN TRADITION

Meanwhile, Clovis resumed his conquest of the patchwork of barbarian principalities in Gaul. By 507, he had subdued the Alamanni, Clothilde's people the Burgundians, and the Goths. In recognition of his victories and his status as a Catholic king, Emperor Anastasius sent envoys from Constantinople granting Clovis the title of honorary consul and effectively adopting him into the imperial family.

Clovis went at once to the holiest place in Gaul—the Basilica of St. Martin in Tours, where he had himself invested with the purple tunic of an emperor and had a Roman military cloak draped over his shoulders. With his own hands he placed a crown on his head; then he displayed himself to his people, decked out as a king in the Roman tradition.

ELIMINATING RIVALS AND KINSMEN

In 507, Sigibert, Frankish king of Cologne, rode out of his city, crossed the Rhine, and in a quiet clearing in the woods had his attendants set up his pavilion. After he had had something to eat and drink, the king lay down on his couch and fell asleep. And as he slept, assassins, sent by his own son Cloderic, crept into the tent and murdered the helpless king.

A FIFTEENTH-CENTRUY MANUSCRIPT ILLUSTRATION DEPICTS THE FOUR SONS OF CLOVIS WHO DIVIDED UP THE KINGDOM AFTER THEIR FATHER'S DEATH IN 511.

It was a vicious crime, but it had not been Cloderic's idea. Clovis had incited the prince to kill his father and seize the power and the wealth now, while he was young enough to enjoy them. After the murder, Cloderic sent a joyful message back to Clovis, "My father is dead, and I have his treasures in my possession, and also his kingdom," he wrote. "Send men to me, and I shall gladly transmit to you from his treasures whatever pleases you."

When Clovis's men arrived in Cologne, Cloderic gave them a tour of old king Sigibert's treasure room. Pointing to one box in particular, Cloderic said, "It was in this little chest that my father used to put his gold coins." Clovis's men asked the new king to show them. As he bent over the chest to reveal its contents, one of the Franks lifted a battle axe and split Cloderic's skull.

Sigibert and Cloderic were the first victims of Clovis's consolidation of power. Now that he had triumphed over his barbarian rivals in Gaul, he set about eliminating potential rivals among his own people. He ambushed and executed the Frankish chieftain, Chararic, and his son. He captured Ragnachar, king of Cambrai, and his brother Ricchar, who were members of Clovis's family.

When the two men were brought before the king with their hands tied behind their backs, Clovis scowled. "Why have you humiliated our family in permitting yourself to be bound?" he asked Ragnachar. "It would have been better for you to die." Then he lifted a battle axe and killed his kinsman himself. Turning on Ricchar he said, "If you had aided your brother, he would not have been bound." Then he killed him, too. By this ruthless policy Clovis ensured that no one would threaten his throne.

St. Gregory of Tours, who recorded all these events in his *History of the Franks*, tells us that at the end of his life, after he had killed off his one-time allies and his relatives, Clovis feigned grief at being all alone. "Woe to me, who have remained as a stranger among foreigners," he said, "and have none of my kinsmen to give me aid if adversity comes."

THE FIRST VIKING INVASION OF ENGLAND: THE SACK OF LINDISFARNE ABBEY

THE LEGACY OF THE VIKINGS IN ENGLAND IS DESTRUCTION. Libraries burned. Rare works of art looted and lost forever. Towns and villages wiped off the landscape. Lives destroyed. And the future of England—the nation that has had an immeasurable impact on the world's ideas about civil rights, representational government, and personal freedom— placed in severe jeopardy.

Some historians have tried to find positive contributions that the Vikings brought to England. But aside from teaching the English a better method of shipbuilding and adding Scandinavian words such as "skate" and "skiff" and "anger" and "muck" to the English language, and giving Scandinavian names to about 1,400 locations in England (places ending in -by, -thorpe, -toft, and -thwaite were originally Viking settlements, while places ending in -town, -borough, and -field were originally English settlements), Viking influence in England was almost nil. With one exception: By annihilating six of the seven English royal families, the Vikings inadvertently transformed the country from a patchwork of little kingdoms into a single realm under one king. And once England was unified, it became a political and cultural powerhouse.

The reason for the Vikings' failure to leave a major, long-lasting impact on English society is a simple one: The English and the Vikings were both of Germanic stock. If a Viking who spoke Old Norse met an Englishman who spoke Old English, they could understand the gist of what each was saying. And although the Vikings were pagans and the English were Catholics, they

TIMELINE

787: ENGLAND IS DIVIDED INTO SEVEN SMALL KINGDOMS, EACH RULED BY ITS OWN KING.

789: THE VIKINGS ATTACK THE ISLE OF PORTLAND IN THE ENGLISH CHANNEL AND KILL AN OFFICIAL FROM DORCHESTER MANOR. THIS IS THE FIRST VIKING ATTACK IN THE BRITISH ISLES.

JUNE 8, 793: VIKING RAIDERS ATTACK THE MONASTERY OF ST. CUTHBERT ON THE ISLAND OF LINDISFARNE, SCOTLAND.

794: JARROW ABBEY IN NORTHERN ENGLAND AND SCOTLAND'S ISLE OF SKYE FALL VICTIM TO THE VIKINGS.

806: VIKINGS STRIKE IONA OFF THE WESTERN COAST OF SCOTLAND, DRAGGING SIXTY-EIGHT MONKS TO THE BEACH AND SLAUGHTERING THEM ALL. THE SITE OF THE MASSACRE IS KNOWN AS MARTYRS' BAY.

---

shared many similar ideas—for example, that a man ought to serve a chief who was generous, noble, and successful in battle.

Consequently, once the Vikings and the English intermarried, and especially once the Vikings began to convert to Christianity, their assimilation into English society was virtually painless. But that integration came decades after the first Viking raid in England. Between 793 and 865, the Vikings were marauders who brought nothing but pain and anguish to the people of England.

Most of the Viking raiders came from the lands we know as Denmark and Norway. The term "Viking" is derived from the Old Norse word for "raider" or "pirate." Since this chapter and the ones that follow focus on raids and invasions in general, we will refer to these raiders and invaders as Vikings.

The Christians of Europe who were on the receiving end of the Viking attacks used a variety of names for the invaders. The English tended to call all Vikings "Danes," although there were plenty of warriors from Norway who invaded England. "Northmen" or "Norsemen" was another common term for Vikings and is the root word of Normandy, the northern French province where many Vikings settled. These settlers, by the way, the French called "Normans." They were also known as "heathen men from the north," or more simply, "heathens."

TIMELINE

832: SHEPPEY ISLAND AT THE MOUTH OF THE RIVER THAMES IS OVERRUN BY VIKINGS.

833: AT CHARNOUTH IN DORSETSHIRE, THE ARMY LED BY KING EGBERT OF WESSEX IS DEFEATED BY A VIKING ARMY.

839: LONDON, CANTERBURY, AND ROCHESTER ARE ALL SACKED AND BURNED BY THE VIKINGS.

851: THE VIKINGS MOUNT A FULL-SCALE INVASION OF ENGLAND,

ANCHORING 350 OF THEIR DRAGON SHIPS IN THE MOUTH OF THE THAMES. WHEN COLD WEATHER COMES, THEY DO NOT RETURN TO SCANDINAVIA BUT SETTLE INSTEAD ON THE ISLE OF THANET IN SOUTHEASTERN ENGLAND.

NOVEMBER 21, 866: SEVERAL THOUSAND VIKINGS LED BY THREE BROTHERS——IVAR THE BONELESS, HALFDAN, AND UBBE——CONQUER THE CITY OF YORK.

870: IVAR CAPTURES AND TORTURES TO DEATH KING EDMUND OF EAST ANGLIA. ALL OF ENGLAND IS OCCUPIED BY THE VIKINGS EXCEPT THE KINGDOM OF WESSEX IN THE SOUTHWEST.

THE FIRST SKIRMISH

The anonymous monk who kept the *Anglo-Saxon Chronicle* wrote in his entry for June 8, 793:

> The pagans from the northern regions came with a naval force to Britain like stinging hornets and spread on all sides like fearful wolves, robbed, tore and slaughtered… priests and deacons, and companies of monks and nuns. And they came to the church of Lindisfarne, laid everything waste with grievous plundering, trampled the holy places with polluted steps, dug up the altars and seized all the treasures of the holy church. They killed some of the brothers, took some away with them in fetters, many they drove out, naked and loaded with insults, some they drowned in the sea.

Many histories of this era declare that the Viking invasions of England began with the brutal attack on the monks at Lindisfarne. In fact, the first incident actually occurred four years earlier at the harbor of Portland in Dorset on England's southern coast. The reeve—the official who managed the local lord's estates—saw three foreign ships in the harbor and men wading ashore.

Thinking they were traders, he rode down to direct them to the lord's manor at Dorchester, where they could receive permission to conduct business in the neighborhood. But before the reeve could speak, the "traders" let fly a volley of arrows, killing him instantly.

This skirmish, though significant as the first encounter between Vikings and English, was overlooked even in the eighth century because it paled in comparison to the massacre of the monks and the destruction of the shrine of St. Cuthbert at Lindisfarne.

THE SLAUGHTER OF CUTHBERT'S MONKS

Lindisfarne Island is not much to look at—about three miles of scrubby land-scape off the coast of northern England, about nine miles south of the Scottish border. Yet for the English this was a place of great sanctity, the cradle of many saints—most famously St. Cuthbert, one of the most beloved figures in the history of the Church in England.

In life Cuthbert had been as renowned for his personal charm as for his personal holiness. He possessed a gentle, persuasive manner that could reconcile the most bitter enemies and bring even hardened sinners back to God. Cuthbert spent twenty-three years at Lindisfarne, first as prior and then as bishop.

After his death, a host of miracles were attributed to his intercession, which ensured St. Cuthbert's continuing popularity and made his tomb in Lindisfarne's monastery church a goal for pilgrims. Consequently, the slaughter of Cuthbert's monks and the ruination of his shrine shocked the English. Writing from the court of Charlemagne, where he ran the emperor's palace school, the English monk Alcuin asked the bishop of Lindisfarne (who somehow survived the raid), "What assurance is there for the churches of Britain if St. Cuthbert, with so great a number of saints, defends not his own?"

"A SWORD AGE, A WIND AGE, A WOLF AGE"

In recent years, it has been popular among historians to rehabilitate the Vikings, emphasizing their genius as shipbuilders and navigators, their impor-tance as the founders of Irish cities such as Dublin and Waterford, their courage as explorers who sailed as far as North America, their contribution to opening up Europe to trade with Asia and the Islamic world. All of this is true.

VIKING DRAGON SHIPS

The Vikings called their longships *drekar*, meaning dragon-headed ships. About one hundred feet long and twenty feet wide, these ships could carry between sixty and eighty men, in addition to weapons and supplies. Viking ships were sleek and fast, fitted out with a large sail as well as banks of oars. But it was the shallow draft of the dragon ships that gave the Vikings a tactical advantage. Unlike larger, heavier vessels that required a harbor, Viking ships could be beached on almost any shoreline or riverbank for lightning-fast raids on neighboring towns, estates, and monasteries.

The secret of the dragon ships was their singular design. Scandinavian shipwrights nailed long, thin planks of oak to a sturdy keel—the main structural element of the ship that stretches along the bottom from the bow at the front to the stern at the rear. After the first planks had been nailed to the keel, subsequent planks were affixed to one another following the clinker method, which means they overlapped. The heaviest part of the ship was the beam, which was affixed to the keel to support the mast. Viking seafarers steered their ships using a single rudder on the right or starboard side of the ship.

Modern-day mariners who have sailed reproductions of Viking ships have found that the ships are not only easy to maneuver, but also fast—a reproduction of a dragon ship such as the Vikings would have used to raid Lindisfarne has been clocked at 14 knots, or about 17 miles per hour.

THIS ELABORATELY CARVED DRAGON HEAD PROW IS TYPICAL OF THE TYPE OF FIGUREHEAD THE VIKINGS MOUNTED ON THEIR LONG SHIPS.

But the Vikings who came ashore at Portland and Lindisfarne were not explorers or merchants or the founders of cities—they were pirates. They came to loot and pillage and enslave, and they killed anyone who got in their way or tried to resist them. Just as there is no denying the Vikings' contributions, it would be a distortion of the historical record to downplay the bloodshed and destruction they wrought on the people of the British Isles and western Europe.

As if they were acting out lines from their own vision of doomsday, the Vikings brought to Christian Europe "a sword age, a wind age, a wolf age. No longer is there mercy among men."

RIPE FOR PLUNDERING

England at the end of the eighth century was a rich prize. While its neighbors, the Welsh and the Scots, were still largely a pastoral people tending herds of cattle and flocks of sheep, living in tribal societies, and employing a barter economy, the English had made the shift to large-scale agriculture and a money-based economy. English farmers produced so much grain that it was possible to stockpile the surplus, which made life in England more secure. The English had also begun to mint gold and silver coins, which made English merchants players in international trade.

Politically, however, England was not at all progressive. The land was divided among seven kingdoms, four major and three minor. The major kingdoms were Northumbria, which extended from the Humber River north along the eastern side of Britain to Edinburgh; Mercia, which controlled almost the entire central portion of the island, from the Welsh border to the North Sea; East Anglia, a boggy territory along England's eastern shore; and Wessex, which included all of southwestern England, including Cornwall.

The three petty kingdoms were Essex, whose greatest city was London; Kent, the region around Canterbury; and Sussex, on the English Channel. Although there were skirmishes among the seven kingdoms, the land, generally speaking, was at peace. And peace permitted the development of the arts, religious life, and education.

From the late seventh century through the eighth century, England's northernmost realm enjoyed a tremendous flourishing in painting, sculpture, architecture, and metalwork that art historians call the Northumbrian Renaissance. It

AN ANONYMOUS MONK KISSES THE FOOT OF ST. CUTHBERT, FAMOUS IN LIFE FOR HIS GENTLE DISPOSITION AND AFTER HIS DEATH FOR HIS MIRACLES.

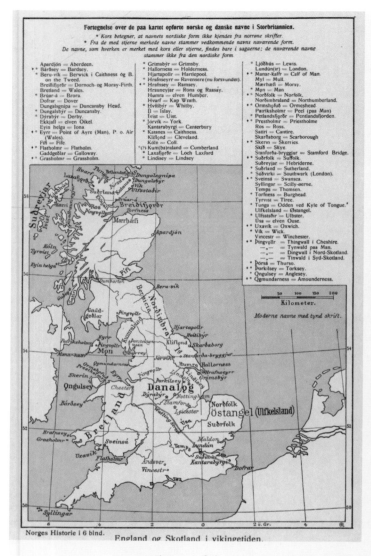

was during this period that some of the most glorious illuminated manuscripts were produced—the Lindisfarne Gospels, the Book of Durrow, and the Book of Kells.

At abbeys and cathedrals around the country, monks opened schools where boys and young men studied history, science, and poetry as well as theology. The English schools enjoyed such a sterling reputation that when Charlemagne decided to open a school at his palace in Aachen, he recruited his teachers from England.

The eighth century was also a period of profound religious devotion, when the lives of monks and nuns were held in high esteem by all classes of English society. This religious devotion, combined with new wealth and a flowering of the arts, expressed itself in lavish gifts to churches, monasteries, and convents. Gospel books received golden covers. Shrines of the saints were plated with silver and studded with precious stones. Bishops presided at Mass holding crosiers of intricately carved ivory. For the Christians of England, these sumptuous displays demonstrated their love for God, His saints, and the Church; it never occurred to them that their generosity would attract the attention of pagans from the northernmost regions of Europe.

Ironically, it was English Christians who suggested—inadvertently—that England was ripe for Viking raids. English merchants, their purses fat with freshly minted gold and silver coins, had begun traveling to Scandinavian ports to purchase furs, walrus ivory, amber, and other valuable commodities that they could sell back home. As they traded, the merchants gossiped about the wealth of their towns, or

A SCANDINAVIAN MAP SHOWS THE EASTERN HALF OF ENGLAND, LABELED "DANALOG," OR DANELAW, WHICH THE VIKINGS CONQUERED AND OCCUPIED.

the treasures in their churches, or the troubles their king was having with his unruly sons or jealous nobles. The Scandinavians listened to these stories with interest.

In Scandinavian society, raiding an enemy's farm or sacking a foreign town was a regular part of life. It introduced teenage boys to the warrior culture, gave men who spent most of the year farming and fishing a taste of adventure, and increased the wealth and reputation of the chieftain who led the raid. Stirred up by the English traders' tales of great wealth "guarded" only by unarmed monks and helpless nuns, the Vikings readied their longships for their farthest raiding voyage yet.

THE END OF IONA

The attack on Lindisfarne in 793 was just the beginning of nearly 300 years of Viking attacks on the British Isles. In 794, the Vikings looted Jarrow Abbey and the Isle of Skye; in 795, they made their first raid on Iona Abbey off the western coast of Scotland.

A center of Celtic scholarship and culture, as well as the site of the shrine of St. Columba, Iona proved to be such a rich target that the Vikings returned again and again. In 806, after looting the church and chapels, the Vikings dragged almost the entire community of Iona—68 monks—down to the seashore and slaughtered them all. Ever since, the spot has been known as Martyrs' Bay. After that massacre in 806, the surviving monks were unwilling to refound their abbey and expose themselves yet again to the fury of the Vikings; they packed up what remained of their possessions and sailed to Ireland.

By 825, however, once again there was a small monastic community on Iona. When rumors reached the island that the Vikings were raiding in the area again, most of the monks fled, taking the relics of St. Columba with them. A handful of monks, along with their abbot, St. Blathmac, refused to go. One morning, not long after the main body of the monastic community had run off, the monks heard the dreadful sound of dragon ships skidding up on the sandy beach, followed by the fierce cries of a Viking raiding party as they leapt ashore. The raiders headed straight for the church where Blathmac was at the altar saying Mass, attended by the remaining monks. The monks the Vikings killed outright. Then, advancing on the abbot, they demanded that he reveal to them the hiding place of the treasures from St. Columba's shrine. Blathmac refused. Raising their swords and axes, the Vikings hacked off St. Blathmac's limbs on the altar steps.

Initially, Viking raids on England were hit-and-run affairs, but after the final attack on Iona in 825, they became more daring. In 832, they overran Sheppey Island; in 833, they destroyed King Egbert's army at Charnouth; in 837, they landed again at Portland harbor, where they scattered an army of Wessex men; in 838, the Vikings ravaged East Anglia and Kent; in 839, they sacked and burned London, Canterbury, and Rochester; in 840, they met the English again at Charnoth and once again defeated them.

Then came 851, when the Vikings mounted a full-scale invasion of England with 350 dragon ships anchored in the mouth of the Thames. From there the raiders from the north sacked London and Canterbury again. Then, rather than return home for the winter as had been their custom, the Vikings settled down for the season on the isle of Thanet.

THE DEATH OF TWO KINGS

The English were not cowards. Time and again, English kings put armies in the field against the Vikings, and sometimes they won. If, from 793 until 851, there were not nearly as many pitched battles between Englishmen and Vikings as one would expect, it is because the Vikings' tactic of "smash, grab, and run back to the ship" enabled them to get safely out to sea long before the local militia could be called up to defend a monastery or town.

Formal battles became common after the invasion of 851, when the Viking strategy shifted from lightning raids to complete conquest that included picking off, one by one, the kingdoms of England (by 851 there were only four kingdoms left: Mercia had absorbed little Essex, and Wessex had gobbled up Sussex and Kent).

Northumbria became the first English kingdom to fall to the Vikings. In late summer 866, a force of several thousand Danes (the English called it "the Great Heathen Army") under the command of Ivar the Boneless and his brothers Halfdan and Ubbe, swarmed into Northumbria. On November 21 they conquered York, the greatest city in the region. Finding the city comfortable and well-fortified, the Vikings decided to remain there for the winter.

In March 867, Ælla, the king of Northumbria, tried to retake York from the Vikings. His assault failed, and the English historians from this period say that Ælla died in battle. The Viking version claims that Ælla was captured alive

THE VIKINGS' SECRET WEAPON

There is a longstanding impression that Viking warriors were tall, blond, and powerfully built, and at least two sources confirm that description.

The German *Annals of Fulda* records that after a battle between the Franks and the Vikings in Saxony, the Franks examined Viking corpses and marveled over "their beauty and the size of their bodies." In 921, an Arab ambassador, Ahmad Ibn Fadlan, stayed for a time among the Swedes and Danes who lived in what is now the Ukraine. He too was impressed by the appearance of the Vikings. Writing in his travelogue, *A Risala*, Ibn Fadlan said, "I have never seen more perfect physical specimens, tall as date palms, blond and ruddy."

Archaeological evidence collected from Viking graves suggests that on average Scandinavians tended to stand five feet eight inches tall—about two to three inches taller than the average Englishman, Frank, or Arab. Furthermore, it was not unusual for Scandinavian nobles and high caste warriors—men who would have had access to a better diet— to be six feet tall. The warrior culture in England, however, was as strong as it was in Scandinavia; a foe who stood a couple inches taller would not have intimidated an experienced English fighting man.

What did scare the English, however, were a group of fighters unique to Scandinavia known as berserkers.

Every society has its military elites—from Achilles' Myrmidons to today's Navy Seals—but the berserkers were not in that class of highly trained, highly disciplined fighting men. They were an out-of-control gang possessed by a kind of battle rage that made them absolutely fearless in the face of the enemy, reckless with their own lives, and capable of inhuman acts of violence.

The Icelandic epic *Egils Saga* tells of a duel between two berserkers. One of the combatants, a man named Egill Skallagrimsson, won the contest by hurling himself against his enemy and tearing out his jugular with his teeth. The *Haraldskvaethi*, a ninth-century poem about the Norwegian king Harald Fairhair, tells how in battle the king always held back his band of berserkers until they were in a state of total frenzy and thirsting for blood—the state at which they would wreak the most damage on the enemy. Yet another saga says that when berserkers charged into battle they "were as mad as dogs or wolves," biting their own shields, killing men with a single devastating blow, but insensible to almost any wound they might receive.

ARCHAEOLOGICAL EVIDENCE SUGGESTS THAT THE VIKINGS WERE TALLER AND LARGER THAN THE ENGLISH.

In searching for the cause of the berserkers' behavior, researchers have suggested everything from hallucinogenic mushrooms to bipolar disorder, but none of these studies have provided a satisfactory, conclusive answer to the maniacal behavior of the berserkers on the battlefield.

STRANGELY UPHOLSTERED CHURCH DOORS

Certainly the English people must have longed for revenge against the Vikings, and according to a story that has been current in southeastern England for centuries, on at least one occasion they got their chance.

They captured a Viking raider who had lingered too long looting the village church. The villagers stripped him naked, strung him up in the churchyard, and flayed him alive. Then they nailed his hide to the church door. Several towns in Essex tell this story, but it is also said that the doors of Worcester Cathedral and even of Westminster Abbey in London were once upholstered with Viking hides.

Although it sounds like a medieval urban legend, several local museums in England claim to possess fragments of these Viking skins. To date only one has been tested—a bit of dried-up epidermis collected from the door of St. Botolph's Church in the village of Hadstock on the Essex/Cambridgeshire border. After examining the scrap researchers at a lab at Oxford University concluded that it was not human skin but ordinary cowhide.

---

and executed in an especially gruesome manner the Vikings called "the blood eagle": the executioner would have cut the king's rib bones away from his spine and splayed them outward, then reached into the cavity, pulled out Ælla's lungs and laid them on his back. The final heaving of the exposed lungs as the victim died were thought to resemble an eagle beating his wings.

In 870 the Great Heathen Army turned its attention to East Anglia, the realm of King Edmund. In 866 Edmund had tried to buy security for himself and his people by presenting the Vikings with a "gift" of hundreds of horses. It appeared initially that the bribe had worked; Ivar accepted the horses and left East Anglia virtually unscathed.

But then he came back, and in exchange for peace in East Anglia Ivar demanded Edmund's complete submission, even to the point of Edmund renouncing Christianity and serving the Scandinavian gods. Edmund, a pious man, rejected Ivar's proposal, gathered his army, and marched against the Vikings. Not only was the East Anglian army crushed, but Edmund was taken alive.

Ivar sentenced Edmund to a prolonged execution. He was beaten with clubs, then tied to a tree and whipped, then turned around and tied again so that he faced his tormenters. A band of Viking bowmen lined up opposite the tree and shot arrows into their prisoner, taking careful aim so none of their shots would be fatal. Finally, when "he was all beset with their shots, as with a porcupine's bristles," but still alive, Ivar had the dying Edmund decapitated.

Afterward, one of the Vikings threw the king's head deep into the forest so the Christians would not be able to bury an intact body. Once the Vikings had moved on, the men of East Anglia came to collect their king's mutilated corpse and even managed to find the head. According to legend, they heard a voice crying, "Here! Here!" Following the sound, they arrived in a thicket where a large gray wolf had Edmund's head between his paws: He had been protecting it from scavenging animals and birds until Christian men could find it.

Seeing what had befallen his fellow kings, Ælla and Edmund, King Burgred of Mercia did not wait for a final confrontation with the Vikings. He abdicated and fled to Rome, where he remained for the rest of his life.

In 870 the Vikings had conquered virtually the entire country; England appeared ready to collapse. The only English kingdom clinging to life was Wessex in the southeast where a 21-year-old king named Alfred had recently come to the throne. To the Vikings, he was just one last petty king to kill; to the English, Alfred was their last desperate hope.

THE LAST KING: ALFRED THE GREAT

I MAGINE A WORLD WITHOUT ENGLAND. NO MAGNA CARTA. No Shakespeare. No Winston Churchill. For about a decade in the late ninth century, such a thing was a very real possibility. The Vikings had swept over England, conquering three-quarters of the country; only Wessex in southern England withstood them, and the odds were excellent that Wessex would fall, too.

A preview of what a Viking England would look like could be seen in Mercia, Northumbria, and East Anglia, the territories already in Danish hands: Towns were smoking ruins; farms that hadn't been occupied by settlers from Scandinavia were desolate, their fields overgrown with weeds, scrubby brush, and saplings; the monasteries were stripped of their treasures, their precious manuscripts burned, shredded, and scattered to the winds, the monks slaughtered or shipped overseas to be sold as slaves.

As for the English people, many of them scratched out a life in marshes and other inaccessible corners of the country, or sought refuge in the hills of Wales. Those who were fortunate enough to scrape together the money for passage to the Continent.

Of all these sorrows, the Viking attacks on the monasteries were the most grievous. Yes, the monasteries were centers of Christian England's religious life, but they were also centers of English culture, civilization, and learning. The monks

UNDER ALFRED THE GREAT, THE VIKINGS WERE CONTAINED AND ENGLAND WAS UNITED UNDER A SINGLE KING.

TIMELINE

849: ALFRED THE GREAT IS BORN AT WANTAGE MANOR IN BERKSHIRE, ENGLAND.

APRIL 23, 871: ALFRED BECOMES KING OF WESSEX, SOUTHWEST ENGLAND.

872: ALFRED BUYS OFF THE VIKINGS. IN EXCHANGE FOR A LARGE SUM OF GOLD, THE VIKINGS PROMISE TO LEAVE WESSEX IN PEACE FOR 5 YEARS.

JANUARY 6, 878: THE VIKINGS MAKE A SURPRISE ATTACK ON THE ROYAL PALACE AT CHIPPENHAM IN WESSEX. ALFRED AND HIS FAMILY BARELY ESCAPE TO AETHELNEY IN THE MARSHES OF SOMERSET.

MAY 878: ALFRED RALLIES THE MILITIA OF SOMERSET, WILTSHIRE, AND WESTERN HAMPSHIRE AND ROUTS THE VIKINGS AT EDINGTON. IN THE TREATY OF WEDMORE, ALFRED AND GUTHRUM, THE VIKING CHIEF, DIVIDE THE KINGDOM INTO TWO REALMS—ENGLAND RULED BY ALFRED, AND THE DANELAW RULED BY THE VIKINGS.

---

produced works of art and music, and in their libraries preserved manuscripts of *Beowulf* as well as the gospels. They also maintained ties with other monasteries in continental Europe, thus keeping England apprised of intellectual and religious trends from as far away as Constantinople and Jerusalem.

Thanks to the Vikings' destruction of so many monasteries the literacy rate in England collapsed, and the country was in danger of entering a true cultural dark age. The man who kept that from happening was King Alfred of Wessex, and his success was so spectacular that he is the only monarch in English history known as "the Great."

THE SURPRISE ATTACK

The alarm came late at night, after the children were in bed asleep, after the food had been cleared from the tables in the banquet and the king, and queen, and their guests were lingering over the wine. A large force of Vikings were battering the gates of Chippenham and storming the defensive wall that surrounded the royal residence and the chapel. Alfred the king and his retainers must have run to the walls, while Ealhswith the queen and her ladies hurried to the nursery to calm and protect the children.

Alfred had grown up at Chippenham. Now that he was king it was one of his favorite residences, particularly for hunting, a sport which Alfred loved. From Chippenham he rode into Selwood Forest to chase the deer and hunt

TIMELINE

885: GUTHRUM BREAKS THE TREATY AND BESIEGES ROCHESTER. ALFRED DECLARES WAR.

886: ALFRED CAPTURES LONDON, ENDING A SEVENTEEN-YEAR-LONG VIKING OCCUPATION OF THE CITY. HE FORCES GUTHRUM TO ACCEPT A NEW TREATY AND BE BAPTIZED.

890: GUTHRUM DIES.

892: A VIKING FLEET FROM FRANCE COMMANDED BY HASTEIN INVADES KENT AND ESSEX.

893: ALFRED'S NAVY DESTROYS THE VIKING FLEET OFF THE COAST OF DEVON.

OCTOBER 26, 899: KING ALFRED DIES AT HIS PALACE IN WINCHESTER.

wild boar and wolves. In winter 878 Alfred and his family had chosen to spend the entire Christmas season at Chippenham. They had just celebrated the Feast of the Epiphany, the day that commemorates the arrival of the Magi in Bethlehem, and marks the official end of the twelve days of Christmas.

It is not known how many English troops were at Chippenham that night, but they were not enough to drive off the Vikings. Seeing that defense was hopeless, Alfred gathered his family and, with a handful of noblemen and warriors, mounted horses and escaped into the forests. It must have been a terrifying moment, galloping to no one knew where, in the middle of a frigid January night, to the sound of the clash of arms and the frantic clanging of the chapel bell at the manor. Riding with the king and queen, bundled in furs were the three royal children: Edward, age seven, and his sisters, six-year-old Ethelfled and four-year-old Elfrida.

As the last independent king in England, Alfred was a natural target for the Vikings. The Danes had tortured to death Ælla, king of Northumbria, and Edmund, king of East Anglia; Burgred, king of Mercia, had forsaken his crown and his people and fled to Rome.

All of England was in Viking hands except Alfred's kingdom of Wessex. For the first six years of his reign, the war with the Danes was inconclusive, with Alfred losing almost as many battles as he won. But in summer 877 Alfred had penned in the Danes at Exeter. When a storm off the Swanage Cliffs destroyed

THE DANES' SURPRISE ATTACK ON CHIPPENHAM WAS A CALCULATED ATTEMPT TO CAPTURE OR KILL THE ONLY ENGLISH KING WHO STILL STOOD IN THE WAY OF TOTAL VIKING DOMINATION OVER ENGLAND.

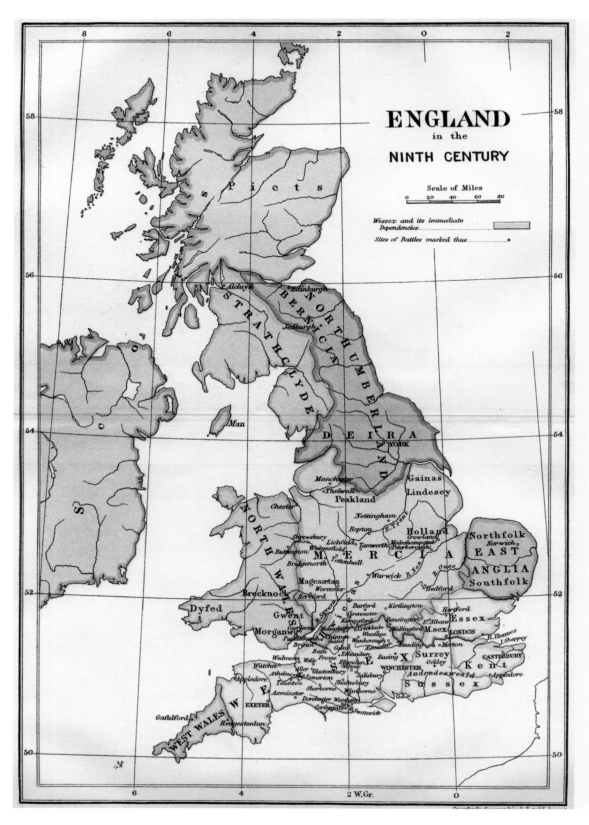

ENGLAND
in the
NINTH CENTURY

Scale of Miles

Wessex and its immediate Dependencies..........

Sites of Battles marked thus..........+

AN UNPRECEDENTED CONQUEST

In the 870s, the Vikings had a stranglehold on England. The evidence is not just in the chronicles; archaeologists have found evidence of the Vikings making themselves at home in England, with hints that they planned to destroy English Christian society and put a Norse pagan one in its place.

Some historians have read the lingering execution of King Edmund of East Anglia not as a martyrdom (as the English interpreted it) but as a sacrifice to the Viking god Odin. In London, in the churchyard of St. Paul's Cathedral archaeologists uncovered a Viking grave slab carved with an image of Sleipnir, Odin's eight-legged horse—could it be evidence that the Vikings were beginning to make Christian holy places their own?

We know that Vikings who wintered in England often made their homes in monasteries or churches, where the large open spaces with lofty ceilings resembled the great timber halls of Scandinavia. Such was the case during the winter of 873–874, when the Vikings, after slaughtering all the monks, moved into St. Wystan's monastery in Repton, Derbyshire. An excavation of St. Wystan's in the 1980s found in the church crypt the remains of many Vikings who died during an epidemic that raged through Repton that winter.

The Viking conquest of England was unprecedented. They had overrun the Orkneys and the Isle of Man, carved out territory along the Irish coast, and moved into Normandy after depopulating the province, but nowhere in western Europe had the Vikings subdued an entire country. Yet beginning with the invasion force that the English called "the Great Heathen Army," it was obvious that the days of sporadic Viking smash-and-grab raids were over and that the Norsemen's new strategy was to seize and colonize England. They brought their wives and their children over from Scandinavia; they built houses or moved into existing English buildings, and they tended the farms of the Englishmen they had just killed or driven off.

A quick glance at the map explains why the Vikings chose England. In terms of both trading and raiding, its location was ideal, putting the Vikings within easy striking distance of Ireland, Scotland, Wales, France, Flanders, and Frisia, only a few days sail from Denmark, and about equidistant from the Baltic and the Mediterranean. The dead of winter, 878, England teetered on the brink of becoming a satellite of Scandinavia.

THIS MAP SHOWS THE FOUR MAJOR KINGDOMS OF ENGLAND OF ALFRED'S DAY——NORTHUMBRIA, MERCIA, EAST ANGLIA, AND WESSEX.

a Viking fleet of 120 ships coming to the relief of the town, the Danes surrendered and withdrew from Wessex back into Mercia. Their surprise attack on Chippenham was a calculated attempt to capture or kill the only English king who still stood in the way of total Viking domination over England.

THE RETURN OF THE KING

Alfred, his family, and a handful of noblemen and warriors fled to the Isle of Aethelney, an oasis of high ground in the marshes of Somerset where, as Bishop Asser, Alfred's friend and biographer put it, they led "a restless life in great distress."

As Alfred and his tiny band of followers clung to life, camping out in midwinter in a swamp, the Vikings completely overran Wessex. With all of England now in Viking hands, it must have seemed like the end of the world. No wonder so many English fled to the Continent.

As a hiding place, Aethelney was ideal. It lay surrounded by deep pools of water, behind thick stands of reeds and tall alder trees. Here Alfred and his men built a fort for security and a causeway so they could find their way through the marsh. It must have been an uncomfortable, primitive life, but there was plenty of food—fish and wild game were plentiful, and on other islands of high ground were isolated farms where Alfred's people could buy or barter with the peasants for bread, milk, and eggs. It's not certain, but from his hidden base Alfred may have led a few guerrilla raids on the Vikings.

Two of the best-known stories about Alfred are set during the Aethelney period. Before leading the men of Wessex against the Vikings, the king entered their camp disguised as a minstrel, and between his songs picked up valuable intelligence.

Better known is the story of Alfred and the cakes. He had just come to Aethelney and begged for shelter in the hut of a poor family. The woman of the house made what in America would be called small loaves of bread (known as "cakes" in England) and set them on the hearthstone to bake. Before she went off to do another task, she told Alfred, who was sitting by the fire cleaning his bow and arrows, to watch the cakes so they wouldn't burn. After the woman left the hut, the king became so absorbed in thought about the disaster that had overtaken him and what he could do to reclaim his kingdom that he forgot to mind the baking. When the woman returned, the room was full of acrid smoke and the cakes were black.

AN ANGRY HOUSEWIFE SCOLDS A DISTRACTED KING ALFRED FOR WORRYING ABOUT HIS TROUBLES WITH THE VIKINGS AND LETTING HER CAKES BURN.

"Quick enough, I warrant, you are to eat them, good and hot," she shouted at the distracted king, "you who do not move to keep my cakes from ruin by the fire!" Both stories were written down about 200 years later. No one knows whether they are true; they may be examples of oral history.

ALFRED'S TERMS FOR PEACE

Around Easter, which came at the end of the March in 878, the king sent messengers to the fyrd, the local militia, in Somerset, Wiltshire, and western Hampshire—the parts of Wessex where Viking control was weakest—commanding them to meet him the first week of May at a landmark in Selwood Forest known as Edgar's Stone. The men who gathered around the stone were astonished to see their king still alive. When he announced that the next day they would march on the Vikings, their astonishment turned to elation.

At Edington, near Chippenham, the house that the Vikings had forced Alfred to abandon five months earlier, the English took their position opposite the Viking camp. The Vikings here were under the command of Guthrum, a chieftain who came to England with the Great Heathen Army in 871. In 872, he conquered Mercia; in 875, he sacked Cambridge; and his systematic attacks on Wessex had culminated in the surprise attack on Alfred's own house.

"Fighting fiercely with a compact shield wall," as Asser describes it, the English broke the Viking ranks. The place they ran to was the fortified royal manor of Chippenham—Alfred's own home, now the Vikings' stronghold in Wessex. But the English pursued the Danes, killing many of them along the way. As the terrified Vikings stumbled through the gates, the English rounded up the horses and cattle that the Vikings had pastured outside the walls.

For two weeks Alfred besieged Chippenham. When the food inside the manor ran out, Guthrum and the rest of the survivors surrendered—on Alfred's terms. In a document known as the Treaty of Wedmore, Alfred and Guthrum agreed on their respective spheres of influence in England. They drew a diagonal line from the Mersey in the west to Maldon in Essex in the east. The division followed, roughly, Watling Street—the English name for the ancient Roman road that ran across England. Alfred's territory was all of southern England, or Wessex, and about half of central England, or Mercia. This territory included two important cities: Winchester, Alfred's capital, and Canterbury, the heart of the Church in England. At a later date, Alfred also acquired London. Guthrum's territory included East Anglia, Northumbria, and the rest of Mercia. This area became known as the Danelaw.

The division of England was only part of the treaty, however. Alfred demanded that Guthrum demobilize his army, and then, with thirty of his leading men, convert to Christianity. Dutifully, Guthrum went through the motions of becoming a Christian, taking the name Aethelstan at his baptism, with Alfred acting as his godfather.

THE ACID TEST

The treaty with Guthrum gave Alfred the breathing space he needed to fortify and revitalize Wessex. As the last outpost of independent England, it was essential for Wessex to have an efficient military.

Throughout his realm, Alfred built strongholds known in Anglo-Saxon as burhs (the origin of the modern English word "borough"). Each held a garrison of about 160 men, plus an undetermined number of servants to do all the cooking, cleaning, and tending of horses. Traditionally the English army moved on foot, but Alfred realized that given the speed with which the Vikings struck English targets, the English must be able to respond quickly, too. The burh garrisons, therefore, were all cavalrymen. For the same reason, the king established his burhs in close proximity—none was more than 20 miles away from another.

IN 886 GUTHRUM, THE CHIEF VIKING WAR LORD IN ENGLAND, CONCEDED DEFEAT AND MADE A COMPLETE SUBMISSION TO ALFRED.

The expense of maintaining the burhs fell upon the local lords, even if that lord was a bishop. (High churchmen had always insisted that they ought to be exempted from such obligations, but in times of crisis English kings compelled the bishops to assume their share of the cost of defending the realm.)

Alfred also reorganized Wessex's army, keeping half of the men on duty at any given time. And although Alfred is famous as the father of the English Navy, kings before Alfred had used war ships. Nonetheless, recognizing that swift ships were just one more advantage the Vikings held over the English, Alfred brought over from Frisia (modern-day Holland) skilled shipwrights to build his new navy.

Responding to the sad state of religious and intellectual life in England, Alfred refounded ruined abbeys and convents, brought over learned monks from France to reestablish schools, and set the example for the revival of literacy in the land by personally translating religious and secular books from Latin into English.

Guthrum gave Alfred seven years to rebuild his kingdom, but then the double-dealing Viking broke the treaty and invaded Wessex in 885 and laid siege to Rochester. But Alfred's new military defensive measures worked. Mobilizing his standing army, his burh garrisons, and his navy, he broke the Danish siege easily, then sent his fleet up the River Thames to capture London.

In 886, after seventeen years of occupation under the Vikings, London was in English hands again. Alfred pressed his advantage by requiring, in a new treaty with Guthrum, that English Christians under Viking rule in the Danelaw enjoy the same legal protections as the settlers from Scandinavia; beaten and humiliated, Guthrum agreed. Four years later, Guthrum, apparently without giving Alfred any more trouble, died in Hadleigh.

ALFRED'S RENAISSANCE

In spite of Guthrum's defeat and death, the Vikings continued to mount sporadic raids on Alfred's territory. But a serious invasion with eighty ships was mounted from France in 892, led by a Viking chief named Hastein who had been terrorizing the inhabitants of the Loire Valley. He ordered part of his force to disembark in Kent, then beached his ships at Benfleet in Essex. Danes from East Anglia and York joined Hastein's army, but once again Alfred's mili-

PREVIOUS PAGE:
WITH HIS NEW NAVY
OF SHIPS BUILT IN THE
DANISH STYLE, ALFRED
WAS ABLE TO FIGHT THE
VIKINGS ON THEIR TERMS
AND DEFEAT THEM.

tary proved its worth. The infantry harried the Vikings, while Alfred's navy destroyed many of Hastein's long ships in a battle off the coast of Devon in 893. After several more reverses on land, Hastein and most of his army retreated up the old Roman road, Watling Street, to Chester.

Bad luck pursued Hastein's army for another three years. The Vikings abandoned Chester in 894 and invaded northern Wales, but the ferocious resistance of the Welshmen and the lack of supplies forced the Vikings to retreat. The next year they attempted to establish a base on the River Lea north of London, no doubt positioning themselves to take the city back from Alfred, but the English hit them so hard that the Vikings had to retreat for safety into the Danelaw, leaving their dragon ships behind. In 896, the Vikings were encamped along the Severn when Alfred attacked again. The Vikings scattered: Some went north to York, and others sailed back to France in hope of easier plunder.

As the sole English king of the old stock, Alfred became an inspiration and arguably even a rallying point for the English, especially for the English in the Danelaw. He had come back strongly from almost certain annihilation, smashed his enemies, reclaimed his kingdom, and made that kingdom so strong it could drive off or defeat every Viking invasion for the rest of his life.

But Alfred also realized that there was more to a nation than military strength. So he revived learning and literature, reformed the English legal code, founded new monasteries to replace the ones destroyed by the Vikings, and brought over monks from the Continent to get the new communities off to a strong start.

Rarely has a country teetered so closely on the brink of destruction than did England in 878. Rarer still has it fallen to one man to bring his nation back from near-disaster. Yet that was the destiny of King Alfred; without him, England as we know it would not exist.

"FLOODS OF DANES AND PIRATES": THE VIKINGS IN IRELAND

NOWHERE IN THE BRITISH ISLES DID THE VIKINGS HAVE a more dramatic impact than in Ireland. They founded the country's first cities—Dublin, Waterford, Wexford, Arklow, Cork, and Limerick. They introduced the first coins to the island. They shifted the focus of Ireland from its cultural and ceremonial heartland around Tara to the east coast, where the port cities the Vikings founded became centers of international trade. They taught the Irish the art of building fine wooden ships. And some historians believe that Iceland was settled by Vikings from Ireland who brought their Irish slaves with them.

TURGEIS THE DEVIL

To the Irish, he was a servant of the devil—a cruel, blasphemous monster who mocked God and the saints in their own sanctuaries. The Irish called this Viking chief Turgeis, although his Norse name was probably Thorgils. No physical description of him has survived; we do not even know anything about his life and career before he came to Ireland. But what he did once he arrived in Ireland was enough to gain him a reputation among the Irish as evil incarnate.

ST. PATRICK, PICTURED HERE IN THE GARB OF A MONK, WAS THE MOST REVERED SAINT IN IRELAND. THE VIKING ATTACK ON HIS SHRINE AT ARMAGH SHOCKED THE IRISH.

 · DE SANCTO PATRICIO · IX ·

Atriauit ōium scothoꝛ
regi te ꝑi paſſione ꝑ
dicaret. ſtāns ante eū
ꝛ appodiauit se super fe
rulam q̄m manu tene
bat et cū̄ pedi regis in

TIMELINE

795–824: IN A SERIES OF RAIDS, THE VIKINGS PLUNDER ISOLATED MONASTERIES ALONG THE IRISH COAST.

C. 839: VIKING CHIEF TURGEIS LOOTS ST. PATRICK'S SHRINE AT ARMAGH, IRELAND.

841: AT A PLACE THE IRISH CALLED DUBH-LINN (THE BLACK POOL) ON THE LIFFEY RIVER, TURGEIS FOUNDS THE TOWN THAT WILL BE DUBLIN.

844: WITH SHIPS FULL OF VIKINGS, TURGEIS LOOTS THE GREAT ABBEY OF CLONMACNOISE. HIS WIFE, OTA, PERFORMS PAGAN RITES FROM THE HIGH ALTAR OF THE ABBEY CHURCH.

845: THE HIGH KING OF IRELAND CAPTURES AND EXECUTES TURGEIS NEAR MODERN-DAY MULLINGAR IN COUNTY WESTMEATH.

It was Turgeis who ransacked Armagh—the holiest place on the island, the Irish Jerusalem. St. Patrick had chosen Armagh as the ecclesiastical heart of Ireland; there he died, and there he was buried. Many of his personal possessions were preserved at Armagh as sacred relics, and around St. Patrick's grave had grown up an impressive religious complex of monasteries, schools, and a cathedral.

In 839 or 840, Turgeis led a Viking attack upon this little holy city. In one respect, it was a typical raid, with Vikings looting everything of value, knocking over the altars, desecrating the tombs of the saints, and slaughtering the monks and their students. But then Turgeis did something so dreadful it was certain to win him a permanent place in the imagination of the Irish: He acted as a kind of Norse high priest, offering prayers and perhaps even animal sacrifices to the heathen gods in the sanctuary of St. Patrick's church.

More acts of sacrilege were to come. In 844, Turgeis was one of the chieftains in the large Viking fleet of approximately sixty ships that entered the mouth of the Shannon River at the site of the present-day city of Limerick. The dragon ships sailed up to Lough Derg, where the Vikings beached them and set up camp. From there, they attacked sacred sites throughout central and western Ireland.

Turgeis selected as his target the great abbey of Clonmacnoise. The place was especially dear to the Irish as a center of scholarship that attracted students

TIMELINE

848: IRISH KINGS SCORE SEVERAL STUNNING VICTORIES OVER THE VIKINGS.

850–853: TWO FACTIONS OF VIKINGS GO TO WAR TO DETERMINE WHICH WILL HAVE EXCLUSIVE RIGHT TO PLUNDER IRELAND. THE VICTOR, OLAF THE WHITE, PROCLAIMS HIMSELF KING AND MAKES DUBLIN HIS CAPITAL.

867: IN THEIR FIRST NAVAL BATTLE, THE IRISH FLEET DEFEATS THE VIKINGS NEAR DERRY.

902: THE IRISH CAPTURE DUBLIN, SLAUGHTERING NEARLY ALL THE VIKING INHABITANTS.

917: A FRESH INVASION OF VIKINGS RECAPTURES DUBLIN.

1014: THE IRISH REPULSE ONE LAST VIKING RAID ON THE ISLAND. FROM THIS POINT ON VIKING SETTLERS IN IRELAND BEGIN TO ASSIMILATE INTO IRISH SOCIETY.

from as far away as France. Furthermore, it was the home of a famous seminary that had produced a host of Irish saints. None of this meant a thing to Turgeis and his Vikings.

After they had killed all the monks and carried back to their ships all the treasures of Clonmacnoise, Turgeis led his wife, Ota, into the abbey church, where he helped her climb up on the high altar. There, surrounded by blood-splattered Vikings, she played the part of a heathen oracle, calling on the Norse gods to give her the gift of prophecy. For the Irish it was too much that the same man should defile Armagh and Clonmacnoise. Turgeis became the focus of their loathing.

THERE WAS NO QUESTION IN KING MAEL'S MIND THAT HE WOULD HAVE TURGEIS KILLED; THE ONLY ISSUE WAS THE METHOD.

TURGEIS'S LEGACY

Consequently, in 845, when the Irish high king, Mael Seachlinn, captured Turgeis near modern-day Mullingar in County Westmeath, the people of Ireland rejoiced. There was no question in King Mael's mind that he would have Turgeis killed; the only issue was the method. After consulting with his inner circle, Mael commanded his prisoner to be bound hand and foot and thrown into Lough Owel to drown.

The simple drowning struck some of the Irish as anticlimactic, so they developed a more elaborate story of how Turgeis died. In this fanciful account, King Mael lures Turgeis and fifteen of his henchmen out to an island in the middle of Lough Owel, where sixteen beautiful Irish women are waiting for them. The Vikings row out the island, and there indeed are sixteen young women, beautifully dressed. As the Vikings embrace them, the young women drop the charade and reveal themselves to be young men in disguise, then draw their daggers and kill Turgeis and his men.

Turgeis's legacy, however, is not the bitter memory of desecrated churches. It is Dublin. In 841, Turgeis came ashore on the east coast of Ireland at a place the Irish called Dubh-Linn ("the black pool") at a convenient fording place across the Liffey River. It was a good spot for a trading settlement, so Turgeis decided to stay. He built houses, surrounded them with a defensive wall, and thereby established the first Viking state in western Europe—with himself as its lord.

PREFERRED VICTIMS

The Irish first felt the wrath of the Vikings in 795, when raiders sacked and burned the monastery on Lambay Island, a little north of the site of Dublin. In 798, the Vikings stormed ashore on St. Patrick's Island, where they were delighted to find not just church treasure but a large heard of fine cattle. By 807, they had worked their way around to the western side of Ireland, where they looted the monasteries on Inishmurray in Sligo and Roscam in Galway Bay. In 821, the Vikings were back on the east coast, picking off the monastic communities on the string of islets in Wexford Harbor.

And in 824, they sailed south to the Skelligs, where they had to work harder than usual for their loot, scrambling up rocky cliffs to the gold-rich churches at the summit. As they retreated to their ships, the Vikings grabbed the superior of the Skelligs, a monk named Etgal. The Irish hoped the Vikings wanted ransom for the holy man; instead, the Vikings amused themselves by starving Etgal to death.

These repeated raids unnerved the monks, who learned to dread calm seas and fair sailing weather. We can get a glimpse into their state of mind via a bit of verse written in the margin of a manuscript by a ninth-century Irish scribe:

The wind is rough tonight,

tossing the white combed ocean.

I need not dread fierce Vikings

crossing the Irish Sea.

Those early Viking raids followed a pattern: Their preferred victims were monasteries on islands or along the coast, places where two or three ships

full of raiders were enough to carry off all the valuables, and where, after a quick strike, they could get away before any local fighting men arrived on the scene. As they learned of richer prizes further inland, the Vikings abandoned their early caution and planned more ambitious raids. In 828, they sailed up the Boyne River to ravage the monasteries along its banks. In 831, they attacked Louth and captured the local king. In 834, they made a daring—and successful—attack on St. Kevin's shrine at Glendalough, high in the Wicklow Hills.

AT CLONMACNOISE ABBEY, THE VIKING CHIEF TURGEIS ENCOURAGED HIS WIFE, OTA, TO PERFORM HEATHEN RITES ON THE HIGH ALTAR OF THE MONASTERY CHURCH.

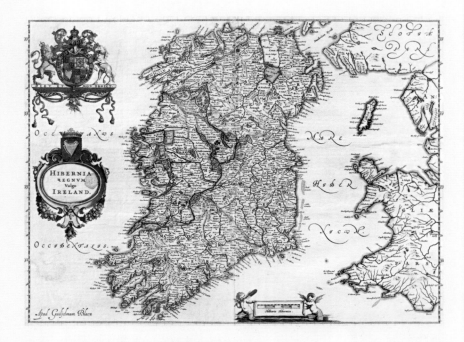

PLUNDER VERSUS RANSOM

Over time the Vikings came to understand that what they considered loot the Irish regarded as irreplaceable objects of great sanctity and immeasurable value. The Vikings were drawn to reliquaries because they were made of gold or silver and usually studded with jewels, whereas the Irish prized what the reliquary contained—the bones or personal belongings of a saint, or a sliver of the True Cross. Typically the Vikings would grab a reliquary, dump out the relic, and carry off the gold or silver chest to be melted down at home, or perhaps given to a member of the family as a trophy. One such example has survived in Scandinavia—a small box made in Ireland in the eighth century to hold a precious relic. The relic is long gone, but scratched on the base of the chest is an inscription in Norse runes dated to the tenth century that reads, "Ranvaik owns this casket." We do not know who Ranvaik was, but we know that she treasured this particular example of Viking plunder.

Yet in spite of the pleasure such loot brought their women, some Viking raiders realized they could get even more gold and silver if they ransomed the shrines, with their relics intact, back to the Irish. The Vikings also learned that there was an even more valuable commodity than shrines in Ireland—the Irish

THE VIKINGS' FAVORITE TARGETS

Ireland's rich deposits of gold, silver, and copper have been mined since ancient times. Precious and semi-precious stones were also found on the island——emeralds, sapphires, amethysts, topaz, freshwater pearls, and "Kerry diamonds." And the Irish have a long tradition, dating at least to 2000 B.C., of producing metalwork of very high quality.

These native materials and skills combined with religious devotion to make the monasteries and convents of Ireland the richest in the British Isles and, as a result, the favorite targets of Viking raiders.

A chronicler in Munster bewailed the "immense floods and countless sea-vomitings of ships and boats and fleets so that there was not a harbor nor a land port nor a dun nor a fortress nor a fastness in all Munster without floods of Danes and pirates." The chronicler went on to report how the Vikings "ravaged [Munster's] chieftainries and her privileged churches and her sanctuaries, and they rent her shrines and her reliquaries and her books."

Archaeologists have discovered many sublime examples of Irish metalwork, stripped from holy places, in Viking graves throughout Scandinavia. How many other comparable works were melted down or lost?

Books were the sole Irish treasure that the Vikings did not prize. Once a book's gold or silver covers had been pried off, the Vikings had no further interest in it. They tossed books into fires, trampled them under foot, or dumped them in the sea or a nearby lake, causing Irish monks to lament the "drowning" of their precious manuscripts.

As the pillage, destruction, and slaughter spread across the country, some Irish monks gathered up their books and fled to the Continent. Many joined monastic communities in France, Germany, Belgium, or the Netherlands, or offered their services as teachers at the schools founded 20 or 30 years earlier by Charlemagne. Other monks chose the missionary life, carrying Christianity to remote corners of Austria and Switzerland. Irish monks had always been wanderers, but this exodus from Ireland was different.

There was a genuine sense among the monks of Ireland that their civilization was on the edge of extinction. If Irish sanctity and scholarship and artistry were to survive, they believed, it would have to be in foreign lands.

themselves. After an attack on Armagh in 869, the Vikings carried off 1,000 prisoners; a raid on Kildare in 886, brought in 280 captives; and in another raid on Armagh in 895, the Vikings captured 710 prisoners. Captives of high rank, such as abbots or noblemen, would be ransomed and some women might be taken as concubines, but the rest the Vikings would sell as slaves, either at home in Scandinavia or in the slave markets along the Baltic Sea.

EARLY VIKING RAIDS FOLLOWED A SIMILAR PATTERN: THEIR PREFERRED VICTIMS WERE MONASTERIES ALONG THE COAST, PLACES WHERE TWO OR THREE SHIPS FULL OF RAIDERS WERE ENOUGH TO CARRY OFF ALL THE VALUABLES AND GET AWAY BEFORE LOCAL FIGHTING MEN ARRIVED.

THE FIGHTING IRISH

All the stories of pillaged shrines and murdered monks can create a false impression that the Irish were easy prey for the Vikings. In fact, the Irish put up a fierce resistance, especially after the defeat and death of Turgeis.

In 848, King Mael led his army against a force of Vikings, defeating them soundly; it is said that at the battle's end 700 Vikings lay dead on the field. Soon thereafter, Olchubur mac Cinaeda, king of Munster, and his ally Lorcan mac Cellaig, king of Leinster, defeated a Viking army near Castledermot in

THE CAPTURE AND ESCAPE OF ST. FINDAN

The story of one of the Vikings' Irish captives has come down to us, preserved in a medieval manuscript that recounts the lives of several Irish saints.

About the year 850, the Norse captured a number of Irish women, possibly an entire convent of nuns. The father of one of these captive women sent his son, Findan or Fintan, to the Norse camp with gold to ransom his sister. The young man barely had a chance to explain the purpose of his mission when some of the Vikings grabbed him, bound him in chains, and carried him off to one of their ships, where they left him without food or water for two days.

Meanwhile, in a conference to discuss the young Irishman's fate, the more prudent Vikings argued that it was shortsighted to mistreat men who came to them with good money to ransom captives. This argument won the day, and the Vikings released Findan and his sister.

Not long after his first brush with the Vikings, Findan's father and brother were killed in a feud with a rival clan. Findan fought his way out of the melee, but his Irish enemies were not willing to let him get away: They paid a band of Vikings to break in on a banquet where Findan was among the guests, and carry him overseas to be sold as a slave. This time, Findan did not escape. Loaded down with chains again, he was sold to a slave dealer and was en route to Scandinavia when the ship made a stop in the Orkney Islands. Somehow, Findan managed to break free and hide on shore until the slavers gave up searching for him and continued on their way.

With his family dead and both Irish and Viking enemies waiting for him at home, Findan decided not to return to Ireland. Instead he traveled to the Continent, made a pilgrimage to Rome, then settled at Rheinau Abbey near Schaffhausen in Switzerland. He spent the last 26 years of his life there, mostly as a hermit, developing a reputation for sanctity among his brother monks and the local people. The Catholic Church venerates Findan as a saint.

THE BATTLE FOR DUBLIN

After the battle of Drogheda, the conflict between Irish and Viking that had once ranged all over Ireland now focused on Dublin.

From a Viking's point of view, Dublin was a gem. Not only did it possess a fine harbor, but it was within easy striking distance for raids against southern Scotland, western England, the Isle of Man, and all of Wales. Unhappily for the townspeople, every Viking chieftain and warrior in Ireland believed he should be king of Dublin. So from the day Olaf the White became king in 853, Dublin endured 49 years of turmoil and bloodshed as one Viking strongman after another tried to take the town for himself.

Five decades of chaos so weakened the Vikings that, in 902, the Irish attacked Dublin and came close to massacring all the Viking inhabitants. The terrified survivors, battered and wounded, scrambled aboard their ships and sailed away.

Then, in 917, Sitric, Olaf the White's nephew, led a fleet commanded by seven of his brothers and cousins in a fresh invasion of eastern Ireland. The decisive battle came outside Dublin on September 14, 919, where the Vikings inflicted a stunning defeat on the Irish, killing five Irish kings and many noblemen. Dublin was back in Viking hands.

Viking Dublin in 919 covered about thirty acres, all set behind defensive walls.

County Kildare, but this was a smaller conflict in which only 200 Vikings were killed. Inspired by these victories, the Irish went on the offensive, and although they did not manage to drive out the Vikings completely, they did push them back to the eastern edge of Ireland.

Fresh trouble came to the country in 850, however, when a fleet of Danish Vikings (the first Viking invaders had been Norwegians) landed at Carlingford Lough in County Down. Almost immediately, the two Viking factions turned on each other, battling on land and sea to determine which would have the exclusive right to pillage Ireland. Meanwhile, the Irish sat back and, wishing a plague on both houses, enjoyed the spectacle of "the Fair Foreigners" (the Norwegians) and "the Dark Foreigners" (the Danes) killing one another.

It housed several thousand inhabitants, almost all of whom were craftsmen, artisans, or merchants. Archaeologists have uncovered the workshops and homes of blacksmiths, weavers, tanners, shoemakers, metalworkers, carpenters, shipwrights, barrel-makers, and even comb-makers, who made their living by catering to Vikings who liked to appear well-groomed.

Outside the walls, the Viking control extended over a large area that included pastures for livestock and fields of grain. Based on the animal bones found in excavations of tenth-century Dublin, the Vikings ate beef almost exclusively, but they did not raise the cattle themselves—Irish annals from this period record that neighboring kings paid their tribute to the Vikings in herds of steers.

As Dublin thrived in the mid-tenth century, the Irish began to settle in the town, too. An Irish poet even praised Dublin's Viking king, Olaf Cuaran (reigned 945–980) as the "good king of Dublin, eager for strong and noble patrimony." By Cuaran's day, the Vikings still had not assimilated into Irish society, but they had made a few concessions: The king had accepted baptism, and the Irish Gaelic names of his daughter and grandson indicate that his family was now firmly Christian. The daughter was called Mael Muire (Muire is Irish Gaelic for Mary) and the grandson's name was Gilla Ciarain (Ciarain is Irish Gaelic for Kieran, the saint who founded the monastery and school at Clonmacnoise).

The Danes had the upper hand in the Viking war until 853, when a Norwegian chief named Olaf the White (Amlaibh to the Irish) brought his great war fleet into Dublin harbor and declared himself king. From the Danes he demanded submission, and from the Irish he demanded tribute money, including *wergeld*, the traditional fine paid by a man's killers, for the death of Turgeis. Impressed by Olaf's strength, the Danes gave him what he wanted, and the Irish followed suit.

As Olaf established himself in Dublin, a new Irish king rose in the north. Aed Finnliaith began his reign with an all-out assault on the Vikings in Meath and the Ulster counties, in which he wiped out all their colonies north of Dublin.

Then Aed assembled a fleet—one of the first in Irish history—and in 867 met the Vikings in battle in Lough Foyle near the site of the present-day city of

Derry in Northern Ireland. The naval battle was a stunning victory for the Irish, and having beaten the Vikings on sea they prepared to hit them again on land, this time outside Drogheda.

To inspire his men and call down the blessing of heaven on his efforts, Aed brought two of Ireland's most sacred relics to the battle—St. Patrick's crozier and a fragment of the True Cross. Flush with their victory at Lough Foyle, filled with hatred for the Viking invaders, and reassured by the presence of the relics, the Irish demolished the Viking army. After their defeat at Drogheda, the Vikings stayed within the walls of Dublin, never again venturing north.

But, not all Irishmen wanted the Vikings gone. In an attempt to grab more power for themselves, or more land, or to even to settle the score with an enemy, some Irish allied themselves with the Vikings. A notorious example occurred in 850 when Cinnaedh, the prince of a petty kingdom, pledged loyalty to the Vikings in Dublin in the hope that together they could crush the north's powerful Ui Neill clan. Cinnaedh's alliance with the heathen foreigners shocked his fellow Irishmen, who looked upon it as a betrayal of Ireland and of the Christian faith.

When Cinnaedh fell into the hands of Maelsechnaill, king of Meath, the consensus that was he deserved death. As a clear sign of their contempt for the traitor, the Irish sentenced Cinnaedh to be drowned in a filthy little stream so shallow he had to be held down in it.

THE MEDIEVAL GLOBAL MARKETPLACE

There has been a trend among historians in recent times to diminish the violent aspect of the Viking incursion in Ireland. This is mistaken: It is undeniable that for the Irish the Viking raids were traumatic, painful events. It could not have been otherwise when so many works of tremendous beauty, sanctity, and cultural significance were wantonly destroyed, and when so many Irish were slaughtered or carried off to slavery.

Bad as the Viking invasions were, however, they did not destroy traditional Irish society; the majority of the Irish preferred life in the country to life in the Viking towns; they gave their primary loyalty to their family and their clan; and the country was still ruled by a host of petty kings.

The Vikings had no interest in genocide, to use a modern term; even if that had been their goal, given the vigor of Irish resistance to the invaders, the Vikings never could have carried off a wholesale massacre. What the Vikings did want was plunder and slaves and land—and they got all three.

But by settling in Ireland they actually brought a few benefits to the Irish, too. At Dublin, Waterford, Wexford, Arklow, Cork, and Limerick, the Vikings established the country's first cities. Before the Vikings came, there had been only embryonic communities at large ecclesiastical centers such as Armagh and Clonmacnoise—little clusters of families and craftsmen who supplied support services to the monasteries.

The Vikings introduced a new concept—the town or city as a thriving, outward-looking commercial center where goods were manufactured or stockpiled for eventual shipment to markets overseas, and that received goods from foreign markets in return. Thanks to the Vikings the Irish began to participate in this early medieval global economy.

But in addition to trading centers the Irish needed currency. The Vikings supplied that, too, establishing a mint to produce the first coins in Ireland. It was the Vikings, then, who guided the Irish as they took their first steps away from their insular, pastoral life and into the international marketplace.

OLAF THE WHITE WAS THE MOST SUCCESSFUL VIKING KING OF DUBLIN. THIS SCENE DEPICTS A LEGEND, THAT OLAF DISGUISED HIMSELF AS A MINSTREL TO INFILTRATE THE ENGLISH COURT.

THE WASTELAND: THE VIKINGS IN THE FRANKISH EMPIRE

IN 885, A VIKING FLEET SAILED UP THE SEINE AND LAID SIEGE TO PARIS.

FRANCE'S PROVINCE OF NORMANDY GETS ITS NAME FROM the Vikings—or the Northmen, as the local inhabitants called them— who drove out the native French population and took the land for themselves.

Within two generations, however, the Vikings had assimilated into French society: They were Christians, they spoke French, and they had forgotten completely the customs of Scandinavia. But they never lost the martial character of their ancestors, and it was this quality that made the Normans the premier fighting force in western Europe for more than 300 years.

The Normans' most famous conquest was England, seized in 1066 by William the Conqueror, great-great-great grandson of a Viking pirate named Rollo. But the Norman influence was felt much farther afield: The magnificent castles that tourists visit in Wales today were built by the Normans; Ireland's 800 years of trouble with its neighbors across the Irish Sea began with a Norman invasion; and the Norman talent for warfare, empire-building, and even art would be felt as far away as Malta and Jerusalem.

TIMELINE

820: VIKINGS FROM DENMARK RAVAGE THE COAST OF NORTHERN BELGIUM.

826: LOUIS THE PIOUS, KING OF THE FRANKS, PERSUADES KING HARALD OF DENMARK TO ACCEPT BAPTISM.

830–840: THE VIKINGS CONDUCT REPEATED RAIDS ON FRISIA (PRESENT-DAY HOLLAND).

840: WAR BREAKS OUT AMONG THE SONS OF LOUIS THE PIOUS. THE VIKINGS TAKE ADVANTAGE OF THE INTERNAL CHAOS IN FRANCE, PLUNDERING ROUEN, ST. WANDRILLE ABBEY, AND NANTES.

865–866: THE FRANKS RALLY, INFLICTING CRUSHING DEFEATS ON THE VIKINGS AT PARIS, CHARTRES, AND LEMANS.

A KISS ON THE FOOT

His name doesn't do the king justice. English historians call him "Charles the Simple" (879–929), which has led generations of students to regard this great-grandson of Charlemagne as a royal fool. In fact, it is a simple case of mistranslation. Charles' Latin nickname was "Simplex," which means straightforward, or lacking in cunning. And in terms of his dealings with the Vikings, Charles was direct, did what had to be done, and struck the best deal possible for himself and his subjects.

Charles knew he could not drive out the Vikings, so he made their leader, Rollo, an offer instead. In exchange for Rollo's oath to defend the Seine River region of France against raids from all other Vikings, Charles granted the entire province of Normandy to Rollo and his followers forever. As gifts go, it was both magnanimous and pragmatic. The Vikings had already devastated the province; scarcely a soul still lived there. It could remain the wasteland of Charles' kingdom, or it could become a bulwark of Vikings against worse Vikings. Once Rollo's Vikings settled the country and the peasants returned, Normandy—as the place came to be called—would flourish again.

Rollo accepted the offer, and in 911 he and Charles signed a formal treaty in which, in exchange for possession of the land and the title Count of Rouen, Rollo swore allegiance to Charles and converted to Christianity. Legend says that after the document was signed, Charles extended his foot for Rollo to kneel before and kiss. No Viking war chief would abase himself in such a way, so

TIMELINE

885: VIKINGS BESIEGE PARIS.

886: THE PROVINCE OF BURGUNDY IS DEVASTATED BY VIKING RAIDS.

900: TO PROTECT TOWNS, MONASTERIES, AND FARMS, DOZENS OF NEW CASTLES ARE ERECTED THROUGHOUT FRANCE.

911: CHARLES THE SIMPLE, KING OF THE FRANKS, GRANTS THE ENTIRE PROVINCE OF NORMANDY TO THE VIKING CHIEF, ROLLO.

1066: NORMAN KNIGHTS, DESCENDED FROM THE FRANKS AND THE VIKINGS, CONQUER ENGLAND.

Rollo ordered one of his men to kiss the king's foot. But the Viking, who had no grasp of the proper procedure, bent down and lifted Charles's foot to his mouth, which caused the king of the Franks to lose his balance and fall backwards on his rear.

A FULL-TIME VIKING

Rollo was an exile from Denmark. His father had been a wealthy nobleman, the lord of many warriors, and a proud man "who never lowered the nape of his neck before any king," according to the Frankish historian Dudo of St. Quentin. When the old man died, he left all his estates to his two sons, Rollo and Gurim, both of whom he had trained to be "vigorous in arms, well-versed in warfare," as Dudo put it.

Unfortunately, Rollo and Gurim's father had offended the king of Denmark. Now that the formidable old man was dead, the king rose up to avenge himself on the sons of his nemesis by leading a full-scale attack on Gurim and Rollo's lands. Gurim was hacked to death in the battle, but Rollo escaped. The Danish king proclaimed Rollo an outlaw, banished him from his homeland forever, and confiscated all of his property.

Like other dispossessed Danes before him, Rollo became a full-time Viking, raiding in England and Frisia (modern-day Holland) before coming at last to France. He was at the Vikings' siege of Paris in 885 and ravaged the countryside of Burgundy in 886. But when he came to the desolate province

of Normandy, Rollo saw his chance to become a great lord as his father had been, but in a new and better country. In honor of the occasion Dudo puts a little speech in Rollo's mouth:

> This land is plentifully furnished with an abundant supply of all the fruits of the earth, shady with trees, divided up by rivers filled with fish, copiously supplied with diverse kinds of wild game, but empty of armed men and warriors," he tells his followers. "We will subordinate this land to our power. And we will claim this land as our allotment.

Once King Charles acquiesced to the inevitable, Rollo and his Vikings settled comfortably in their new home. As the surviving Frankish inhabitants returned, the Vikings intermarried with them, converted to Christianity, and adopted French customs so thoroughly that by the middle of the tenth century it was difficult in this land of the Northmen to find anyone who still spoke Norse.

THRONGS OF MERCHANTS

The riches of England and Ireland, fine as they were, paled in comparison to the wealth of the Frankish Empire. Initially sponsored by Charlemagne—arguably the greatest, most influential monarch of the Middle Ages—the land we know as France (and its satellite states that spilled over into western Germany, Belgium, and Holland), grew fabulously wealthy, with everyone from barons to archbishops embracing the new capitalist economy.

Dazzled by what money could buy, knights and noblemen refused to accept wheels of cheese or baskets of eggs from their tenants—they wanted the rent paid in silver coins. Abbots and noblemen whose lands bordered navigable rivers began to hold weekly markets at which merchants sold everything from humble cooking utensils to shimmering silks from Asia to eager shoppers. The monks and aristocrats on whose estates the market was held received a percentage of the sales.

When Charlemagne was alive, traders from Denmark and other Scandinavian lands had been among the throngs of merchants who sailed up and down the great rivers of France. Then, in 820, Danes of a different kind beached thirteen long ships on the Flemish coast in northern Belgium; they began to

FRANCE'S KING LOUIS THE PIOUS ATTEMPTED TO NEUTRALIZE THE VIKINGS BY CONVERTING THEM TO CHRISTIANITY.

PRIVATE ARMIES

Some historians have sought to diminish the impact of the Viking raids on the Frankish Empire, and they have a point. Viking attacks here were sporadic and, aside from Normandy, Viking attempts at settling in the realm Charlemagne built were not successful.

It's very likely that the Franks, disorganized though they were politically, still mounted a stiff resistance to the Vikings. That said, for the Frankish monks and laity whose monasteries were ransacked or whose towns were burned, a Viking raid would seem like the end of the world. "All take flight," one ninth-century Frankish chronicler wrote. "Few are those who cry, 'Stop! Resist! Fight for your country, your children, and your nation!' "

And it would have been difficult in many circumstances for the Franks to put up a good fight against the Vikings. First, the rivers of France became the Vikings' highways to some of the richest prizes in the empire, and there was no way to barricade the waterways to keep the Vikings out. Second, Charlemagne had designed his army to fight large-scale battles; it had no experience responding to the lightning raids that were the Vikings' specialty.

Truly, the destruction the Vikings wrought in France's western provinces was significant. Repeated attacks on the northern French coastal province of Brittany persuaded many of the province's noble families to seek refuge in the kingdom of Wessex in southern England and the protection of King Aethelstan. The Vikings killed or drove off so many peasants in Aquitaine, one of the gardens of France, that weeds grew in the streets of desolate villages and the wilderness began to reclaim once-fertile fields, orchards, and vineyards. Normandy was hit so hard and so often that it took one hundred years for the province to recover.

Before the Vikings arrived, the monasteries of Tours, Corbie, St. Denis, St. Bertin, St. Vaast, and Ferriéres had all operated schools along with scriptoria where books were copied and disseminated throughout the Frankish Empire. So many learned monks and scholars and copyists were slaughtered by the Vikings that literacy in western France went into decline.

THESE SUPERB PANEL PAINTINGS DEPICT FOUR SCENES FROM THE LIFE OF ST. BERTIN, WHOSE MONASTERY WAS LOOTED BY THE VIKINGS IN 860.

Cy comencent les gestes z histoires le Roy cha
le chauf premierent coment les filz secobati
contre lui z coment ilz fuirent desconfiz te

maraud across the country in the usual way, but the Franks rallied and drove them off before the Northmen could do much damage. The raiders enjoyed better success at Poitou, where they looted towns and monasteries and then sailed off, their boats heavy with plunder.

The reaction of Charlemagne's son and successor, King Louis the Pious, to the raids was singular: True to his name, he launched an ambitious missionary effort to Denmark, hoping to neutralize the Northmen by converting them to Christianity. The campaign enjoyed a major coup in 826 when King Harald of Denmark, along with his wife and son, all accepted baptism; at the ceremony, Louis acted as Harald's godfather. Unfortunately, Harald's claim to the throne was hotly contested in Denmark; the year after his conversion, Harald and his family were driven out of the country. The following year, Harald, backed by the Franks, led an army into Denmark to regain his throne, but the new king, Horik, trounced Harald on the battlefield and sent him running back to the safety of Louis's realm.

THE SILVER OF DORESTAD

In the 830s, the Northmen's attacks on the Franks' empire began in earnest. Their chief target at this time was Frisia, the coastal flatlands that stretched from Holland up to the Danish border. In early spring of 834, they attacked Dorestad, the site of one of the royal mints. After stealing all the silver, they destroyed the town, massacred almost the entire population, and then carried off the survivors. In 835, the Northmen came back to Dorestad and stole the fresh supply of silver. They returned again in 837, when they burned the rebuilt town, marauded through the countryside, and then, as a condition of leaving, demanded even more silver from the Frisians.

A Frankish fleet patrolling Frisian waters would have deterred the Northmen or engaged them in battle, but as Louis did not have a navy, the Frisians were virtually defenseless. And adding insult to injury, Louis discovered that one of the pirates ravaging Frisia was his one-time ally and godson, Harald.

THE WAR OF THE THREE BROTHERS

At Louis's death in 840, a nasty power struggle erupted among his three sons— Lothair, Louis the German, and Charles the Bald. Louis had tried to satisfy all

AT FOUNTENOY-EN-PUISAYE IN 841, LOTHAIR I FOUGHT HIS TWO BROTHERS, LOUIS THE GERMAN AND CHARLES THE BALD, FOR CONTROL OF CHARLEMAGNE'S EMPIRE.

three of the contenders by granting lands to each: Lothair, as the eldest son, was named emperor and was granted Italy and the lands from the North Sea south to the Mediterranean through the Rhine and Rhone valleys; Louis the German received the eastern lands, covering Saxony and Bavaria, and Charles the Bald received almost all of France other than what belonged to Lothair.

None of the princes welcomed the settlement; all of them wanted to be sole emperor of all the lands conquered by their grandfather Charlemagne. The result was a civil war that weakened the empire at the precise moment when it needed all its strength to resist the Northmen. At this critical moment, as if to prove just how foolhardy an emperor he would be, Lothair granted the island of Walcheren off the Frisian coast to his family's old nemesis, Harald. Lothair may have believed he was placating a ruthless foe, but Harald and his fellow Vikings capitalized on their new possession by using Walcheren Island as a launching pad for recurring invasions of Frisia until the land was completely in their hands.

In June of that same year, Lothair met Charles and Louis in battle at Fontenay-en-Puisaye in the province of Burgundy in eastern France. The old chroniclers claim that the armies were evenly matched, with about 150,000 men on each side. At the end of the day, Lothair was chased off the field, leaving behind approximately 25,000 dead men, including many of the finest, most experienced warriors of the Aquitaine, the wealthy, militarily powerful province that covered almost all of central and southern France.

The Northmen had been observing the internecine warfare among the Franks, and now, within a few weeks of the battle of Fontenay, they struck one of the richest and weakest points in the empire—Normandy. First fell Rouen, the capital of the province. Then the Vikings overran the nearby monastery of St. Wandrille near the mouth of the River Seine. These calamities were followed by the ravaging of Quentovic, an especially prosperous center of trade just south of Boulogne, and the plundering of the Breton port of Nantes.

CASTLES AND CAVALRYMEN

Under Charlemagne, the Franks were so accustomed to long periods of peace that in many towns they had dismantled the old defensive walls erected by the Romans and used the stone to build new churches. Now the Franks put church construction on hold and began to build castles and fortified towns.

THE RISE OF THE ARISTOCRACY

Long after the Vikings had stopped marauding in France, the lords kept up their castles and maintained their garrisons. It was the beginning of the militarization of French society, in which every knight and baron had a private army he could mobilize to defend his own interests against those of his neighbors. In the centuries that followed, this development would create a class of aristocrats jealous of their independence and weaken the authority of the French king.

The monks of Vezelay moved out of their unprotected abbey in the river valley and into a fortified monastery they built at the summit of a nearby hill. A baron named Wilfrid the Hairy built a fortified town and invited the local populace to move in—on certain conditions: One day a week, they must work on maintaining the fortifications, and, if the Vikings attacked, all men of fighting age were obliged to serve in the garrison. Similar castles and strongholds sprouted all over France; by the year 900, there were twenty castles just in the neighborhood of Chartres.

But castles were useless without fighting men to defend them. For many years, abbeys and cathedrals had funded small bands of armed men to fulfill their obligation to provide the king with soldiers in time of war. Now the aristocracy adopted this model, hiring experienced soldiers and training new recruits to man their newly built castles. To be able to respond to swift Viking raids, these small private armies had to be fast. Consequently, most of them trained as cavalry so they could reach the attackers quickly.

NORMANDY WAS HIT SO HARD AND SO OFTEN THAT IT TOOK 100 YEARS FOR THE PROVINCE TO RECOVER.

AN EXODUS OF MONKS

Monasteries had always been the Vikings' prime target. These houses of prayer were stuffed with gold and silver, and "guarded" by men who on principle would not raise a hand to defend themselves or their valuables. But if monks could not fight, they could run away. After the initial Viking onslaught of the 830s, the monks learned the virtue of flight.

In 845, the monks at the abbey of St. Germain on the Seine received a warning that Viking ships had been spotted down river. They packed their books and sacred vessels and the relics of St. Germain into their boats and sailed away to safety. The Vikings must have been frustrated when they arrived to find the church and treasury empty. But the wine cellar was intact, so the Vikings emptied that instead.

In 860, the monks of St. Bertin also received a timely warning that Vikings were coming. But as the entire community packed up to go, four monks, hoping for martyrdom, refused to join the exodus. Once again the Vikings' plans had been frustrated—in this case, the raiders had intended to carry off the abbot and other senior monks for ransom; instead they found four elderly monks of no particular rank. In an attempt to squeeze some profit out of a bad situation, the Vikings chose the healthiest looking monk as the most likely prospect, but when they nudged him toward the ship, the monk threw himself to the ground crying that he would not go, that he wanted die in his abbey and be buried among his brothers. To get him up and moving the Vikings poked him with the butt of their spears, then pricked him with the spear points. Their sport got out of hand, however, and the Vikings beat and stabbed the obstinate monk to death.

The monks of the monastery of St. Philibert were in an especially vulnerable position, located as they were on the island of Noirmoutier just south of Brittany. Every year during the raiding season, from 819 to 836, the monks collected their treasures, including the relics of St. Philibert, and traveled to a safe location on the French mainland. After the raiding season was over and the Vikings had returned north to Scandinavia, the monks went home. In 843 the Vikings decided to winter on Noirmoutier, thereby forcing the monks to make other arrangements. Ultimately the monks of St. Philibert decided not to return to their island but to settle instead at Tournus in Burgundy.

BRIBES AND RANSOM

Following the pattern they had found successful in England and Ireland, the Vikings alternated between violent raids and accepting bribes to leave a place in peace—for the time being. About the year 845, the monks of the abbey of St. Wandrille paid a Viking raiding party six pounds of silver to

leave them in peace, but in 852 a different band of Vikings attacked and plundered St. Wandrille, burning the entire abbey complex to the ground. At the abbey of St. Denis, the monks scraped together enough money to ransom sixty-eight members of their community, as well as some laypeople the Vikings had captured.

But in 858, another band of Vikings sailed up the Seine to St. Denis, seized the abbot Louis and his brother Gauzlin, and demanded an enormous ransom for the life of the man of God: 686 pounds of gold and 3,250 pounds of silver. The chroniclers assure us that the Vikings got their price, thanks to an order from Charles the Bald that the churches of France should empty their treasuries and strip the shrines of their saints to liberate the abbot of St. Denis and his brother.

Over time the Vikings learned that they would find choice captives for ransom if they attacked a cathedral or important monastery on a holy day when the leading families in the region would be present at Mass. They also became audacious in their demands for bribes: They swore to the king of the West Franks, Louis the Fat, to leave his entire realm unharmed in exchange for 12,000 pounds in gold and silver. Somehow Louis raised the sum, and the Vikings went away.

THE FRANKS' SUCCESSES

This lust for huge amounts of gold and silver does not mean the Vikings had lost their fighting spirit. They were still fearsome warriors, especially on the sea, where they defeated the Frankish navy in every battle.

On land, too, they were impressive. It was common for a large Viking army to split up into many groups that would strike different places simultaneously, thus elevating the level of panic among the Franks. They were not afraid to travel over rough terrain, through forests or marshes, where the Franks did not like to go.

But in two respects the Franks had the upper hand. Their swords were superior to Viking swords: Frankish weapons were heavier than Viking swords and featured a crossguard at the base of the blade that protected the swordsman's hand. And the Franks wore chain mail into battle, whereas the closest thing the Vikings had to armor was the leather overshirt.

Indeed, the Franks scored many victories on land. In 865, in battles around Chartres and Paris, the Franks killed more than 700 Vikings; in 866 near Lemans, about 400 Vikings died fighting the Franks; and some sources from the period claim that between 880 and 882, the Franks slaughtered 15,000 Vikings. This degree of resistance in France and the easy pickings just across the English Channel, probably explains why the Vikings did not make any settlements in France outside Normandy.

NORMANS IN JERUSALEM

The Normans will always be best remembered for their triumph over the English at the Battle of Hastings, but in 1016, before they ever considered mounting an invasion across the English Channel, Norman knights became the driving force that expelled the Saracens from Sicily, Malta, and southern Italy. The Normans liked these warm, southern lands and decided to stay to forge a new kingdom for themselves. Their subjects were Sicilians, Greeks, Moors, and Jews, and out of all these influences emerged a Norman-led cultural renaissance. A century earlier, their ancestors had been notorious for smashing or stealing objects of great beauty; now, in Monreale and Palermo and Cefalu, Normans were commissioning extraordinary works of art and architecture from some of the finest artists in the Mediterranean world.

Even more ironic is what occurred in 1095, when Pope Urban II called for a crusade to liberate Jerusalem. Immediately the Normans took a leading role, bringing hundreds, perhaps thousands, of the finest fighting men to the gates of Jerusalem. They even found time to carve out yet another new kingdom for themselves in Syria, with Antioch as its capital. The descendants of cruel heathens who had slaughtered monks and defiled sanctuaries were now hailed as the liberators of the Holy Sepulcher and the champions of Christendom.

THE RESURRECTION OF HASTEIN: THE VIKINGS IN THE MEDITERRANEAN

THE MEDITERRANEAN SEA WAS THE ONE PLACE IN EUROPE the Vikings learned to avoid. Unlike England, Ireland, northern France, and the Ukraine, there was a power along the inland sea the Vikings could neither frighten nor defeat. That power was the Moors.

Concentrated along northern Africa and in Spain and Portugal, the Moorish empire possessed a war machine that made Europe and Byzantium nervous. The Moors had invaded the Iberian Peninsula from present-day Morocco in 711 and within eight years had conquered Spain and Portugal (in contrast, it would take the Spanish and the Portuguese 700 years to get their countries back).

In 732, the Moors thundered across the Pyrenees into France. They got as far as Tour, about 150 miles south of Paris, when they were turned back in an epic battle against the Franks, led by Charles Martel, "the hero of the age," as the historian Edward Gibbon called him. The de facto ruler at a time when the Frankish kings had become very weak, Charles was also a skillful commander who had already enjoyed victories over at least four different Germanic nations before he fought the Moors. By crushing the army of Emir

AT THE BATTLE OF TOURS IN 732, THE FRANKISH WARLORD, CHARLES MARTEL, DEFEATED THE MOORS AND SAVED WESTERN EUROPE FROM MOORISH CONQUEST.

Abdul Rahman (who was killed in the battle) and driving the survivors back across the Pyrenees, Charles saved western Europe from Moorish conquest.

South of the Pyrenees, the Moors were still a major military power. The Vikings they regarded as a nuisance, but a destructive, disruptive one that could not be ignored. That is why, in the wake of Hastein and Bjorn's raids on southern Spain in 859, the emir of Cordoba built the first Moorish fleet to fight and beat the Vikings on their own turf. One crushing loss to the Moorish navy was all it took for the Vikings to learn their lesson: The surviving dragon ships limped northward, never to return to the Mediterranean.

TIMELINE

711–722: THE MOORS, MUSLIM INVADERS FROM NORTH AFRICA, CONQUER ALMOST ALL OF SPAIN AND PORTUGAL.

844: THIRTY BOATLOADS OF VIKINGS ATTACK AND CONQUER SEVILLE IN SOUTHERN SPAIN. THEY PLUNDER THE SURROUNDING COUNTRYSIDE UNTIL THE MOORS DRIVE THEM OUT.

C. 849: TWELVE-YEAR-OLD BJORN, A DANISH PRINCE, IS SENT TO LIVE WITH HASTEIN TO LEARN HOW TO BE A VIKING RAIDER AND WARRIOR.

SUMMER 859: IN NORTH AFRICA, HASTEIN AND BJORN TAKE CAPTIVES TO BE SOLD IN THE SLAVE MARKETS OF IRELAND.

Charles Martel saved western Europe from the Moors, and the Moors saved the Mediterranean world from the Vikings.

A MORAL DILEMMA

The men on the battlements could scarcely believe what they were hearing. In front of the main gates of the city lay a man on a litter, surrounded by a small band of Vikings. "Open the gates!" their spokesman shouted. "Our lord is very ill and wants to be baptized before he dies."

Earlier that same day in 859, when sixty two dragon-prowed ships sailed into the harbor of Luna on the western coast of Italy, the alarm bells had rung, the people in the suburbs had raced for the safety of the city, and the garrison had barred the gates and taken their posts on the walls, bracing themselves for a Viking attack. Instead of an assault, however, they were faced with a moral dilemma: As Christians, could they turn away a dying man who asked for salvation? So the soldiers sent their own messengers to the count who ruled the city and the bishop to let them decide what was to be done. Meanwhile, the Vikings waited patiently at the city gates.

After a quick conference, the count and the bishop agreed to admit the Vikings. They sent a guard of soldiers to escort them to the cathedral, where the bishop baptized the sick man—his named was Hastein—and the count served as his godfather. Throughout the ceremony, Hastein's attendants

TIMELINE

WINTER 859–860: FROM THEIR WINTER QUARTERS ON THE FRENCH RIVIERA, THE TWO VIKING CHIEFS LEAD SUCCESSFUL ATTACKS ON THE FRENCH CITIES OF NIMES, ARLES, AND VALENCE, AS WELL AS PISA IN ITALY.

860: HASTEIN AND BJORN RAID THE ITALIAN TOWN OF LUNA, MISTAKING IT FOR ROME.

861: THE VIKINGS SAIL FOR HOME BUT FIND THEIR WAY BLOCKED AT THE STRAIT OF GIBRALTAR BY A MOORISH FLEET. ONLY TWENTY VIKING SHIPS MAKE IT THROUGH THE BLOCKADE.

c. 965–971: THE VIKINGS OCCUPY GALICIA IN NORTHWEST SPAIN UNTIL A SPANISH ARMY COMMANDED BY COUNT GONSALVO SANCHO DRIVES THEM OUT.

c. 950–1204: THOUSANDS OF VIKINGS TRAVEL TO CONSTANTINOPLE TO ENLIST AS MERCENARIES IN THE BYZANTINE ARMY.

---

remained quiet, solemn, and respectful. As for Hastein, he feigned a mix of piety and weakness. When the baptismal rite was concluded, the Vikings lifted the litter and bore their newly christened lord back through the town and out to his ship. Once the Vikings were gone, the guards barred the gates again—just to be on the safe side.

"A LEWD, UNBRIDLED, CONTENTIOUS RASCAL"

Details about Hastein's life are hard to come by. He was probably a Swede. He must have been an experienced, respected Viking leader otherwise he never could have raised a fleet of 62 longships in 859 for a raiding voyage into the Mediterranean. A typical longship held between thirty and forty men, which would have place Hastein in command of about 2,400 Vikings. William of Jumieges, a Norman monk and historian, described the scene:

> On the appointed day, the ships were pushed into the sea and the soldiers hastened to go aboard. They raised the standards, spread the sails before the wind, and like agile wolves set out to rend the Lord's sheep, pouring out human blood to their god Thor.

We do not know what Hastein looked like, but another Norman monk and historian, Dudo of Saint-Quentin, writing more than one hundred years after

the fact, left us an assessment of his character. Dudo described Hastein as "accursed and headstrong, extremely cruel and harsh, destructive, troublesome, wild, ferocious, infamous, destructive and inconstant, brash, conceited and lawless, death-dealing, rude, everywhere on guard, a rebellious traitor and kindler of evil, a double-faced hypocrite, an ungodly, arrogant, seductive and foolhardy deceiver, a lewd, unbridled, contentious rascal."

Dudo was not exaggerating. Hastein's raids in northern France had been so destructive that King Charles the Bald bought him off by handing over to Hastein the city of Chartres. The Viking chief had no use for a town, so he sold it to a Frankish count named Theobald. In Brittany, Hastein made a more practical peace treaty with Count Salomon, promising to cease all raids on the province in exchange for a payment of 500 cows.

About ten years before the voyage to the Mediterranean, Ragnar Lodbrok, the king of Sweden and Denmark, had placed his son twelve-year-old son Bjorn in Hastein's care, instructing him to teach the boy how be a proper Viking warrior. Bjorn became Hastein's most trusted lieutenant and joined him on the Mediterranean raid. By then he had acquired a nickname—Bjorn Ironside, because, the Vikings said, his mother Aslaug had cast a spell that made the young man invulnerable on the battlefield.

THE VIKING RAID IN THE MEDITERRANEAN

After days of digging beneath Seville's walls, a handful of Vikings set fire to the wooden beams that held up the tunnel, and then sprinted outside to watch the result. The burned beams gave way, the tunnel collapsed, and with a thunderous crash, a section of Seville's defensive walls fell and 1,000 battle-crazed Viking warriors surged into the city. Moorish soldiers who had manned the walls now retreated at a full run to the citadel, the only refuge within Seville strong enough to withstand the Vikings.

Unable to breach the citadel walls, the Vikings gave up the attempt and set about looting the city. They took their time, spending a week amassing treasures from the palaces of the Moorish aristocracy and the houses of the city's wealthy silk merchants. They rounded up the strongest and most attractive men and women of Seville—Moors and Christians—for future sale to slavers and herded the weeping throng down to their ships on the Guadalquivir River.

HASTEIN LED INTO THE MEDITERRANEAN A FLEET OF SIXTY TWO VIKING LONG SHIPS SIMILAR TO THIS ONE, DEPICTED IN A TWENTIETH-CENTURY TAPESTRY.

The year was 844. In preparation for their first raid on Spain, the Vikings had beached their fleet of thirty ships on Isla Menor at the mouth of Spain's Guadalquivir River. From their base camp on the island, the Northmen attacked Seville, where the plunder proved to be so rich the majority of Vikings established a branch operation in the ransacked city, riding out on horseback to raid the surrounding towns and shipping their spoils and captives down to Isla Menor. For six weeks, the Vikings lingered in the battered city, giving the Moors ample time to regroup and launch a counter-offensive.

The Moors called the Vikings "Majus," derived from the Persian word "magus" for a priest of the Zoroastrian religion, a sect renowned for fire-worship. Magus also is the source for the English words "magi," "magic," and "magician," but among the Moors Majus meant "heathen."

As the Vikings took their time stripping the countryside around Seville, Abdurrhaman II, emir of Córdoba, gathered his army. He sent small units to ambush Viking raiding parties, while he led the main force to Seville where he took the Vikings by surprise. He captured 500 Vikings, so many that there was no room to hang them all on the city gallows; to accommodate the overflow, the Moors strung up Vikings from palm trees.

To celebrate his triumph (and perhaps to intimidate the recipient) Abdurrhaman sent 200 Vikings heads to a friend and ally in Tangiers. Meanwhile, the Vikings, who escaped the Moors' counterattack, were surrounded and stranded on Isla Menor, where they and their captives were starving. They sent a message to the emir with an offer: The Vikings would release all their captives in exchange for a guarantee of safe passage out of Spain, as well as a quantity of food and fresh clothes. Abdurrhaman paid the "ransom," taking great pleasure in seeing the Vikings depart and having his captive people returned to him.

AT THE CONCLUSION OF HIS "FUNERAL," HASTEIN LEAPT OFF THE BIER AND WITH HIS VIKINGS MASSACRED THE CONGREGATION IN THE CATHEDRAL OF LUNA.

The first Viking incursion into the Mediterranean had ended badly, but word spread among the Northmen of the wealth of the towns, the abundance of food and wine, the fruit and livestock in the countryside, and the warm climate, all of which made the region irresistible to other Vikings. Fifteen years later, Hastein and Bjorn took what they considered to be a virtually invincible fleet of 62 long ships into the Mediterranean to plunder the southern paradise.

BACK FROM THE DEAD

Once safe on his ship, Hastein climbed off his "sickbed" to put in action the next step of his scheme. After nightfall, his messenger called on the count and the bishop bearing the sad news that Hastein had died. On his deathbed he asked for one more favor—that the bishop offer his funeral Mass and then bury him in the cathedral monastery. Without a moment's hesitation, the bishop agreed and set a time for the funeral the next day.

Meanwhile, the story of the bloodthirsty Viking who had converted on his deathbed and now would be buried in the cathedral had spread to every household in the city. The next morning, a grave procession of fifty Vikings, each dressed in long, dark-colored robes, passed slowly into the city bearing

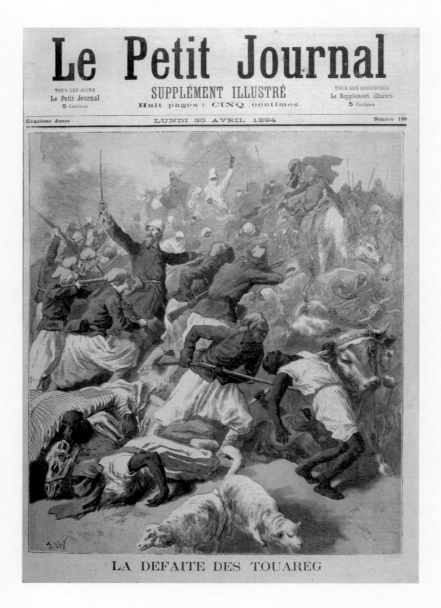

Le Petit Journal

SUPPLÉMENT ILLUSTRÉ

TOUS LES JOURS
Le Petit Journal
5 Centimes

Huit pages : CINQ centimes

TOUS LES DIMANCHES
Le Supplément illustré
5 Centimes

Cinquième Année   LUNDI 30 AVRIL 1894   Numéro 180

LA DEFAITE DES TOUAREG

THE TUAREGS, SHOWN HERE IN A NINETEENTH-CENTURY BATTLE, WERE THE "BLUE MEN" OF NORTH AFRICA WHOM THE VIKINGS CAPTURED AND SOLD AS SLAVES IN IRELAND.

Hastein's corpse on a bier. Lining the streets the entire way from the gates to the cathedral door stood the entire throngs of onlookers.

On the broad steps of the cathedral stood the bishop robed in elaborate black vestments, his golden crosier clasped in his left hand. Beside him was the count, and all around them stood a large number of priests and monks, as well as a crowd of altar boys, each one bearing a tall, lighted candle.

After blessing the corpse with holy water, the bishop led the grieving band of Vikings, along with a large crowd of curious townspeople, into the cathedral. Inside the crowd filled the nave, the monks filed into the choir, and the priests and altar took their places in the sanctuary. When the funeral Mass was over, the bishop gestured to the Vikings to follow him to the burial place.

Suddenly Hastein leapt off his bier, drew his sword, and before anyone in the church could react, killed the bishop. Turning on the count, who was too astonished to defend himself, Hastein killed him, too. As several of Hastein's men ran down the nave to bar the church doors, the rest of the Vikings threw off their mourning robes, pulled out their weapons, and attacked the defenseless congregation. In the bloody free-for-all that followed, the Vikings spared only a few young men and women who would fetch a good price at the slave market.

There must have been some prearranged signal, perhaps the tolling of the bell at the conclusion of the funeral, because as the fifty Viking "mourners" spilled out of the cathedral, their nearly 2,000 comrades leapt off their ships and charged into the city. For the rest of the day they killed and looted and took prisoners. When they had filled their ships with as many captives and as much loot as the boats could hold, the Vikings set fire to Luna and sailed away.

The sack of Luna had been a brilliant success except in one respect—the Vikings had attacked the wrong city. Somewhere during their adventures they had heard Christians speak of Rome as a great city of white marble buildings where every church and monastery held a fortune in gold and silver and precious jewels.

No Viking had ever plundered Rome, but Hastein and Bjorn intended to be the first. They knew Rome lay in the country of Italy near the coast of the Tyrrhenian Sea, but they had no directions more specific than that. When they entered the Gulf of Spezia on Italy's western shore and saw a lovely city of white marble churches behind high defensive walls, they assumed the town must be Rome, and poor Luna's fate was sealed.

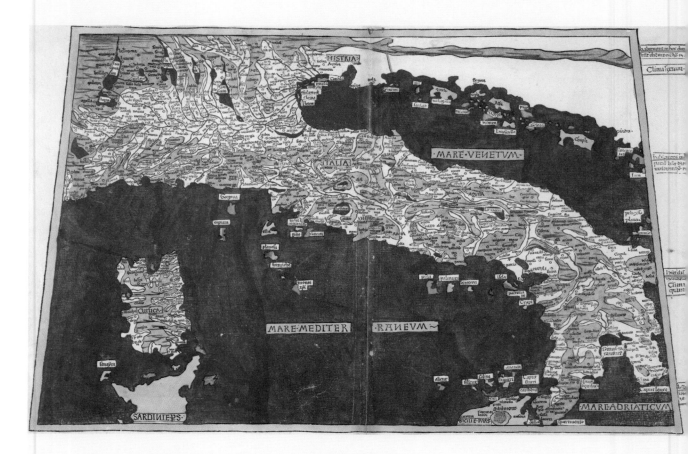

VIKINGS ON THE RIVIERA

"Blue men!" the slave trader bellowed. "Black Men!" A fascinated crowd of Vikings and Irish gathered around the auction block, staring at the strange men up for sale, fresh off a Viking ship from the Mediterranean. It was a late summer day in one of the port towns the Vikings had founded on the Irish coast, but compared to their homeland near the equator, the Africans must have found this strange island cold and damp. While the Africans shivered and the Irish stared, the auctioneer began taking bids from eager Viking buyers.

The "blue men" were probably tattooed Tuaregs, members of the Berber ethnic group found in modern-day Libya and Algeria. The "black men" were probably sub-Saharan Africans and may already have been slaves of the Moors of North Africa when the Vikings captured them.

In the summer of 859, Bjorn and Hastein led their fleet of sixty-two ships up the Guadalquivir River to Seville, hoping to have better luck than the first Viking raiders. In fact, they did much worse. The Moorish garrison defended their city with primitive flamethrowers that used a simple hand pump to spew burning naphtha that consumed ships and roasted men. After a disorderly retreat down the river, Bjorn and Hastein retaliated by plundering and burning the towns Algeciras and Cabo Tres Forcas in the province of Cádiz. Next they sailed to North Africa, where they seized their exotic slaves. Which North African towns they attacked or what success they enjoyed, aside from the captives, is unknown.

With winter coming, the Vikings made a seasonal camp in the south of France. The weather was still good, so they attacked Nîmes, Arles, and Valence. When the Franks sent an army against them the Vikings retreated to a new location—the Côte d'Azur on the French Riviera—from which they sacked the town of Pisa in Italy. It may have been from captured Pisans that the two Viking chiefs first heard of Rome.

For two years, the Viking fleet ricocheted around the Mediterranean, from southern Europe to northern Africa and back again. Hastein and Bjorn may even have attempted an assault on Alexandria in Egypt—there are rumors of such an attack, but nothing definitive in the records from the period. By 861, Bjorn and Hastein were ready to return home. As they drew close to the Strait of Gibraltar, they found their way blocked by a Moorish fleet. The Moors had never had a navy before, but after the last attack on Seville they built one specifically to crush the famous seafarers. The Vikings had generations of experience in naval warfare, but the Moors trumped it with their flamethrowers. Of the approximately sixty ships Bjorn and Hastein took into battle, only twenty managed to fight their way through to the Atlantic.

The Moors had adopted the flamethrower after the Byzantines had used it on them a century or so earlier. It was a heavy metal tube with a hand-operated pump. It operated just like the modern-day water cannons children play with in the summer. The tube was filled with a flammable chemical and then, by employing the pump, spewed liquid fire on one's enemies. Like the Byzantines, the Moors had found that the flamethrower was especially effective when used

HASTEIN KNEW ROME LAY NEAR THE TYRRHENIAN SEA ON THE WESTERN COAST OF ITALY, BUT HE MISTOOK LUNA FOR THE ETERNAL CITY.

THE MOORISH CONQUEST OF SPAIN

Islam gave the Arabs what they had never had before—a cohesive idea, bigger than any tribe or clan, around which all the tribes and clans could rally. Once they had been poor desert wanderers; now they were the chosen people of God. The truth of this statement was confirmed by the Prophet Muhammed, whose successful wars against his opponents convinced the Arabs that if they united against a common foe, they were virtually unstoppable.

After the death of Muhammed in 632, the Arabs found themselves in an interesting political situation. The two greatest empires in the region, the Persian and the Byzantine, had just finished a prolonged, destructive war that left both sides exhausted. Recognizing an opportunity to expand their power and their new religion, the Arabs swept down upon Persia, Syria, and Egypt. Worn out by their last war, the inhabitants barely put up a fight: The greatest lands in the Near East fell into the Arabs' laps. Then from Egypt the Arabs moved westward, conquering about half of North Africa.

In the year 710, Wittiza, the king of Spain, died. Wittiza had belonged to the Arian Christian sect, which the Catholic establishment viewed as heretical. Unwilling to see another Arian on the throne, the Catholic bishops of Spain, in a hastily organized ceremony, crowned a Catholic nobleman named Roderic king.

Wittiza's outraged relatives fled to North Africa to seek the protection of a Spanish Arian count named Julian, who ruled the region around present-day Ceuta in Morocco. To drive out Roderic and install an Arian king in Spain, Julian invited or perhaps hired to fight for him an army of Muslim Moroccans—Moors—led by a general named Tariq ibn Zayid. Julian even offered his own ships to ferry the Moors across the Strait of Gibraltar to Spain.

With Julian serving as his guide, showing him the best harbors, the richest towns, and all the other secrets of Spain, Tariq enjoyed the kind of advantage that rarely comes to an invader. There was one other advantage that Count Julian overlooked but that Tariq saw at once: Spain was a divided nation. Catholics and Arians were at each other's throats, and even within King Roderic's own family there were relatives who felt they deserved to be king. On July 19, w711, at the Battle of Guadalete at the southernmost tip of Spain, Tariq's Moorish army defeated and virtually

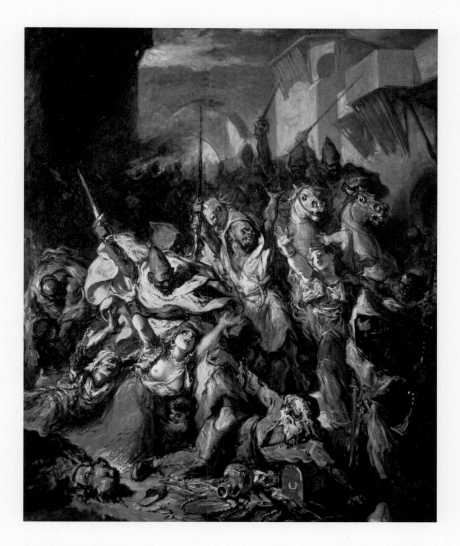

massacred Roderic's army. Roderic probably died in the carnage, but his body was never recovered.

Encouraged by news of such a promising beginning, the Moorish governor of North Africa sent reinforcements to Tariq. Capitalizing on the dissension in the country and the treachery of the Spanish, as well as on the Muslims' own sense of invincibility, Tariq conquered all of Spain and Portugal within five years. The only holdout was the Christian kingdom of Asturias in the northwest corner of the country.

against enemy ships, as they were built of wood and caulked with pitch. At the first spurt of flaming liquid a wooden ship would burst into flame.

After Hastein and Bjorn's near escape from the Moorish fleet, the Vikings steered away from the Mediterranean but continued to raid the Atlantic coast of Spain. In the late 960s, the Vikings sacked eighteen cities in the little Christian kingdom of Asturias on the Bay of Biscay. They captured the town of Santiago de Compostela, looted the shrine of St. James, killed the bishop Sisenand, and finding the country to their liking, decided to stay. For three years the Vikings occupied Galicia, living off the local population, and sometimes taking captives to sell as slaves, until in 971 a Galician count, Gonsalvo Sancho, raised an army and drove the Norsemen out.

The Vikings settled extensively throughout northern Europe, but they found no place for themselves in the Mediterranean—with one exception, the city of Constantinople. These Vikings, however, did not come to the great city through the Strait of Gibraltar; they traveled south on the rivers of Russia and the Ukraine to the Black Sea, where Byzantine generals recruited them to serve the emperor as mercenaries. The Byzantines liked to think of themselves as the heirs of the old Roman Empire, and in this respect at least they were imitating the caesars who had used barbarian warriors to buttress the strength of Rome's legions.

Contact between the Byzantines and the Vikings who had settled in and around Kiev must have begun no later than the early ninth century, because we know that in 839 Emperor Theophilus persuaded Viking chiefs, or "Rhos," as he called them, to let him hire some of their fighting men. Communication between the Vikings in the Ukraine and the Byzantines became more frequent after Olga, Princess of Kiev, and then her grandson, Vladimir, converted to Christianity.

THE VARANGIAN GUARD

By the late tenth century, there was a large Viking detachment serving in the Byzantine army—at least 6,000 men, each of whom had sworn a personal oath to fight in defense of the emperor. They were called the Varangian Guard, Varangian coming from two Old Norse words that mean "to swear an oath."

When Emperor Basil II attacked the rebel general Bardas Phocas, he brought the entire Varangian Guard with him. In the final battle, as Phocas's soldiers ran from the battlefield, the Varangians chased them down and, as one Byzantine chronicler put, "cheerfully hacked them to pieces." After that day, Basil made the Varangians his personal bodyguard—a function the Varangians performed for succeeding generations of Byzantine emperors.

Eventually, the Varangian Vikings converted to Christianity and adopted Greek as their first language. But they clung to some of their traditions. They had a preference for using axes in battle and a weakness for heavy drinking—although in Constantinople they drank wine rather than mead or ale. Their drunkenness was so conspicuous that when King Eric the Good of Denmark made a state visit to the Byzantine court in 1103, he delivered a speech to the Varangians, saying they were giving their countrymen a bad name and urging them to moderate their drinking.

There was one more thing the Varangians remembered—the runic alphabet of their homeland. Rune graffiti has been found on columns and other monuments in Constantinople (present-day Istanbul), as well as on a pair of marble lions that were once in Athens but are now displayed in Venice.

In 1204, when the men of the Fourth Crusade were persuaded to sack Constantinople rather than march to the Holy Land to liberate Jerusalem, the only section of the city that was not overrun by the Crusaders was the part defended by the Varangians. After that final victory, the Varangians disappear from the historical record. In the entire Mediterranean world, Constantinople was the only place where Vikings made a lasting impact.

THE BLOOD OF HEROES: IRISH AND VIKINGS AT THE BATTLE OF CLONTARF

FOR NEARLY 1,000 YEARS, THE BATTLE OF CLONTARF, FOUGHT between the Irish and the Vikings outside Dublin on Good Friday, April 23, 1014, has been celebrated as the defining event in the story of medieval Ireland. Traditionally the battle is seen as the climax of two centuries of Irish resistance to a brutal, heathen invader. According to this version of the story, at Clontarf the Christian Irish drove the pagan Viking horde out of Ireland for good.

It wasn't at all like that. In the first place, the Viking king of Dublin, Sitric Silkenbeard, was as Catholic as the Irish king, Brian Boru. Sitric is believed to have founded Dublin's first cathedral, Christ Church; the coins he minted bore the sign of the cross; and in the years after the battle, Sitric made two pilgrimages to Rome.

WHILE PRAYING IN HIS TENT, KING BRIAN BORU WAS KILLED BY A VIKING WHO HAD FLED THE BATTLEFIELD.

For all the misinformation and myth that has accumulated around Clontarf, it was nonetheless an important moment in Irish history. The Irish who assembled outside Dublin on that Good Friday most certainly wanted to keep Dublin and all the other cities along the eastern and southern coasts of their island that had been founded and were still occupied by the Vikings.

But it was not to defend their faith and reassert their freedom that the Irish had gone to war; under the Vikings, Dublin, Waterford, Wexford, Arklow, Cork, and Limerick had become thriving centers of international trade. They generated an enormous amount of wealth, and with wealth came political power and influence. The Irish wanted all that entirely under their control. They had come to see that the commercial economy introduced to the island by the Vikings was preferable to the rural, pastoral economy that had been the mainstay of Ireland for centuries. That is one reason why the Christian Irish waged war on the Christian Vikings.

The other reason was Brian Boru's desire to make Ireland a unified nation under a single strong king—specifically, himself. He had spent his long reign of thirty-eight years conquering or consolidating the many tiny kingdoms of Ireland; by 1014 he was master of three quarters of Ireland, as well as six of the seven Viking towns in the country. Only northern Ireland and Dublin still held out against him.

TIMELINE

926: BRIAN BORU IS BORN INTO AN IRISH ROYAL FAMILY THAT RULES COUNTIES LIMERICK AND CLARE.

C. 964: BRIAN AND HIS OLDER BROTHER MATHGAMAIN SACK THE VIKING PORT TOWN OF LIMERICK.

976: VIKINGS AND THEIR IRISH ALLIES ASSASSINATE MATHGAMAIN. BRIAN BECOMES KING OF MUNSTER.

1002: THE IRISH KING OF CONNAUGHT ABDICATES AND SURRENDERS HIS CROWN TO BRIAN.

996: BRIAN CONQUERS THE IRISH KINGDOM OF LEINSTER.

"POISONOUS, MURDEROUS, HOSTILE"

Vultures screamed overhead as the men lined up for battle. At one end of the field, their backs to the walls of Dublin, stood the Vikings, "shouting, hateful, powerful, wrestling, valiant, active, fierce-moving, dangerous, nimble, violent, furious, unscrupulous, untameable, inexorable, unsteady, cruel, barbarous, frightful, ready, huge, prepared, cunning, warlike, poisonous, murderous, hostile," as the adjective-loving author of the chronicle, the *Comgadh*, described them.

Arrayed against them were the Irish, "full of courage, quick, doing great deeds, pompous, beautiful, aggressive, hot, strong, swelling, bright, fresh, never-weary, terrible, valiant, [the] victorious heroes and chieftains and champions" of Ireland.

In terms of weapons, the Irish and the Vikings were equally matched: Both sides carried words, battle-axes, spears, and daggers. By this point the Vikings had begun to go into battle wearing heavy armor. The Irish were more lightly protected with metal collars around their necks and shoulders, and "crested golden helmets" on their heads.

Of the 7,500 men who rode onto the field of Clontarf under Brian's banner, the core of the army were the king's most loyal men from Munster, his home province. They were supported by fighting men from Connaught and a mixed band of Norse and Irish warriors recruited in Limerick and Waterford.

Sitric also had about 7,500 men fighting for him, including Irishmen under Maelmurda, the former king of Leinster, who hoped to reclaim his kingdom by leading a rebellion against Brian, and Vikings from the Scottish isles

IN THE HEAT OF BATTLE BRIAN'S SON MURCHAD STRIPPED THE VIKING EBRIC OF HIS MAIL SHIRT, THEN STABBED HIS HALF-NAKED ENEMY TO DEATH.

TIMELINE

1005: DURING A PILGRIMAGE TO THE TOMB OF ST. PATRICK AT ARMAGH, BRIAN ADOPTS A NEW TITLE, "EMPEROR OF THE IRISH."

1012: THE DEPOSED IRISH KING OF LEINSTER FORMS AN ALLIANCE WITH SITRIC, THE VIKING KING OF DUBLIN, TO REBEL AGAINST BRIAN.

APRIL 23, 1014: BRIAN BORU DEFEATS THE IRISH REBELS AND THEIR VIKING ALLIES AT THE BATTLE OF CLONTARF OUTSIDE DUBLIN. AT THE END OF THE BATTLE, BRIAN IS MURDERED. THE VIKINGS MAKE NO MORE RAIDS ON IRELAND. THOSE VIKINGS WHO REMAINED BECOME ASSIMILATED INTO IRISH SOCIETY.

THE SLAVE TRADE IN IRELAND

Often overlooked in accounts of the Vikings in Ireland is their reintroduction of slavery and the slave trade.

There had been slaves in pre-Christian Ireland, the most famous being St. Patrick, who at age 16 was captured by Irish raiders and sold to a chieftain in northern Ireland. After seven years as a slave, Patrick ran away and escaped back to his home in Britain. Understandably, St. Patrick became a fierce opponent of slavery. One of the few surviving authentic documents written by Patrick is a blistering letter addressed to a British warlord who had raided Ireland and carried off into slavery dozens of newly baptized Irish Christians. It's possible that St. Patrick's hatred of the slave trade influenced the Irish to give it up; certainly, by the time of the first Viking raids in the eighth century, slavery had died out in Ireland.

Initially the Vikings had taken their Irish captives overseas to be sold in Scandinavia or in the slave markets along the Baltic Sea. Once the Vikings settled in Ireland, however, they kept some of their Irish captives as slaves in Ireland. The Irish took it as a cruel insult, reducing their freeborn countrymen to slavery in their own land. As retaliation the Irish began a small-scale slave trade—but they bought and sold only Viking warriors captured in battle.

---

led by Sigurd the Stout, earl of the Orkneys, and Vikings from the Isle of Man led by Brodir, a renowned warrior.

The presence of so many Vikings on the battlefield surprised Brian. The night before, his scouts had reported seeing the Vikings climb into their long ships and sail away. Brian went to sleep that night elated, certain of an easy victory in the morning. But the Vikings had not deserted. Their "flight" was a ruse. They sailed a short distance away, then came ashore and prepared for battle, far from the eyes of Brian's scouts. At dawn on Good Friday the Irish awoke to find 3,000 armed Vikings on the field and an additional 3,000 Irishmen from Leinster fighting under Maelmurda. Inside Dublin were another 1,000 fighting men. And standing on the ramparts for a bird's-eye view of the coming battle was Sitric.

ST. PATRICK HAD FIRST COME TO IRELAND AT AGE 16 AS A SLAVE, AN EXPERIENCE THAT MADE HIM A LIFE-LONG OPPONENT OF SLAVERY.

Brian, on the other hand, was surrounded by family that day. His brother Cuduiligh, his son Murchad, his grandson Tordhelbach, and his nephew Conaing were all in command of various divisions of Brian's army. The king himself, at age 88, was too old and feeble to fight. He took his place on a ridge where he could observe the battle in safety. Nearby his tent was pitched, with a single servant to attend him.

Both the Irish and the Vikings adopted identical battle formations—the shield wall. Men of the front rank stood shoulder to shoulder, their shields overlapping to create a solid wall that their enemies—everyone hoped—could not penetrate. It is not known which army rushed the other first, but it would have been a near-suicidal charge as men hurled themselves against that wall of wood and metal and muscle, hacking at their enemies from above, stabbing up at them from below, trying to break the formation.

THE UNEXPECTED HEIR

A heady mix of hatred, ambition, and envy shaped the character of Brian Boru. He was born in 926, the younger son of the royal family of a minor Irish kingdom known as Thomond whose lands embraced most of the counties of Limerick and Clare. Because the River Shannon runs through these counties, for one hundred years the Vikings had sailed their long ships up the Shannon to pillage Thomond's monasteries and burn the halls of its kings. As a little boy, Brian survived one of these Viking assaults on the family's stronghold; his mother, though, was killed in the attack.

By 964 Brian's father was dead, too, and his older brother, Mathgamain, was king. Dissatisfied with the insignificance of his kingdom, Mathgamain longed for something grander. He laid claim to all of Munster, the province that covers the southwestern quarter of Ireland, by capturing the kingdom's chief fortress, the Rock of Cashel.

Maelmuad, the deposed king of Munster, tried to drive Mathgamain out by forging an alliance with the Vikings at Limerick, the city that stood at the mouth of the Shannon, within easy striking distance of Mathgamain's home territory. Mathgamain and Brian raised their own army and met the men of Munster and the Vikings at a place called Sulchoid in County Tipperary.

A vivid (if not always accurate) account of Brian's life, *Cogadh Gaedhel re*

THE VIKINGS RE-INTRODUCED SLAVERY TO IRELAND. SOME IRISH CAPTIVES THEY SOLD OVERSEAS, BUT MOST GALLING TO THE IRISH WERE THE IRISH SLAVES THE VIKINGS KEPT IN IRELAND.

Gaillaibh, or *The Wars of the of Irish Against the Foreigners*, tells how at Sulchoid "a fierce, bloody, crimsoned, violent, rough, unsparing, implacable battle" was fought between the rival kings. But it was the Vikings, led by their chief, Ivar, who gave up the fight first. They fled the field, running for the safety of Limerick's walls, with Mathgamain and Brian pursuing them. At Limerick, the Irish overwhelmed the Viking defenses, then set about looting the rich town.

"They carried off their jewels and their best property," the *Codagh* says, "and their saddles beautiful and foreign, their gold and silver, their beautifully woven cloth of all colors and of all kinds." Once all the valuables were safely stowed outside the town, the brothers' army set fire "to the fort and to the good town, [reducing everything] to a cloud of smoke and to red fire." Then the men of Thomond rounded up the town's survivors, "their soft, youthful, bright, matchless girls; their blooming, silk-clad young women; and their active, large, and well-formed boys." On a hill outside Limerick, the Irish assembled their prisoners; all those who were strong enough to bear arms Mathgamain and Brian had killed; the rest they sold into slavery.

UNEXPECTEDLY GENEROUS TERMS

Both Maelmuad and Ivar escaped the carnage at Sulchoid and Limerick. Several years later, they invited Mathgamain to a peace conference. It was an ambush in which Mathgamain was murdered.

Brian, now in his mid-fifties, inherited the crown and the obligation to avenge his brother. First he attacked the Vikings at the rebuilt town of Limerick, killing Ivar and Ivar's heir. Then he hunted down Maelmuad and killed him. With his brother's assassins dead, Brian was ready to make peace on unexpectedly generous terms. He permitted the Viking settlers to remain in Limerick and made an alliance with Maelmuad's son, Cain, marrying his daughter to the young prince. Cain, grateful to escape with his life and get a princess in the bargain, continued as Brian's most loyal ally for the rest of the king's life.

With his powerbase in Munster secure, Brian began to move against the kingdom of Leinster in the east and Connaught in the west. His ambition was to clear away the clutter of petty kingdoms in his homeland and become king of all Ireland.

Taking a lesson from the Vikings, Brian sent his ships up Ireland's rivers on lightning strikes against inland targets. For towns and fortresses along the coast Brian adopted a classic pincer movement, sending in his navy to hit the enemy head-on, then bringing his infantry up to attack the enemy's rear. It took fifteen years for Brian to subdue Leinster and Connaught, but in the end he won, thanks to his unconventional strategy of deploying both ships and land troops against his enemies.

The kings of Leinster and Connaught, who stuck to the traditional Irish method of fighting only on land, were not prepared for Brian's new, Viking-inspired style of warfare. In fact, Brian employed the same method to capture all the Viking cities in Ireland. The sole holdout was Dublin, but the city's Christian Viking king, Sitric Silkenbeard, seeing the way the wind was blowing, offered his allegiance to Brian without a fight.

Perhaps the loss of his independence chafed, perhaps Brian demanded too much tribute money—we do not know the cause, but in 999, Sitric rebelled against Brian. It was a puny uprising that Brian crushed easily. Sitric fled north into the territory of the Ui Neills.

BRIAN'S COMPLICATED FAMILY TREE

For generations, the Ui Neills had been the most prominent, most powerful royal house in Ireland. Brian Boru's campaign to become sole king in Ireland had weakened the Ui Neill; royal families that had once been loyal to them were now clients of Brian. In their ancestral territory—the northern province of Ulster—the Ui Neills were still independent, but they were not willing to antagonize Brian. They gave Sitric no help.

With no other option, Sitric went to Brian, begged for clemency, and offered his allegiance once again. And once again Brian showed generosity to a defeated foe: In exchange for Sitric's loyalty, Brian permitted him to remain king of Dublin, and Brian gave his daughter Slaine to be Sitric's wife.

With the Sitric-Slaine wedding, the ties between Sitric and Brian became more complicated. Brian's queen at the time was an Irish princess, Gormlaith, the sister of Maelmorda, the ex-king of Leinster, deposed by Brian himself. Gormlaith had had three husbands in succession. By Olaf Cuaran, king of Dublin, she bore Sitric. At Olaf's death she married Mael Sechnaill, the former high king of Ireland and Brian's chief rival. After her marriage to Mael was annulled, Gormlaith married Brian, bearing him a son, Donnchad. Sitric Silkenbeard, then, was Brian's vassal, his stepson, and his son-in-law.

EMPEROR OF THE IRISH

After Sitric's pledge of fealty, Brian enjoyed several years of peace during which he consolidated his power. In 1005, Brian made a pilgrimage of thanksgiving to Armagh, where St. Patrick lay buried. In the monastery church he left twenty ounces of gold on St. Patrick's altar. Before leaving the shrine Brian commanded his secretary to document his visit and his offering in the shrine's record book, *The Book of Armagh*. At his king's direction, the secretary used the new title Brian had given himself, *imperator Scottorum*, emperor of the Irish.

It was not such a daring claim. Brian was the most powerful man in Ireland, the greatest king the island had ever known. In addition to ruling over the provinces of Munster, Connaught, and Leinster, as well as all the Viking towns, he had been granted the title of high king, thus adding a certain ceremonial cache to his status as Ireland's supreme political strongman. Granted, Ulster in the north still was still not under his control, and the most of the little kings whom he had dispossessed were still alive and deeply resentful, yet Brian Boru was in a better position now than at any time in his military career.

In 1012, one of the kings Brian deposed, Maelmorda, ex-king of Leinster, formed an alliance with Sitric, raised an army, and rebelled against Brian. To his dismay, Brian learned that one of the instigators of the revolt was his wife, Gormaith, Maelmorda's sister and Sitric's mother. Her motives have not come down to us, but apparently Gormlaith felt a stronger sense of loyalty to her brother and son than to her husband. Brian imprisoned Gormlaith, then began a series of quick, destructive little raids on the villages around Dublin to frighten any Irishmen who considered joining Sitric and Maelmorda.

Gormlaith must have been a cunning woman, because even in prison she hatched a new scheme. Somehow she got an appeal to Sigurd Lodvesson, also known as Sigurd the Stout, the Viking earl of the Orkney Islands, begging him to come free her from her cruel husband. She made the same offer to a well-known Viking warrior from the Isle of Man named Brodir. In her letters Gormlaith offered both men the same deal: If they freed her and killed Brian, she would become her hero's wife, bringing Dublin as her dowry. For Gormlaith's sake and a chance at becoming king of the richest prize in Ireland, Sigurd and Brodir joined Sitric and Maelmorda's rebellion.

HAND-TO-HAND COMBAT

The battle of Clontarf raged all day in the fields west of Howth and along the River Liffey. Initially, the Vikings and the Leinster men had the upper hand, but once the shield walls had broken up, the fighting became hand-to-hand, and the Irish began to drive their enemies back toward the river and farther back to Dublin Bay.

Brian's grandson Tordelbach was fighting right on the banks of the Liffey when a blow to the head knocked him unconscious; he fell into the water and drowned. The author of the *Comgadh*, though, claims that Tordelbach dragged three Vikings down with him.

Meanwhile, Brodir attacked the left flank of Brian's army, where the king's brother Cuduiligh was in command. Initially the Vikings drove the Irishmen back, but then Brodir and Cuduiligh came face to face. In the ferocious one-on-one match that ensued, Cuduiligh battered Brodir's armor, knocked him to the ground, and was ready to strike the death blow when Brodir scrambled up and ran.

During Brodir's desertion, Brian's son Murchad led his men into the fray. This division of Irish was considered the best fighters in Brian's army—and they were almost all distantly related to the king. Unable to withstand an assault from Cuduligh and Murchad's men, Brodir's Vikings broke ranks and ran for their ships.

In the center, Sigurd and Maelmurda were fighting Brian's men from Munster. A Norse legend says that the Vikings had with them an enchanted battle standard of a raven, woven by Sigurd's mother, that guaranteed victory to the side that possessed it but also guaranteed death to whoever held the banner. According to the story, the Vikings dropped the standard, and no one was willing to touch it—except Sigurd, who raised it high as Murchad came straight at him.

It's said that Murchad, 63 years old at the time, rode into battle bearing a sword in each hand, in the style of an Irish hero of old. In single combat with

INSPIRED BY THE SPEED AND MANEUVERABILITY OF VIKING VESSELS, BRIAN BORU BUILT HIS OWN FLEET OF LONG SHIPS.

Sigurd, he smashed the Viking earl's helmet, knocking it off his head, then hacked at Sigurd's throat, killing him. A Viking named Ebric, one of the men Sigurd had brought from Scotland, rushed on Murchad, slashing him with his sword. Murchad grabbed Ebric's coat of mail, pulled it over his head, and then stabbed the Viking three times with his sword. As he began to fall, Ebric pulled out his dagger and slashed open Murchad's belly. Both men dropped to the ground, Ebric dead, Murchad mortally wounded. Brian's son and heir died the next day.

THE VIKINGS' NATURAL INHERITANCE

With Sigurd dead and Brodir gone from the battle, the Vikings began to retreat. Their only escape route lay across a single small bridge, which created a bottleneck of panicky men. As the desperate Vikings pushed and shoved to get across the river, the Irish bore down on them; it was a slaughter.

Those Vikings who managed to get across the bridge found no escape there either. Before the battle, following their usual practice, the Vikings had beached their ships along the Liffey above the high water line. But an unusually high tide had lifted the boats and carried them into midstream. The Vikings dove into the water to swim to their boats, but the weight of their armor dragged them down to the river bottom. More long ships lay offshore in Dublin Bay, and a number of Vikings tried to swim to those ships, too.

From the battlements of Dublin, Sitric and Slaine watched the carnage. As the frightened Vikings made their frantic dive into the sea, Slaine remarked that in this fight they had "gained their natural inheritance," a snide reference to the Vikings as pirates who were getting what they deserved. Sitric smacked her.

AN OLD MAN, ALONE

Brian Boru did not witness his victory. He had watched the beginning of the battle and then retired to his tent. As the Irish were slaughtering their enemies, Brian knelt on a cushion before his crucifix, praying from the book of psalms.

Passing through the woods outside the king's tent, still trying to find some way to reach safety, was the fugitive Brodir with two companions. The Vikings saw Brian in his tent at the same moment the king's attendant spotted the Vikings. He shouted a warning to Brian that armed enemies were outside. "It is not to do good to thee that they come," Brian replied.

Seeing the old man alone with his psalter and his crucifix, Brodir's companions assumed he was a Catholic priest, but Brodir recognized the Irish king. Gripping his "bright, gleaming, trusty battle-axe" he rushed into the tent and split Brian's skull. The old king fell dead.

A Norse saga, *The Story of Burnt Njal*, claims that an Irish warrior named Wolf the Quarrelsome made it his mission to track down Brian's killer. When he found Brodir, he made a small slit in the Viking's belly, tacked one end of his intestines to a tree, then dragged Brodir around and around, until all his entrails were wound about the trunk.

THE HIGH PRICE OF VICTORY

It's estimated that 4,000 of Brian's men and 6,000 men from the combined forces of Sitric, Maelmorda, Sigurd, and Brodir fell at Clontarf. It was the highest number of Viking dead ever recorded in a single battle in Ireland and became a source of pride among the Irish ever after.

But also among the dead were Brian, his son Murchad, his grandson Tordelbach, his nephew Conaing, his brother Cuduiligh, and countless princes and lords from the royal and noble clans of Munster. Monks from Armagh escorted the bodies of Brian and Murchad, and the head of Conaing (he must have been decapitated in battle and his body never found) to St. Patrick's church, where they held a twelve-day wake for the dead.

Donnchad, Brian's son by Gormlaith, inherited but could not keep the "empire" his father bequeathed to him. One by one the minor kingdoms split away, reasserting their independence. In the end, Donnchad was king only of Munster. Mael Sechnaill, the high king whom Brian had deposed, maneuvered successfully to become high king again. And Sitric remained king of Dublin.

The Battle of Clontarf was a victory for the Irish, but it did not unify Ireland as Brian had hoped, nor did it consolidate Irish rule in the hands of a single king. It did, however, give birth to a stirring legend of a pitched battle in which the Irish reclaimed their island from a despised invader. It is a story that would inspire generations of Irish rebels as they fought to drive the English from Ireland.

THE END OF THE VIKING AGE: THE BATTLE OF STAMFORD BRIDGE

A T A SCRUFFY LITTLE WOODEN BRIDGE OUTSIDE THE CITY of York, King Harold of England crushed a Viking invasion and put an end to almost three centuries of piratical raids from Scandinavia. It should have been what the English call "a famous victory," and to a point it was. But although he was triumphant against the Viking invaders, a little more than two weeks later Harold would be killed trying to fight off Norman invaders led by William the Conqueror.

The Battle of Stamford Bridge is one of the great "what if" moments in history. If Harold and his army had not had to race north to York to drive out the Vikings, wouldn't they have been fresh enough and strong enough and had sufficient numbers of men to defeat William at Hastings? The answer is, "maybe." But had the Normans been defeated, history and the world map would be very different today.

THE BERSERKER AT THE BRIDGE

The English had never seen anything like this berserker. At nearly seven feet tall, he dwarfed even Norway's towering king, Harald Hardrada. He wore a

coat of chain mail that fell almost to his knees, and in his massive hands he held a huge battle-axe.

The sole survivor of the Viking rear guard, he had taken his position at the far side of the narrow wooden bridge that spanned the Derwent River near the village of Stamford, seven miles east of York. Behind him, on the other side of the bridge, the panicked Norsemen were scrambling to get in battle formation. Before him was arrayed the English army, keen to thunder across the bridge and start slaughtering the invaders. The only thing in the English army's way was this one anonymous berserker.

A handful of English soldiers rushed him; with a few powerful swings of his axe, the giant killed them all. Another band of Englishmen attacked him, and he killed all of them, too. English archers fired a volley of arrows at the Viking, but the arrows were deflected by his chain mail armor.

While the berserker was busy dispatching yet a third group, an English soldier gathered some companions and slipped away to the river, following along its banks until they found a small boat. Taking care to paddle quietly

TIMELINE

1016: KING AETHELRED THE UNREADY DIES. THE ENGLISH ACCEPT AS THEIR KING CANUTE, KING OF DENMARK, WHO HAS CONQUERED ALMOST ALL OF ENGLAND.

1042: CANUTE DIES WITH NO HEIR TO SUCCEED HIM. AETHELRED'S SOLE SURVIVING SON, EDWARD THE CONFESSOR, IS CROWNED KING OF ENGLAND.

1053: KING EDWARD'S BROTHER-IN-LAW, HAROLD GODWINSON, BECOMES EARL OF WESSEX, MAKING HIM THE SECOND MOST POWERFUL MAN IN THE REALM.

1064: HAROLD IS SHIPWRECKED ON THE COAST OF FRANCE. LATER, WILLIAM, DUKE OF NORMANDY AND LATER, KNOWN AS WILLIAM THE CONQUEROR, WILL ALLEGE THAT WHILE HAROLD WAS HIS GUEST HE SWORE TO SUPPORT WILLIAM'S CLAIM TO THE ENGLISH THRONE.

and stay on the far side of the Derwent, out of the Viking's sight, they came at last to the bridge. When the rowers had maneuvered the boat under the bridge, directly beneath the berserker, the English soldier thrust his spear through a gap in the bridge's floorboards, rammed the spear point into the Viking's groin and up into his abdomen, then wrenched it out again. Bellowing in agony and gushing blood, the berserker fell to the ground, mortally wounded.

With a loud cheer, the English army surged forward, leaping over the body of the giant as they stampeded across Stamford Bridge. The date of the final, decisive English victory over of the Vikings was September 25, 1066.

THE CONFESSOR

ST. EDWARD THE CONFESSOR DIED CHILDLESS, THEREBY SETTING OFF THE RIVALRY BETWEEN EARL HAROLD AND DUKE WILLIAM THAT RESULTED IN THE NORMAN CONQUEST.

Nine months before the Stamford battle, England's devoutly Christian king, Edward the Confessor, died. His generosity to the poor, gifts to the Church, and lifelong chastity convinced the English people that their king had been a saint; they began to refer to him as "Edward the Confessor" (a confessor is a saint who did not die a martyr). When Edward was young, many people who knew him expected he would become monk; no one imagined he would ever be king, for the simple reason that Edward had eight half-brothers, all of whom came ahead of him in the line of succession.

TIMELINE

JANUARY 5, 1066:
EDWARD THE CONFESSOR DIES
CHILDLESS. THE LEADING NOBLEMEN
OF ENGLAND CHOOSE HAROLD
GODWINSON AS THEIR KING.

SEPTEMBER 25, 1066: AT STAMFORD BRIDGE
NEAR YORK, THE ENGLISH SCORE
A DECISIVE VICTORY OVER VIKINGS,
PUTTING AN END TO ALMOST
300 YEARS OF VIKING RAIDS AND
INVASIONS.

OCTOBER 14, 1066:
WILLIAM, DUKE OF NORMANDY,
INVADES ENGLAND. AT THE BATTLE
OF HASTINGS HE DEFEATS THE
ENGLISH, SLAYS HAROLD, THEN
MARCHES ON LONDON, WHERE HE
CLAIMS THE ENGLISH CROWN FOR
HIMSELF.

Edward's father was King Aethelred the Unready, a direct descendant of Alfred the Great, and like his noble ancestor, Aethelred experienced a reign marred by almost continual warfare with the Vikings. (By the way, Aethelred's title "the unready" is actually a mistranslation of an Old English word: *unræd* means "ill-advised," not "unready").

Tragically, in Aethelred's case, the Vikings gained the upper hand, the Anglo-Saxon royal family was displaced, and England's next king was a Viking, Canute I. Also known as Canute the Great, Canute was a Dane who by force of arms, skillful manipulation of his political allies, and just plain good luck became supreme ruler of England, Denmark, Norway, and a slice of western Sweden and northern Germany. For twenty years, Canute reigned over England, and at his death his three sons stood ready to establish a Danish dynasty in England. But just like all of Edward's older brothers, death claimed Canute's sons, one by one. The death of Canute and all his heirs gave the Anglo-Saxon royal family an opportunity to regain their throne, and the next man in line for the crown was Edward the Confessor.

Since age ten, Edward had been living quietly in Normandy among his mother's relatives; now the leading nobles and bishops of England invited him home to become their king and reestablish the Anglo-Saxon royal line. The year was 1042, and Edward was thirty-seven years old.

As the sole surviving son of England's King Aethelred the Unready, Edward was indisputably the heir to the throne. But he had been away from home for 27 years. He had no allies among the English powerbrokers. He did not know whom among the nobles, bishops, and abbots he could trust. And he had no political experience of government.

During Canute's reign, Earl Godwin of Wessex had become the most powerful Englishman in the country; Edward would need Godwin's support if he hoped to rule effectively. An alliance with Godwin would not be a simple matter, however, because just six years earlier, to prove his loyalty to Harald, Canute's son and heir, Godwin had seized Edward's younger brother Alfred and blinded him so brutally that the English prince had died of his wounds. But political expediency demanded that Edward put aside feelings of family loyalty and his natural impulse for vengeance. And so, shortly after his arrival in England, Edward married Earl Godwin's daughter Edith, who was about thirteen years old at the time.

Edward and Edith had no children. After his canonization as St. Edward the Confessor, it was said that the king so envied the life of monks that he made a private vow to remain a virgin; although they were technically husband and wife, Edward and Edith lived as chastely as a brother and sister. It is also possible the couple was infertile or incompatible, or that Edward was homosexual. All of this

ST. EDWARD THE CONFESSOR DIED CHILDLESS, THEREBY SETTING OFF THE RIVALRY BETWEEN EARL HAROLD AND DUKE WILLIAM THAT RESULTED IN THE NORMAN CONQUEST.

is sheer speculation, of course; the only fact we possess is that Edward produced no heir. When Edward died on January 5, 1066, all of England wondered whether he had promised the crown to any man in particular.

Edward's brother-in-law and the Earl Godwin's son, Harold Godwinson, 44 years old, had been at the deathbed of the king. He said that before Edward died he had named Harold as his successor. This scenario does appear likely because the Witan, the assembly of the most prominent men in the kingdom (and a forerunner of the English Parliament), immediately threw its support behind Harold, even arranging for him to be crowned king the very next day.

And in every respect Harold was an excellent choice for king of England. He had been raised in a family that knew how to wield political power. As earl of Wessex, East Anglia, and Hereford he was the preeminent nobleman in the land. He had fathered five sons, so barring a repetition of the disasters that overtook all of Edward the Confessor's half-brothers, continuity would return to the English royal family. And he was the kind of man other men followed: He had courage, eloquence, and a sharp wit; he was tall, good-looking, and physically strong—once, alone and with his bare hands, he pulled two men out of a pool of quicksand. In the absence of any member of Edward's family, Harold Godwinson was a good choice for king of England.

THE PERJURED MAN

Across the English Channel was a man who insisted that he was a member of the English royal family and that the throne of England by right was his. Duke William of Normandy, about 38 years old, was the illegitimate son of one of Edward the Confessor's first cousins. As the contender with a true, if tainted, claim by blood to the English crown, William had been looking for an opportunity to assert his right; in 1064 he got his chance.

News reached William that his rival, Harold Godwinson, had been shipwrecked on the coast of northern France and seized by Count Guy of Ponthieu, who expected that King Edward and the Godwins would pay a large ransom to get the second most powerful man in England back safe and unharmed. Duke William frustrated his vassal's plans by commanding Guy to turn Harold over to him.

William treated Harold as an honored guest, even inviting him along on a military expedition against the Bretons. Some historians believe that by taking Harold along on a military campaign, William was showing his rival the strength and skill of his cavalry and infantry.

After his men trounced the Bretons, William brought Harold back to Normandy where he made him an offer: If Harold swore a solemn oath on the relics of saints recognizing William's right to succeed King Edward, William, once he was king of England, would make Harold richer and more powerful than he was now. Behind the generous offer was an unspoken threat: If Harold refused to take the oath, he would be locked up in a Norman dungeon. Harold had no choice; he placed his hands on the reliquaries and swore in the presence of witnesses that William was Edward the Confessor's heir.

Did Harold mean what he said at the oath-taking ceremony? Probably not. In the first place, he could maintain that the oath was not binding because he had made it under duress. In the second place, why would Harold, who at Edward's death would be militarily and politically the most powerful man in England, quietly step aside so a Norman duke could become king?

Furthermore, it is likely that William understood this perfectly, that he purposely had put Harold in the awkward position of swearing falsely, so that when Harold repudiated his oath at some future date, William could use it as just one more reason to invade England. All that would come later, of course. In the meantime, William kept up the charade of the gracious host, and sent Harold home, loaded down with expensive gifts.

In fact, there was an heir who had a better claim to the title "king of England" than Harold or William—Edward the Confessor's grand-nephew, Edgar, known as the Aetheling, or Prince. After the death of Edgar's father, Edward brought the boy and his two sisters to the royal palace, where he raised them. If Edward had lived longer, Edgar undoubtedly would have been his choice as successor, but when Edward lay dying in 1066, Edgar was about fourteen years old. England needed a man as king, so Edward passed over the boy and chose Harold Godwinson to succeed him.

A TYRANT IN THE FAMILY

At a time when English noblemen were *non grata*, Earl Godwin had become the Danish king Canute's trusted advisor. By 1064, Godwin's son Harold had ingratiated himself with Edward the Confessor and stood an excellent chance

of becoming the childless king's successor. In this family of skillful politicians, the odd man out was Harold's younger brother, Tostig, Earl of Northumbria. He had no finesse. He alienated the thanes, the noblemen of Northumbria, by murdering two of their own who were guests in Tostig's house—a violation of a promise of safe conduct and a gross affront to the Anglo-Saxon code of safeguarding the lives of one's guests.

When the thanes objected, Tostig responded with more acts of tyranny. The thanes countered by rising up against their earl. England could not afford such turmoil in Northumbria, a wealthy province and home to York, the kingdom's second most important city. In an effort to sort out the mess, Harold met with the thanes. Persuaded that his brother was unfit to rule, he recommended, reluctantly, that Edward the Confessor strip Tostig of his earldom and banish him.

Over the next two years, Tostig did all he could undermine Edward, Harold, and England. He went to William of Normandy and offered to help him seize the English throne; William declined the offer. Then he got a small fleet of ships and harried Sandwich, Norfolk, and Lincolnshire, but was driven away by Earl Edwin of Mercia and his younger brother Earl Morcar. Finally Tostig approached the King of Norway, Harald Hardrada, with an offer to help him become king of England. Hardrada found it an interesting proposal; by the time Edward the Confessor died in the first days of 1066, Hardrada had become convinced that he was the legitimate heir to the English crown.

Harold and William each had a reasonable claim to England; Hardrada's claim, one the other hand, was wildly implausible. It went like this: Harthacanute, king of Denmark and England and the last son of Canute the Great, had made a treaty with Magnus, king of Norway, swearing that if he died without a male heir to succeed him, the crown of England would pass to Magnus. Harthacanute did die without producing a son, but throughout his reign, rebels and rivals kept Magnus tied down in Norway. He, too, died without ever having a son and without having asserted his right to the English crown. At Magnus's death, his uncle, Hardrada, declared that he was the natural heir of Magnus' realm—and that realm included England. So in September 1066, with 300 long ships, approximately 7,000 warriors, and the exiled Earl Tostig in tow, Hardrada mounted what would be the last Viking invasion of England.

The Vikings came ashore on the northeast coast of England at Scarborough; in the classic Viking style, they looted the town and then burned it. With the treasures of Scarborough safe aboard the ships, Hardrada directed his fleet down the River Ouse to an obscure place called Riccall where he beached some of the long ships and anchored others in the shallows. Here the Vikings prepared to move against York, about a fifteen-mile march away.

SPLINTERED SHIELDS AND SHATTERED SKULLS

Edwin and Morcar, the brothers who had defeated Tostig once before, were the first noblemen to prepare to resist the Viking invasion. Each man would have been able to bring his personal army of 200–500 men, known as house-carls—members of the earls' households who were experienced warriors of unquestioned loyalty.

Edwin and Morcar also called up the fyrd, the militia composed of free peasants, as well as recruits from York, which brought their fighting strength up to about 3,000 men. That the earls had been able to assemble a respectable army within days of first sighting the Norwegian fleet indicates that the English had developed an efficient system for getting fighting men into the field.

The two armies met at a place called Fulford. The earls chose ground that looked easy to defend; on their right was the River Ouse, on their left was a marsh, while meandering across the field between marsh and river was a stream, the German Beck. Edwin commanded near the river, and Morcar near the marsh. In the first clash between Englishmen and Vikings, Morcar's men gained the upper hand, bogging down the Vikings in the muck of the swamp. Hardrada sent in more men, putting additional pressure on the center of the English line as well as Edwin's position along the river. Under this two-pronged attack the English battle lines wavered, and now Hardrada entered the fight.

A powerfully built man who stood nearly six and a half feet tall, Hardrada rushed into the fight swinging his massive battle-axe in a wide, deadly arc that smashed English shields and splintered English skulls. Protecting the king were Hardrada's picked men who formed a semicircle of shields and spears around their lord, keeping would-be attackers at bay while also keeping themselves clear of his death-dealing axe. The center, weakened by Hardrada's attack, collapsed, followed almost immediately by the retreat of Edwin's men from

their position beside the Ouse. Again the Vikings pressed their advantage, and now Edwin's men broke ranks completely and ran for the safety of York.

At the other end of the field, Morcar's men were pinned down, with Vikings assaulting them on three sides and their backs to the marsh. Yet the English fought on, even as they were being driven back into the swamp where, exhausted, knee-deep in mud, and unable to flee, about 500 Englishmen were slaughtered by the Vikings. Somehow Earl Morcar escaped the massacre.

From Fulford, the Vikings marched on York, which surrendered immediately. Hardrada demanded hostages and provisions, and then settled down with Tostig to plot their next move.

THE SUNBATHERS

While Edwin and Morcar fought the Vikings, King Harold Godwinson was in London preparing to repel an attack from Normandy where Duke William—at the moment known as "the Bastard" but soon to be called "the Conqueror"—had assembled his fleet to invade England and seize the English throne for himself.

The news that the king of Norway, accompanied by Harold's outlaw brother, had landed in Yorkshire and burned Scarborough to the ground created a dilemma for the English king: Would he have time to rush north and drive out the Vikings before William arrived in England? A violent storm that blew up in the English Channel and wrecked part of the English navy made the decision for Harold—if he had lost ships to the storm, so had William. Gambling that it would take time for the Normans to repair and refit their battered fleet, Harold called out his private army and then sent messengers speeding to West Mercia and East Anglia with orders that the fyrd should meet him on the road to York.

Although the English almost always fought on foot, they rode to war on horseback. London is approximately 220 miles from York, and Harold and his mounted army covered the distance in only four days, arriving at a place called Tadcaster, a few miles outside York, on September 24. After a night's rest, on September 25, Harold and his army rode east to the Viking camp at Stamford Bridge.

The weather was hot, and after their victory at Fulford and the capitulation of York, the Vikings were spending a leisurely day beside the River Derwent. Some were swimming, and others had stripped off their clothes and were lying in the sun. Suddenly someone among the sunbathing Vikings saw a bright flashing light at the crest of the hill overlooking the bridge—it was the sun reflecting off thousands of English helmets and spear points. As Harold and his army came into view, the astonished Vikings scrambled to their feet. None of them had armor, few of them had weapons, and some of them were naked or nearly so. The men on the north side of the bridge, the side closest to Harold, ran for the opposite shore.

To cover their retreat, Hardrada ordered a small party of warriors to take up positions on the north side of the bridge and hold off the English as long as possible. In their first charge the English killed the Viking rear guard quickly

EDITH SWAN-NECK, HAROLD'S QUEEN, DISCOVERS HER HUSBAND'S BODY ON THE HASTINGS BATTLEFIELD.

enough—all except the berserker with the axe. Once he was dead, the English crossed to the south shore and lined up for battle.

There is a story of King Harold riding close to the Viking lines to parlay with his brother, Tostig. If he left Hardrada's service right now, Harold swore to grant him a full pardon and restore his rank and lands to him. Tostig shouted back a question—"What would Harold give Hardrada?" Harold replied that usually he gave his enemies six feet of earth, but since Hardrada was taller than most men, he would allow him seven feet of English ground. Then Harold ordered his men to attack.

Lacking armor and sufficient weapons, the Vikings were at a disadvantage. Hardrada had sent riders back to the ships to bring up reinforcements, but the

AT THE BATTLE OF HASTINGS IN 1066 THE INVADING NORMANS KILLED KING HAROLD, DROVE THE ENGLISH FROM THE FIELD, THEN WENT ON TO CONQUER ALL OF ENGLAND.

WILLIAM THE CONQUEROR

Before he was known as "the Conqueror," William was known as "the Bastard." His father, Duke Robert of Normandy, had taken an undertaker's daughter as his mistress. Duke Robert never married the woman (her name was Herleva), but did recognize his illegitimate son and, while William was still a child, named him his heir. In 1035, Duke Robert died, and 7-year-old William was suddenly Duke of Normandy.

With William too young to rule on his own and no one trustworthy willing to rule temporarily in his name, Normandy descended into chaos. Violent crime escalated, neighboring knights and nobles stole the duke's property, several members of Duke Robert's family were murdered in bloody feuds, and finally, in 1047, the Count of Brienne tried to seize all of Normandy for himself. By this time William was 19 or 20 years old; he enlisted the help of the king of France and drove the count from Normandy. Then William set about restoring law and order.

In 1053, he married Matilda of Flanders; they were happy together, although physically they were mismatched—William stood more than six feet tall and became obese as he aged, while Matilda stood only four feet two inches tall and always remained petite.

William claimed that his childless cousin, Edward the Confessor, had promised he would inherit the throne of England. Most modern historians believe Edward never said any such thing. The Norman invasion of England, was a calculated gamble on William's part. But after he killed Harold and defeated the English army at Hastings in 1066, William stopped at nothing to consolidate his power in England.

With great brutality, within 5 years William subdued the entire country. He killed or scattered almost all the English nobility, giving their lands to Normans. He introduced feudalism to England, which made the English peasants little better than slaves. And although he kept traditional English laws on the books, he sought every opportunity to mangle and exploit them for his own purposes. The English monk who wrote the *Anglo-Saxon Chronicle* characterized William as "stern beyond all measure to people who resisted his will." Yet the England that exists today is a direct product of William the Conqueror.

Vikings at Stamford Bridge could still expect hours of hard fighting before help arrived. When the reinforcements did reach the battlefield, they proved to be little help: After running about sixteen16 miles from Riccall in the late summer heat, the Vikings were physically exhausted; they fell easily before the English swords.

Tostig was killed that day, and so was Eynstein Orre, leader of the reinforcements from the ships. Hardrada died when an English arrow pierced his throat. As the Vikings retreated to Riccall, the English harried them the entire way, leaving a trial of corpses from Stamford Bridge to the River Ouse where the Vikings had beached their fleet. Of the 300 ships and 7,000 men Hardrada had brought to England, approximately 750 men in 30 ships returned home to Norway.

Two weeks after his return to London, Harold and his army were on the move again. William of Normandy was about to land his invasion force of 600 ships at Hastings. The Battle at Stamford Bridge had weakened Harold's army; nonetheless, when the English and the Normans faced off against each other on October 14, 1066, the fight could have gone either way. Traditionally it's believed that the decisive moment came when Harold was killed by an arrow in the eye. Without their king, the English abandoned the field.

William moved against London, meeting little or no resistance—which proved to be the case in most of southern England. Resistance was stiffer in northern England; it took William six years to put down the rebellions that flared up in the northern counties. Although he had been crowned king of England on Christmas Day, 1066, it was not until 1072 that he had the realm firmly under his control.

THE AFTERMATH OF THE CONQUEST

The repercussions of the Norman victory at Hastings have been felt for at least 800 years, from India to Ireland to Canada. Norman aggression did not end in England: The Normans conquered Wales, reducing an independent kingdom into an English satellite. They invaded Ireland, setting off 800 years of Irish-English hostilities. But the primary power struggle would be between England and France.

As king of England and duke of Normandy, William had one foot in Britain and another in France. This was further complicated a century later when his descendant, Henry II, married the French heiress Eleanor of Aquitaine, who brought along whole French provinces as her dowry.

The kings of France could not tolerate having large swaths of their country in Englishand hands, and the kings of England would not relinquish lands that brought them great wealth and made them a power on the Continent. The tension between England and France, which often broke out in long, nasty wars, endured into the nineteenth century. By then, their contest to gain the upper hand had spread across the globe: In the eighteenth century, England, seized France's colonies in India and Canada; as revenge, France helped the American colonies break free from England. And it all began with an English victory over the Vikings at Stamford Bridge.

VENGEANCE ON HER MIND: OLGA OF KIEV

TERRITORIALLY VAST, RICH IN RESOURCES, AND POLITICALLY unpredictable, Russia—even without its satellite nations from Soviet days—is a major power broker in the modern world. Hundreds of ethnic, racial, and religious minorities dwell within its borders, but they are all Russian citizens. And we can trace the origins of that arrangement not to the ancient native inhabitants of the lands we know today as Russia and the Ukraine, but to the Vikings.

About the year 800, ships, mainly from Sweden, began to sail down the broad rivers that are still the highways of Russian and Ukrainian commerce. These Swedes came to trade, but once they saw how the inhabitants of this vast land were divided into small, militarily weak tribal bands, they decided to stay on as conquerors.

In short order, they subdued tiny communities of Slavs, Finns, and countless other ethnic groups to form the beginnings of the Norse-Slavic kingdom. As for the larger tribes in the neighborhood—the Magyars and the Khazars—who put up a stronger resistance, the Vikings simply avoided them. By 850, the Vikings dominated a huge swathe of what would be Estonian, Russian, and Ukrainian territory that stretched from the Baltic to the Black Sea. This was the beginning of a new

IN 862 ROURIK, OR RURIK, A WARLORD FROM SWEDEN, FOUNDED THE VIKING DYNASTY THAT RULED KIEV.

ROURIK
I.ᴱᴿ

*il monta sur le trône en 862, ré-
gna 17. ans et mourut en 879.*

TIMELINE

C. 800: VIKINGS SAIL DOWN THE RIVERS OF THE UKRAINE AND RUSSIA.

C. 850: RURIK, A DANE, BECOMES THE FIRST VIKING RULER OF THE UKRAINE REGION THAT WILL BECOME KNOWN AS KIEVAN RUS. HE ESTABLISHES HIS CAPITAL AT NOVGOROD.

C. 880: RURIK'S BROTHER-IN-LAW, OLEG, SUCCEEDS HIM AND MOVES THE CAPITAL TO KIEV.

903: OLGA MARRIES IGOR, HEIR AND GRANDNEPHEW OF RURIK.

941: IGOR LEADS A NAVAL ASSAULT ON CONSTANTINOPLE.

945: THE DREVLIANS, ONE OF THE TRIBES CONQUERED BY THE KIEV VIKINGS, REFUSE TO PAY ANY MORE TRIBUTE TO IGOR AND ASSASSINATE

---

kingdom the historians refer to as Kievan Rus. Kiev was the town that became the Viking capital. Rus, the root of the word Russia and Russians, is harder to identify, but it probably is derived from a local term for the Vikings.

The first ruler of Kievan Rus was a Danish warlord named Rurik. He was a Viking of the old school who had raided towns and monasteries in England, northern France, along the mouth of the Rhine, and throughout the North Sea. As the founder of a Viking-Slavic dynasty and of Russia itself, Rurik assumed nearly mythical status in Russia's history. He was the chieftain who put an end to the region's petty wars and compelled hostile clans and tribes to recognize him as their overlord, the prince of Kiev. In later centuries, the czars routinely claimed to be descended from Rurik.

Of all the lands where the Vikings settled, Kievan Rus was undoubtedly the richest in natural resources. The rivers and lakes teemed with fish, the immense forests were filled with all kinds of wild game for meat and furs, the rich, black soil of the vast, open steppes made virtually any type of agriculture easy. The land around the city of Kiev, for example, was so fertile that it supported large commercial vegetable gardens. Even metallurgy was made simple thanks to large deposits of iron ore that lay just beneath the surface, and sometimes right on the ground, in boggy areas. And with so much grassland, the region's tribes became expert cattle and horse breeders.

The inhabitants were also shrewd traders. The rivers that brought the Vikings into the country also brought merchant ships bearing damascene steel weapons from Arab lands; spices, jewels, and silk from China; gold, glassware,

HIM. TO AVENGE HER HUSBAND, OLGA USES TREACHERY, MURDER, AND OPEN WARFARE AGAINST THE DREVLIANS.

946–955: OLGA LAUNCHES A SERIES OF REFORMS TO MAKE THE RULE OF KIEVAN RUS LESS AUTOCRATIC.

955: WHILE ON A DIPLOMATIC MISSION IN CONSTANTINOPLE, OLGA CONVERTS TO CHRISTIANITY.

956: OLGA INTRODUCES CHRISTIANITY TO KIEV, BUT THE MISSIONARY EFFORT IS LARGELY A FAILURE.

JULY 11, 969: OLGA DIES. HER SON SVYATOSLAV, A PAGAN, SUCCEEDS HER AS PRINCE OF KIEV.

and fruit from Byzantium. For Vikings who came from a place where the growing season was short, food could be scarce, and luxury items rare and expensive, the lands that lay along the Dnieper, the Don, and the Volga rivers must have appeared to be an earthly paradise.

THE ASSASSIN'S AMBASSADORS

It was commonplace during the Middle Ages for royal widows to receive offers of marriage while they were still in mourning. What made Olga, princess of Kiev's case remarkable was that the marriage proposal came from the man who had murdered her husband.

The messengers had barely brought Olga the tragic news of her husband's death when an embassy of twenty distinguished chiefs from Mal, the prince of the Drevlians, arrived at Olga's gates. They assumed that Olga, as a widow with a young son, would be feeling frightened and vulnerable, and this assumption made the Drevlian ambassadors bold. Once they were shown into the princess's presence, they admitted candidly that their people had indeed assassinated Olga's husband, Igor. Pushing the bounds of good sense as well as good taste, they asserted that Igor deserved what he got, that to the Drevlians he was "like a wolf, crafty and ravening." But why dwell upon the unhappy events of the past, they said, when Prince Mal was so eager to make Olga his wife?

Whatever sense of outrage she may have felt at this moment, Olga suppressed it. Forcing herself to appear agreeable, she replied, "Your proposal is pleasing to me. Indeed my husband cannot rise again from the

RURIK ASSUMED NEARLY MYTHICAL STATUS IN RUSSIA'S HISTORY. HE WAS THE CHIEFTAIN WHO PUT AN END TO THE REGION'S PETTY WARS AND COMPELLED HOSTILE CLANS AND TRIBES TO RECOGNIZE HIM AS THEIR OVERLORD, THE PRINCE OF KIEV.

"THE FILTHIEST OF GOD'S CREATURES"

Olga came from Pskov, a town on the Velikaya River, about twenty miles from the contemporary border between Russia and Estonia, where her Viking ancestors had settled a generation or two earlier. In 903, she married Igor, the prince of Kiev and grandnephew of Rurik. No description of her has come down to us, although some sources refer to her as "Olga the Beautiful." In 921, an emissary from the caliph of Baghdad, Ahmad Ibn Fadlan, visited Olga and Igor's realm. He was impressed by the Rus of Kiev, their height, their superb physiques, their yellow hair and ruddy complexions— which is as close as we can get to a general description of Olga.

In other respects, however, the Rus failed to live up to Ibn Fadlan's standards. Good looks aside, the Arab declared that his hosts were "the filthiest of God's creatures. They have no modesty in defecation and urination, nor do they wash after pollution from orgasm, nor do they wash their hands after eating."

Though he conceded that the Norse did wash their hands and face every morning, he found the way they did it utterly repulsive. "Every morning a girl servant brings a great basin of water; she offers this to her master and he washes his hands and face and his hair—he washes it and combs it out with a comb in the water; then he blows his nose and spits into the basin. When he has finished, the servant carries the basin to the next person, who does likewise. She carries the basin thus to all the household in turn, and each blows his nose, spits, and washes his face and hair in it."

---

dead." Of course, she would want time to consider the prince's offer. If the ambassadors returned the next day she would give them her answer. Smiling, the Drevlians agreed, and bowing deeply they left Olga's citadel. Once they were gone, Olga ordered her servants to go outside and dig a deep ditch beside the stronghold.

By morning the pit was finished, and soon thereafter the Drevlian ambassadors returned, dressed in their finest garments, a token of respect to the woman who, they were certain, was about to consent to be their princess. Rather than speak of marriage, however, Olga commanded her guards to drag the Drevlains

outside and toss them into the pit. From the edge of the hole Olga called down to the ambassadors to ask how they were enjoying their visit to Kiev.

"Our case," they cried, "is worse than Igor's!" Then Olga gestured to her servants and they began to shovel dirt into the ditch, burying the twenty ambassadors alive.

GREEK FIRE

As Prince of Kiev, Igor continued his family's campaign to expand its personal empire by subjugating more tribes and wringing as much tribute out of them as possible. His campaigns were successful, and this success must have gone

RESIDENTS OF A
SLAVIC TOWN GREET
THE GRAND DUKE OF KIEV,
A DESCENDANT OF RURIK
THE VIKING.

καιπομεγγρωπικορευπωπλοκσαμπαχεωσαφαεται· καιπωχωρισωπροσορμιζεταιπωβρυ
δεωρ· εκωπερτηκονπακαιτριακοσιωρσωρσωιραμεμοπωπλοίωρ· πολεμικωσπεκαισιπαρχων
δετουβασιλικουσολουκαπαρχοντεσ· τικπουπωρεπαμσκοπεσελδωμ· μυκποσεπαπιτερπαιραω
λοχοϊωτοισεχαπίοισ· καιπωαιφιμιζωκαπαπλημξαμεχοι· πολλαουμεραμπαδρομσεσχοι
πωγγικωρ· Ηρασδεκαιπωσκλαφωπρωπολοωτπυρί·

πολερωμωμ πυρπολ ΤΟΝΤΩΝΕΝΗΛΗΠΛΟΝ·

Ολιχωμπαρπελωοξεωγρνομεμωρπωπαδοιο· καιπροστομκολπωρπωρβλαμρλαμρλαμαπαραιεσε

---

to Igor's head, because in 941 he launched a naval attack on Constantinople. With about 1,000 ships, he sailed for the capital of the Byzantine Empire.

Whether by intent or by sheer luck, Igor's timing was flawless: The Byzantine army was away, fighting the emperor's enemies in the distant eastern provinces, and the imperial navy was far from home, with half the ships patrolling the Mediterranean and the other half patrolling the Black Sea.

As Igor's armada advanced, Emperor Romanos sent desperate messages to all his commanders to return home at once. Meanwhile, the city's shipbuilders worked night and day to make seaworthy the only warships available—fifteen leaky hulks that were rotting in the harbor. By the time the Kievan ships cruised into the Bosphorus, the reconditioned Byzantine "fleet" had been patched up and was ready to sail.

THE BYZANTINES' SECRET WEAPON WAS GREEK FIRE, A HIGHLY FLAMMABLE LIQUID THEY SPRAYED UPON THEIR ENEMIES USING A PRIMITIVE TYPE OF FLAMETHROWER.

As the first rank of Igor's fleet bore down on them, the Byzantine sailors brought out their secret weapon—Greek fire. Using a kind of primitive but effective flamethrower, they sprayed the flammable liquid on the Kievan ships, which instantly burst into flames. The precise chemical composition of Greek fire remains a mystery, but we do know that it was a dark, sticky liquid, that water could not extinguish it, and in fact, that water caused the fire to flare up and intensify. Chemists have suggested it might have been made with quicklime or naphtha, but the formula has never been found nor replicated in a modern laboratory.

As ship after ship erupted in flames, Igor ordered the rest of his navy to turn and run. The Byzantines let them go.

IGOR'S NARROW ESCAPE

Fearful, frustrated, and itching for revenge, Igor's army sailed back into the Black Sea. At Bithynia, in modern-day northern Turkey, they drew up their ships and stormed ashore, slaughtering the inhabitants without mercy. They were especially cruel to Christian priests and monks, some of whom they used for target practice, while others they killed by hammering iron spikes through their skulls.

If Igor had been wise, he would have let his men blow off steam for a few days in Bithynia, then got them back on their ships and returned home. Instead, he and his army lingered, looting more towns and skewering more monks. Then, one morning, Igor emerged from his tent to find the Byzantine fleet in full battle array just offshore, and blocking all escape routes. When Igor tried to run the blockade, the Byzantines spewed Greek fire at him again. Almost the entire Kievan navy went up in flames; hundreds of men were burned alive on the decks of their ships, and hundreds more leapt into the sea, where they continued to burn.

Igor and a handful of followers escaped, but surviving members of his army were bound and dragged back to Constantinople, where they were led through the streets and executed en masse before a cheering throng of citizens.

A WOLF AMONG THE SHEEP

By attempting to seize Constantinople, Igor overextended himself. His father, Oleg, had begun the process of conquering the petty tribes of what is now the Ukraine, forcing them into a feudal relationship in which the tribal chiefs recognized Oleg as their overlord and paid him annual tribute. It was the beginning of a family dynasty, but more important, of centralized authority in Russia. Back in Kiev after learning a hard lesson, Igor once again took up again the task of subduing more local tribes and collecting more tribute.

One of Kiev's client tribes, the Drevlians, had always been troublesome. During Oleg's life, they had tried to break free from his authority, and at his death, they staged a full-scale rebellion (which failed).

Having been defeated down twice, the Drevlians kept quiet through most of Igor's reign. Then, about the year 943, they stopped sending their tribute money to Kiev. Igor sent messages promising dreadful punishments if the Drevlians did not submit; the Drevlians' Prince Mal sent back messages brimming with scorn and defiance. Finally Igor had had enough.

In 945, he assembled an army and marched on Iskorosten, the Drevlians' chief town (today known as Korosten on the Uzh River). For all his bravado Mal was unnerved by the sight of the Kievan army; rather than risk battle and possible annihilation, he submitted to Igor's authority once more and handed over the gold.

While marching back to Kiev with his men, Igor convinced himself that for all the trouble they had caused him, the Drevlians ought to pay a penalty on top of the usual tribute. Ordering his army to continue home and taking only a handful of bodyguards with him, he turned back to Iskorosten. Boldly he reentered the city and demanded more gold from Mal. The Drevlian prince begged permission to withdraw to consult with his advisors and learn how much gold remained in the treasury. Once he was behind closed doors Mal said to his councilors, "If a wolf comes among the sheep, he will take away the whole flock one by one unless he be killed."

Moments later, a large detachment of Drevlian soldiers attacked Igor and his men. The bodyguards were all slain, but Igor was taken alive and dragged outside. According to the Byzantine historian Leo the Deacon, some of the Drevlian troops threw Igor to the ground and held him there while others "bent down two birch trees to the prince's feet and tied them to his legs; then they let the trees straighten again, thus tearing the prince's body apart."

With Igor dead, Mal saw his chance to become the prince of Kiev, with all the tribes paying homage and tribute to him. All he had to do was marry Olga and dispose of her young son, Igor's heir. What could be simpler?

A NICE HOT BATH

Olga's servants were still packing down the dirt over the ambassadors' mass grave when she sent a message to Prince Mal expressing her delight with his marriage proposal and her eagerness to meet him.

Although the twenty ambassadors he had sent were all fine men, out of regard for her rank as princess of Kiev she required a grander escort to bring her to Iskorosten. She urged Mal to send the most noble men of his court to Kiev, so that when she arrived at Iskorosten she would be surrounded by the best of the Drevlian nation. Impressed by Olga's sense of propriety, not to mention how effortlessly his scheme was progressing, Mal sent his most exalted nobles to Kiev.

Upon their arrival, Olga was the model of warmth and hospitality. She even offered the use of her private bathhouse to the Drevlian nobles so they could unwind and tidy up after their long ride. Once the last Drevlian had entered the bathhouse, Olga's servants locked and barricaded the door, then set fire to the building. As the Drevlian lords roasted in the bathhouse, Olga sent yet another message to Mal. She was on her way, but she had one last request: She wanted to honor Igor's memory by weeping over his grave and then holding the customary funeral feast for Mal and his courtiers. Would the prince make the arrangements?

Olga, accompanied by a large entourage of her own people, was still some distance from Iskorosten when Mal rode out to greet her. Where, he wanted to know, were his ambassadors and the noble escort he had sent her? Olga replied that in her eagerness to meet him, she had rode ahead. The besotted prince believed every word.

Both Drevlians and Kievans went at once to Igor's grave, where Olga shed dutiful tears while her servants heaped up the traditional burial mound over their prince's torn body. With the funeral rites completed, Mal led Olga and her retinue to his hall for the funeral feast. Seated at the tables were several hundred of the Drevlian nation's wealthiest and most influential men.

Acting as hostess, Olga made the rounds of the tables, keeping everyone's cups filled with mead. The Drevlians were in such high spirits that they didn't notice that no one in the Kiev party was drinking. Hours later, when Prince Mal and his Drevlians were stupefied with drink, Olga's men drew their daggers and killed every Drevlian in the hall.

SATED AT LAST

Incredibly, Olga's thirst for vengeance still was not satisfied. With her followers she rode hard back to Kiev, assembled her army, and marched on Iskorosten.

The reappearance of this bloodthirsty woman outside their city terrified both soldiers and civilians. They sent out envoys, who promised to pay

öλΓω

any amount if Olga would spare the people, but she rejected all offers of ransom; she wanted the utter destruction of the Drevlians. As the envoys retreated back into their doomed city, Kievan archers fired volley after volley of flaming arrows into Iskorosten. One by one the wooden houses burst into flames; as the city became an inferno, the Drevlians threw open the gates and streamed out onto the plain, pleading for mercy. They found none. The Drevlians who survived the massacre were rounded up and sold into slavery.

With her enemy's city in ashes, and his people dead or enslaved, Olga felt content and returned home to Kiev.

DURING A VISIT TO CONSTANTINOPLE OLGA, SEEN HERE STANDING TO THE LEFT OF THE EMPEROR, CONVERTED TO CHRISTIANITY.

A STATESWOMAN IN KIEV

Happily for the Ukraine and Russia, Olga's gifts extended beyond novel of methods of destroying her enemies. Certainly she could not countenance the assassination of a prince—particularly if the prince in question were her own husband—yet she could see that there existed serious flaws in the autocratic way Igor had ruled.

The tribal chiefs and subject princes bitterly resented digging into their personal hoards every year to keep the peace with Kiev, so Olga abolished the collection of tribute money. In its place she instituted a tax paid by every household in her realm. She also restored to local princes the authority to deal with local crimes and lesser administrative issues in their own territory. These were clever moves by which Olga made the tribal lords willing participants in her government rather than disgruntled and rebellious subjects. By instituting these reforms, Olga restored to the chiefs and princes a degree of autonomy that noblemen enjoyed elsewhere in Europe and Asia. One thing was still lacking—an idea or system that would unify the tribes. To achieve it, Olga made the most daring move of her political life.

In 955, Olga traveled to Constantinople, ostensibly on a mission to ensure peace and trade between Kiev and the Byzantine Empire. Most likely she traveled south to become a Christian.

A tiny Christian population already existed in the Kievan lands; a document dating from about 945 even mentions their church, dedicated to St. Elias. The overwhelming number of Olga's people, however, clung to various pantheons of gods—the Slavic gods were different from the Turkic gods, who were distinct from the Norse gods. Christianity would unite the people of Kiev in a single faith and make them part of the cultural and ideological mainstream of western Europe and Byzantium. So in Constantinople, Olga asked to be instructed in the Christian faith. At her baptism in the glorious Church of St. Sophia she took the name Helena, in honor of the Byzantine empress who may have served as her godmother on the occasion.

On her return to Kiev, Olga brought priests, Bibles, icons, and everything else necessary to establish the Church in her lands. Her conversion enhanced the status of the local Christians, and she built several churches in Kiev, her old hometown Pskov, and in various other cities of her realm, but her attempt to convert her people was almost a complete failure. The vast majority of the tribes rejected Christianity.

Even Olga's son Svyatoslav refused to be baptized, telling her candidly that he and his warriors regarded Christianity as a feeble religion, with its emphasis on patience, forgiveness, and turning the other cheek. If he became a Christian, Svyatoslav said, he would lose forever the respect of his men. Olga died on July 11, 969, heartbroken by her people's rejection of Christianity.

Olga was correct—Christianity would have unified her people. Furthermore, it would have strengthened their ties to the wealthy and powerful Byzantine Empire. And although she went to her grave thinking herself a failure, the Catholic and Orthodox Churches have taken a more charitable view of Olga, revering her as the first to try to establish Christianity in the Ukraine and Russia.

Both churches address her as Saint Olga, but the Orthodox have honored her with a more exalted title, "Equal to the Apostles," in recognition of her efforts to establish the gospel in pagan lands, just as Christ's twelve apostles had done 1,000 years earlier.

THE PRINCE WHO MADE KIEV CHRISTIAN: VLADIMIR OF KIEV

OLGA OF KIEV'S BAPTISM WAS AN ACT OF TREMENDOUS consequence for the lands that would become the Ukraine and Russia, even if she went to her grave lamenting that she had failed to convince her people to become Christians.

By becoming Christian, the Ukraine and Russia were aligning themselves with Europe rather than Asia. Although their liturgy and religious life were Byzantine rather than Roman Catholic, and the government of these lands was autocratic to an extent that empire-builders like Charlemagne could only dream of, Ukrainian and Russian Christians felt themselves to be in some way heirs to the legacy of ancient Greece and imperial Rome. After the fall of Constantinople to the Turks in 1459, Russian Christians referred to Moscow as "the third Rome," the natural inheritor of the mantle of imperial and religious authority.

In spite of a host of political, cultural, and religious traditions that are to this day decidedly non-Western, the Judeo-Christian, Greco-Roman traditions of the West constitute the Ukraine and Russia's strongest ties. It began with the baptism of Olga, but it became permanent with the baptism of her grandson Vladimir.

AS A CONDITION FOR MARRYING THE BYZANTINE EMPEROR'S SISTER, VLADIMIR, PRINCE OF KIEV, AGREED TO BE BAPTIZED.

THE MAN IN THE CLEAN TUNIC

In the early spring of 972, John Tzimiskes, emperor of Byzantium, astride a magnificent mount, magnificent himself in his jeweled crown and golden armor, waited to meet the prince of Kiev. Clustered around him on the southern bank of the Danube were the members of his entourage, a small crowd of nobles, generals, clergy, and eunuchs. They were all watching a small boat make its way across the river. Inside it were just a handful of men—Svyatoslav, prince of Kiev, and a few followers, who sprawled comfortably in their seats as their prince rowed the boat himself. The Byzantine historian, Leo the Deacon, has provided us with a vivid portrait of Svyatoslav's personal appearance.

"He was of medium height—neither too tall, nor too short. He had bushy brows, blue eyes, and was snub-nosed; he shaved his beard but wore a long and

TIMELINE

EARLY SPRING, 972: PRINCE SVYATOSLAV, SON OF IGOR AND OLGA, IS AMBUSHED AND KILLED BY THE TURKIC TRIBE OF THE PECHENEGS.

972: HIS SON YAROPOLK WAGES WAR AGAINST HIS BROTHER OLEG, WHO DIES OUTSIDE ISKOROSTEN. HIS OTHER SON, VLADIMIR, FLEES THE COUNTRY.

980: VLADIMIR RETURNS TO KIEVAN RUS WITH A SCANDINAVIAN ARMY, KILLS YAROPOLK, AND BECOMES PRINCE OF KIEV.

988: THE BYZANTINE EMPEROR BASIL II ASKS FOR VLADIMIR'S HELP IN CRUSHING A REBELLION.

bushy moustache. His head was shaven except for a lock of hair on one side as a sign of the nobility of his clan. His neck was thick, his shoulders broad, and his whole stature pretty fine. He seemed gloomy and savage. On one of his ears hung a golden earring adorned with two pearls and a ruby set between them. His white garments were not distinguishable from those of his men except for cleanness."

Svyatoslav was a Kievan prince of the old school. One by one his neighbors would accept Christianity: Poland's Prince Miesko in 966, Denmark's King Harald Bluetooth in 974, King Olaf Trygvasson of Norway in 976, and Duke Geza of Hungary in 985. Nonetheless, Svyatolsav remained decidedly, even aggressively, pagan.

And it wasn't just in religion that Svyatoslav had kept up the old ways; like Rurik, Oleg, and Igor, he had a genuine hunger for more power, more territory, and more tribes he would keep under his thumb. Igor and Olga had consolidated the power of Kievan Rus; now Svyatoslav was eager to use that strength to create an empire that stretched from Kiev to the Caspian Sea.

Standing in his way were the Khazars, a powerful nation based along the Volga River. Years earlier, Rurik and Oleg had worked out a go-along-to-get-along relationship with the Khazars by recognizing nominally the king, or khagan, as their overlord. In return, the Khazars refrained from interfering with Kiev's expansion, as long as it did not infringe on Khazar territory. The arrangement kept peace between Kiev and the Khazars for three generations, yet Svyatoslav chaffed under it; he was determined to conquer the Khazars.

EVEN IN ITS CLOTHING THE BYZANTINE COURT EXCEEDED ANYTHING KNOWN IN KIEV. THE WOMAN IN THE LOWER PANEL GIVES A SENSE OF WHAT THE EMPEROR'S SISTER, ANNA, WOULD HAVE WORN.

TIMELINE

989: VLADIMIR ACCEPTS BAPTISM AS A CONDITION FOR MARRYING THE EMPEROR'S SISTER, ANNA.

990: VLADIMIR RETURNS TO KIEV WITH ANNA AND MANY BISHOPS AND PRIESTS TO BEGIN THE CONVERSION OF HIS PEOPLE TO CHRISTIANITY.

990–1015: VLADIMIR BUILDS CHURCHES; FOUNDS MONASTERIES, CONVENTS, AND SCHOOLS; ESTABLISHES CHARITABLE INSTITUTIONS; AND OUTLAWS THE DEATH PENALTY.

1015: VLADIMIR DIES WHILE EN ROUTE TO PUT DOWN A REBELLION.

IGOR AND OLGA HAD CONSOLIDATED THE POWER OF KIEVAN RUS; NOW SVYATOSLAV WAS EAGER TO USE THAT STRENGTH TO CREATE AN EMPIRE THAT STRETCHED FROM KIEV TO THE CASPIAN SEA.

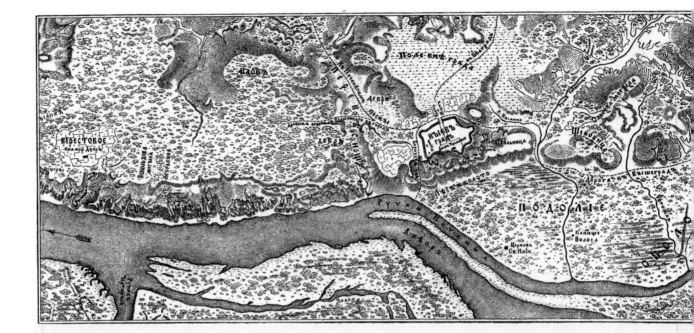

In 963, after giving them fair warning—he always sent his enemies a courier who always bore the same message, "I am setting forth against you"—Svyatoslav marched against the Khazars. The campaign lasted six years, concluding in 969 with the capture and destruction of Atil, the Khazars' capital city. A traveler who saw Atil's ruins soon after the battle said, "No grape or raisin remained, not a leaf on a branch."

Because they were successful, Svyatoslav's aggressive policies worried the Byzantines, so much so that Emperor John invited the prince to a parley where they could hammer out a treaty. Svyatoslav's contempt for the Byzantines extended only to their religion; he knew they were a power he could not overcome, and he came to the parley ready to be agreeable. In exchange for friendly relations with Byzantium, Svyatoslav agreed to rein in his imperial ambitions, leave the southern Crimea alone, and even withdraw his troops from the Balkans.

The conference on the Danube had been a triumph for the emperor; he left the meeting with everything he wanted, and then fate handed him a little bit more. As Svyatoslav made his way home, he was ambushed by an enemy tribe, the Pechenegs. They killed Svyatoslav, decapitated him, and presented his head as a trophy to their king, who had the skull made into a drinking cup.

THE HEIRS

Svyatslav's three sons, Yaropolk, Oleg, and Vladimir, learned of their father's death from the battered, bloodied handful of the prince's retainers who escaped the Pechenegs' ambush.

In a scene right out of King Lear, the sons agreed to divide their father's kingdom in three: Yaropolk, as the eldest, inherited Kiev; Oleg received the Drevlian lands; Vladimir got Novgorod. As an illegitimate son (his mother had been one of Svyatslav's slaves), Vladimir was lucky to get anything at all; no one would have objected if his half-brothers had divided their father's estate between the two of them alone. Secretly each of the princes longed to be sole ruler of the kingdom, and once the scheming started, the balance of power among the brothers began to shift.

One day in 972, while out hunting, Oleg shot and killed one of Yaropolk's retainers, mistaking him—he said—for a poacher. Whether this was an accident or not, Yaropolk chose to view it as an expression of Oleg's contempt, and all the excuse he needed to declare war on his younger brother. Their armies clashed outside the city of Iskorosten, where years earlier their Grandmother Olga had exacted her revenge on her husband's murderers.

Yaropolk's army scattered Oleg's men, and in the panicky retreat back to the city Oleg lost his footing on Iskorosten's drawbridge, fell into the water-filled moat, and drowned. The men of Kiev fished Oleg's body out and carried it to Yaropolk, who dutifully shed crocodile tears over the corpse.

Rather than wait for his brother to pick a fight with him, Vladimir fled the country. He went to his relatives in Scandinavia, where he hired an army, and then in 980 he returned to Kievan Rus to seize the crown for himself. The brothers' war didn't last long. One by one, Vladimir captured the important cities that lay along the road to Kiev. When a message came, supposedly from Vladimir, that he was willing to negotiate a peaceful settlement, Yaropolk accepted the invitation, seeing it perhaps as his only chance of holding on to some shred of power. The invitation was a trap; Vladimir's henchmen assassinated Yaropolk.

Vladimir skipped the charade of feigning grief over the death of his brother; instead he rode to a convent where Yaropolk's wife had taken refuge. Years earlier, she had been a nun in a convent in Bulgaria. Svyatoslav, while raiding the country,

AFTER SVYATSLAV'S DEATH, YAROPOLK, THE ELDEST OF HIS THREE SONS, INHERITED KIEV, SHOWN HERE.

had looted the convent and, struck by the beauty of this particular nun, carried her back to Kiev, where he forced her to marry his son, Yaropolk. Now the poor woman's nightmare repeated itself as pagans battered down the convent gates, raced through the cloister, seized her, and dragged her off to be raped by Vladimir and then forced to marry him.

During his pagan period, Vladimir acquired seven wives and assembled a large harem. The ancient sources claim he had 800 concubines and that he divided them up into groups and housed them in the major cities and towns of his realm so that, no matter where he was, he could enjoy a wide variety of female companionship. The number may be inflated, but it is certainly true that Vladimir kept concubines and that the size of his harem impressed his people.

Not long after he seized power, Vladimir erected a huge temple in Kiev in which he placed idols of all the Slavic gods—and all the idols of all of neighboring Turkic tribe's gods, too, perhaps just to be on the safe side. To consecrate his temple, Vladimir revived an old custom: human sacrifice. He chose the victims himself—Theodore, a proven warrior, and Theodore's young son, John. As the names suggest, Theodore and John were Christians. Perhaps by his choice of victims Vladimir meant to intimidate the tiny Christian community of Kiev, or he may have seen a kind of poetic justice in offering to the gods two men who had renounced the old religion to follow Christ. Whatever his reasons, Vladimir's actions undoubtedly would have horrified his grandmother Olga; Vladimir's father Svyatoslav, on the other hand, would have been proud.

THE RELUCTANT BRIDE

By Vladimir's day, the conquest of neighboring tribes was his family's most firmly established tradition. He secured his southeastern border by subduing the tribes in the region known today as Slovakia; he conquered the Lithuanian tribes along the Nieman River so he would have easy access by water to the Baltic Sea; and he waged war against the Bulgars, who contested Kiev's access to the Volga River.

Vladimir's conquests made him the most powerful prince his dynasty had ever known, and with power came a form of prestige that barbarian kings

A PORTRAIT OF EMPEROR BASIL II SHOWS HIM ATTENDED BY SAINTS AND ANGELS, AS MEN OF VARIOUS NATIONS FALL DOWN AT HIS FEET, WHILE CHRIST PRESENTS HIM WITH A HEAVENLY CROWN.

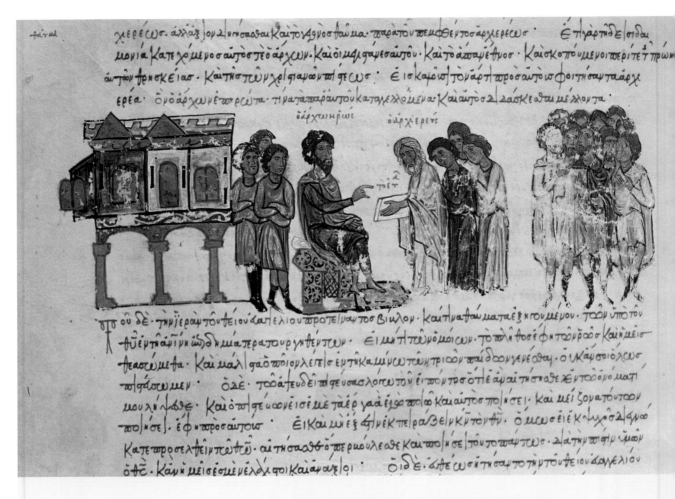

ὁ ἄρχημρωι   ὁ ἄρχιερεύς

secretly desired but never liked to admit—recognition from Christian monarchs. After Vladimir's successful campaign in Slovakia, King Boleslav of Poland signed a treaty with him to keep the Kievan warlord from encroaching on the borders of his kingdom.

But the greatest honor came in 988 when envoys arrived from Constantinople. Emperor Basil II was being troubled by an upstart named Bardas Phocas who was threatening Constantinople. In return for Vladimir's help, Basil promised give his sister Anna to Vladimir in marriage. The prince accepted the offer, called up 6,000 of his men, and at Abydos on the Asian side of the Hellespont crushed the emperor's enemies and killed Bardas Phocas. Now that Vladimir had kept his side of the bargain, it was time for Basil to keep his; in some ways, however, the emperor found that waging war against a rebel was simpler than arranging his sister's marriage.

AMBASSADORS FROM VLADIMIR DISCUSS THE TERMS OF THE PRINCE'S MARRIAGE AND CONVERSION TO CHRISTIANITY WITH EMPEROR BASIL II.

Basil and Anna were "Porphyrogenetes," or "born in the purple," a title that meant they had been born in the imperial palace in Constantinople—a circumstance that held special, even sacred, significance in the Byzantine Empire. Generally speaking, it meant a Porphyrogenete could only marry a Greek of the highest rank.

Basil's promise to give his sister to Vladimir raised a host of problems, not to mention a firestorm of outrage among the clergy and nobility of Constantinople. It was unthinkable to marry a Porphyrogenete to a polygamist heathen who indulged in human sacrifice and kept a small army of concubines. Anna joined the howls of protest, accusing her brother of selling her like a slave. But neither the outrage of his bishops and nobles nor the bitter tears of his sister would dissuade Basil. He was determined to have Vladimir of Kiev as his ally; besides, as a condition for marrying Anna, Vladimir had promised to convert to Christianity.

Meanwhile, Vladimir kept the pressure on Basil by sweeping through the Byzantine province of Crimea, conquering a string of cities, including Kherson, one of the wealthiest towns in the region. There he waited to see what Basil would do. He did not have to wait long: Anna, amid a procession of Byzantine dignitaries, appeared at the city gates, ready to submit to a marriage with Vladimir. The bishop of Kherson first baptized the prince of Kiev and then married the unhappy couple. After the ceremonies had been concluded, Vladimir, as a gesture of his good faith, returned Kherson to his new brother-in-law the emperor as a bridegroom's gift.

THE MAKINGS OF A SAINT

No doubt everyone from Anna to Vladimir's generals to the ladies of his harem were convinced that the prince's conversion was a sham, that he would never abandon his old ways. They were surprised, then, when Vladimir recruited bishops and priests to travel back to Kiev with him, and spent a small fortune on liturgical vessels, icons, and relics.

More surprises came once the prince, his Christian wife, and their entourage of clerics arrived in Kiev in spring or summer of 990. Vladimir ordered his grand temple to the gods destroyed and had the idol of Perun, the chief god of the Kiev pantheon, tied to a horse's tail and dragged down to the Dnieper, where it was dumped in the river.

Then he ordered the entire population of Kiev, including every member of his retinue, to report to the river where every bishop and priest was kept very busy performing baptisms. The final shock came when Vladimir dismissed his seven wives and hundreds of concubines. By now everyone understood their prince intended to make Kiev a Christian land.

A QUESTION OF SINCERITY

The question ever since Vladimir's day has been, how much of his conversion was politically opportunistic, and how much of it was sincere? Though there were unquestionable advantages to adopting Christianity and spreading it throughout his territories, there is evidence that baptism brought about a genuine change of heart in Vladimir.

After his return to Kiev, the prince who murdered his brother and raped his sister-in-law went about providing free meals daily at his own residence for the sick and the needy. When it occurred to him that some were too weak to get to the palace, "he arranged that wagons should be brought in, and after having them loaded with bread, meat, fish, various vegetables, mead in casks, and kvas, he ordered them driven through the city. The drivers were under instructions to call out, 'Where is there a poor man or a beggar who cannot walk?' To such they distributed according to their necessities." Even more surprising was an unexpected alteration Vladimir made to the laws of the realm—he outlawed the death penalty.

Vladimir also lavished money on creating a Christian infrastructure in his realm. On the site where his grand pagan temple had stood, he built a church dedicated to St. Basil, the name he had taken at his baptism. The next church he built was dedicated to the Dormition (or Assumption) of the Holy Virgin; it became known as the "Tithe Church" because Vladimir gave one-tenth of his income for its maintenance. He also established schools, monasteries, and convents. By the time of his death in 1015, Vladimir's program of Christianizing the lands of Kiev was so successful that there were seven bishops administering seven dioceses in the kingdom.

A TASTE FOR EMPIRE-BUILDING

The significance of Vladimir's conversion is hard to overestimate. He opened his lands to influence from western Europe and Byzantium. He brought a new code of law, a new set of morals, a new style of art and architecture, even a new calendar into his realm. He also brought in an alphabet—for the first time Kiev would have a written language. Vladimir was giving his people, one could even say imposing upon them, an entirely new civilization.

From the perspective of western Europeans and Byzantines, by adopting Christianity, at least parts of Roman law, and promoting literacy, Kiev became part of their civilized world. Such recognition brought new respect to Kiev and its rulers, who were no longer viewed as barbarians but as fellow Christians and potential political allies and trading partners.

In spite of everything he surrendered at his baptism, there was one thing that Vladimir did not give up—his independence. He would not become a vassal of the Byzantine emperor. He wanted the Church in his realm to be independent, too. Almost from the beginning, what would become the Ukrainian and Russian Orthodox Churches jealously guarded their autonomy, never offering more than the most perfunctory (and artificial) tokens of obedience to the supposed head of their Church, the Patriarch of Constantinople.

And there was another thing that Vladimir's descendants clung to: The Russians never lost their taste for the empire-building that began on a small scale with Rurik. With the collapse of the Byzantine Empire in the mid-fifteenth century, the Russian czars saw themselves as the natural heirs of the emperors, which only accelerated their taste for expanding their borders. This hunger for land is something the Russian government, no matter who is in power, has never lost. Even today the leaders of post-Communist Russia dream of reclaiming at least some parts of the old Soviet Empire—at the very least the Ukraine, where Russian Christian civilization was born.

SPITTING ON THE EMPEROR: THE MONGOLS IN CHINA

THE NUMBERS ARE STAGGERING. GENGHIS KHAN CONQUERED thirty countries, ruled over approximately fifty million people, and governed an empire that covered between eleven and twelve million square miles—an area larger than all of the United States, Canada, Mexico, the nations of Central America, and the Caribbean islands combined.

Renowned primarily as a conqueror, Genghis was also an inspired empire builder. For efficiency, he consolidated the dozens of jealous, piddling city-states in the steppes and forests of eastern Europe into the Russian nation. He did the same thing in south Asia, uniting Manchuria, Tibet, the Uighur lands of Turkistan, and a kingdom known as Xi Xia near the Gobi Desert with the anemic kingdom of the Jin Dynasty to create the world power we know as China. As historian Jack Weatherford put it, Genghis Khan's "architecture was not in stones, but in nations."

There is, of course, another side to Genghis and the Mongols: everywhere they rode they brought death on an epic scale and unprecedented destruction. Some historians believe that during the Mongol conquest of China, approximately 50 million Chinese—about the half the population—were killed

TIMELINE

1162: GENGHIS KHAN IS BORN NEAR THE SITE OF THE PRESENT-DAY CITY OF ULAANBAATAR IN MONGOLIA. HE IS GIVEN THE NAME TEMUJIN.

1170: TEMUJIN'S FATHER DIES. THE TRIBE ABANDONS GENGHIS, HIS MOTHER, AND HIS SIX BROTHERS AND SISTERS ON THE STEPPE.

1175: TO BECOME HEAD OF THE FAMILY, 13-YEAR-OLD TEMUJIN MURDERS HIS ELDER BROTHER.

outright, died of starvation or disease, or were sold into slavery. News of the Mongol massacres spread to Europe, where the Benedictine monk and historian Matthew Paris trembled in his monastery in England, and deep-sea fishermen in Denmark refused to leave port, afraid that they might run into the Mongols on the high seas. (In fact, the ocean was the one place the Danes would have been safe—the Mongols never did learn to sail.)

Without minimizing the brutality of the Mongols, it must also be said that as emperor Genghis was far-sighted. He laid the groundwork of a global economy, encouraging merchants and traders from China, Persia, and other Asian lands to market their goods in the Middle East, Africa, and far-off Europe. In return, he welcomed merchants from the west into his empire. The free trade agreements that exist today between many Western nations and China have their origin in the international commercial contacts that Genghis Khan promoted 800 years ago.

AN ARROW IN THE BACK

It had taken the Chinese ambassadors many weeks to reach the camp of Genghis Khan in Mongolia. Emperor Zhangzong had died, and Weiwang was now "the Golden Emperor" in Beijing. Custom demanded that, upon hearing this news, Genghis make an act of submission to the new emperor by dropping to his knees before Weiwang's envoys and striking the ground with his forehead.

Genghis received the ambassadors in his large, lavishly furnished felt tent. They delivered their message and then waited for the Mongol khan to perform the traditional *kow-tow*. Instead Genghis kept his seat, turned his head to the south, the direction of the Golden Emperor's capital, and spat. As the Chinese envoys stood there speechless, Genghis launched into a tirade. "Is such an

TIMELINE

C. 1186–1206: BY WARFARE AND NEGOTIATION, TEMUJIN BECOMES SOLE LORD OF ALL FIFTY TRIBES OF THE MONGOLS.

1208: GENGHIS REFUSES TO MAKE THE TRADITIONAL KOW-TOW IN HONOR OF CHINA'S NEW EMPEROR. INSTEAD HE LEADS AN INVASION OF CHINA.

MAY, 1215: AFTER A 3-MONTH SIEGE, THE MONGOLS SMASH THEIR WAY INTO BEIJING, CHINA'S CAPITAL.

imbecile worthy of the throne?" he shouted. "Shall I abase myself before him?" Frightened, the ambassadors scurried out of the tent.

On the day in 1208 when Genghis metaphorically spat in the face of the Jin emperor, he was 46 years old and had been the khan of the Mongols for twenty-one years. His early life had been plagued with so many troubles and dangers that he was lucky to be alive at all. He was born in spring, 1162, near the Onon River in Mongolia, not far from the site of the present-day Mongolian capital, Ulaanbaatan. His father, Yesugei, was a minor tribal chieftain; his mother, Hoelun, had been married to another man when Yesugei saw her and carried her off to be his second wife. At birth, his parents named the future Genghis Khan Temujin, derived from the Mongol word for "inspired" or "creative." The child was about eight years old when, in 1170, Yesugei died, poisoned by an enemy tribe. He left behind two wives and seven children, all under the age of ten.

The family had been living with another small clan led by Targutai, known as the Fat Khan. With no adult male to protect them or hunt for them, Yesugei's widows and children were now a liability—the Fat Khan did not have the resources to feed them. Targutai decided to abandon Yesugei's family on the steppe. As the Fat Khan and his clan rode away, one old man scolded Targutai for his heartlessness; Targutai plunged his spear into the old man's chest.

But the family survived: Hoelun foraged for berries and roots, and Temujin, who could already use a bow and arrow, hunted rodents and other small animals. They found help at last from distant relatives of Yesugei who brought Hoelun and her family into their camp. But a new problem presented itself: In the absence of an adult male, Temujin's elder half-brother, Begter, became head of the family. He could do as he wished, take whatever he wanted, and he lorded his position over Temujin. Under the Mongol code, Begter, although only an

adolescent boy, also had sexual rights to Hoelun—either within or outside of marriage. Bullying Temujin could endure, but he would not tolerate the idea of Begter as his stepfather. So one day Temujin and his younger brother Khasar took their bows and went hunting for Begter. Finding him alone out on the steppe, the brothers fired almost simultaneously. Khasar's arrow struck Begter full in the chest; Temujin's arrow buried itself in Begter's back. As the boy toppled over, his half brothers walked away without even looking to see whether he was already dead or would bleed to death. Begter was twelve or thirteen at the time, while Temujin was about eleven years old, and Khasar nine or ten.

WALKING OVER CORPSES

From their watchtowers on the walls of Xingqing (in what is now the Ningxia Hui Autonomous Region in northern China), the Tangut guards gave the alarm. The Mongols were in sight, but there was something odd about their appearance. Marching in a disorderly, unmilitary mass before the Mongol horsemen was a huge crowd of what must be infantry—but the Mongols never used infantry.

As the Mongol horde drew closer to the walls, the garrison saw that the "infantry" was an immense throng of wailing Tangut peasants, and they were not marching, they were being driven forward by the Mongols. When the weeping mob reached the moat surrounding the gates, those in the front ranks stopped, teetering on the brink, but they could not stand there long. With their whips and their spears the Mongols urged the peasants in the rear forward.

As the Tangut soldiers watched, the first rank of peasants toppled into the moat, followed by the peasants behind them, and then the peasants behind them. The Mongols drove all their captives forward until the moat was packed solid with bodies; then hundreds of Mongols carrying scaling ladders charged forward over the causeway of corpses and stormed the Tangut town.

Genghis's first target was Xi Xia in present-day northern China; this was the kingdom of the Tanguts, a nation closely related to the Tibetans. Most of the Tanguts were farmers and herders, but there were Tangut cities and fortresses, too, and a standing Tangut army of about 150,000 men.

In 1208, when Genghis led his Mongols into Xi Xia, his only experience of warfare had been cavalry charges across the open steppes. He did not have the equipment to batter down stone walls; he had never encountered a moat

TEMUJIN, SURROUNDED BY HIS SONS AND GENERALS, IS ELECTED CHIEF OF THE MONGOLS AND TAKES A NEW NAME, "GENGHIS KHAN," WHICH MEANS "THE GREAT EMPEROR."

before; he did not know how to conduct a siege. But Genghis was resilient; he invented new tactics to fit the situation. The simplest method, Genghis found, was to surround a town, cut off its food supply, and wait for starvation to take its toll on the defenders. At one Tangut city, Genghis put his men to work digging an enormous ditch to divert the river that filled the town's moat. The Mongols, who had no trained engineers with them, succeeded in channeling the river away from the town, but it broke the ditch's banks and swept away most of the Mongol camp. Nonetheless, Genghis realized the river-diversion tactic would be useful once his men learned how to utilize it safely; he sent out an order to take captive any Tangut engineers the army happened to encounter.

Outside the Tangut towns, the Mongols swept over the farms and villages of Xi Xia, raping, killing, and burning. After the first fury of a raid, the Mongols collected all stores of food, rounded up all the livestock, enslaved the strongest surviving Tanguts, and sent all their plunder north to enrich their families back in Mongolia. These raids served as an object lesson for the Tanguts. At the beginning of a siege, Genghis sent messengers to the town with a promise and a threat—if the town surrendered, the inhabitants' lives would be spared; if the town resisted him, Genghis would give his men free rein to do what they had done to all those outlying farms—massacre the population and reduce the place to ashes. He fulfilled that threat so often and so completely that in 1207 the Tangut emperor, Li An-Chuan, surrendered his kingdom to the Mongols and married one of his daughters to Genghis. The Great Khan's next target was the Chinese kingdom of the Jin Dynasty.

"INTREPID, SANGUINARY, AND CRUEL"

By 1206, Genghis was lord of the Central Asia plateau, the vast land-locked region of steppes and desert north of China. It had taken him almost two decades to defeat, outmaneuver, or negotiate a settlement with the fifty or so Mongol tribes; now in an all-tribe assembly they elected him their chief. They called him "Genghis Khan," which means "the Great Emperor." Although individually they probably still referred to themselves by their tribal names—Merkits, or Uighurs, or Naimans—outsiders knew them collectively as "the Mongols."

Genghis's achievement was remarkable—no one had ever managed to bring peace to the contentious tribes of Central Asia, let alone unite them all under a

GENGHIS'S MONGOL CAVALRY ATTACKS A TANGUT TOWN, CAUSING PANIC INSIDE THE CITY.

single ruler. In fact, Genghis's reign was a first in Mongol history. They had always been an independent group, with each clan going its own way, refusing to answer to anyone. Genghis put an end to Mongol individualism by founding an imperial dynasty that lasted for centuries and also by promulgating a legal

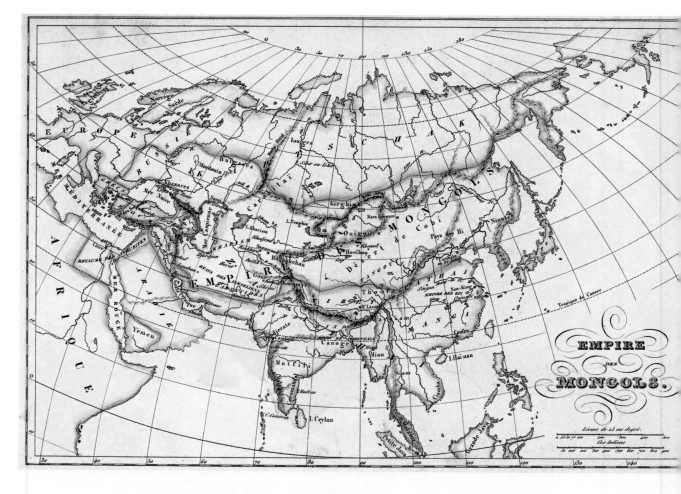

code called the Yassa, in which all Mongols were bound to obey "The Sky God," Genghis said "has appointed me to rule all the generations living in felt tents."

The most detailed physical description of Genghis to come down to us was recorded when he was about sixty years old. The Persian historian, Minhaj al-Siraj Juzjani, tells us Genghis was "tall… of vigorous build, robust in body, the hair on his face scanty and turned white, with cats' eyes." Juzjani goes on to describe the complex facets of Genghis's character: "possessed of dedicated energy, discernment, genius, and understanding, awe-striking, a butcher, just, resolute, an overthrower of enemies, intrepid, sanguinary, and cruel."

"THEY ANNIHILATE EMPIRES"

Even the Mongols were astonished when they captured Beijing. The capital of the Golden Emperor was enclosed within twenty-six miles of massive walls.

GENGHIS KHAN RULED OVER AN EMPIRE THAT COVERED APPROXIMATELY TWELVE MILLION SQUARE MILES AND EMBRACED ABOUT THREE BILLION PEOPLE.

There were twelve enormous gates, ninety towers, and the city itself was divided into four distinct walled and heavily fortified towns, each of which the Mongols would have to take in turn before Beijing would be theirs.

Yet against all odds, in May 1215, after a three-month-long siege, the Mongols smashed their way into the capital thanks to the Chinese siege engines built for them by captured Chinese engineers. Catapults hurled huge stones that pulverized the defensive walls, and flaming liquids in clay pots that shattered on impact, causing whatever they struck to explode in flames. Once the Mongols broke through, they raped the women of the imperial court, killed the throngs of eunuchs who had served Weiwang, looted the treasures of the Golden Emperor, then set the palace on fire—it burned for a month.

In 1208 China was divided into two great kingdoms, the realm of the Jin Dynasty in the north and the realm of the Sung Dynasty in the south. The Jin were descended from a tribe known in the thirteenth century as the Jurchen but better known today as the Manchu. The Jin emperor ruled from Beijing (known at the time as Zhongdu, or the Central Capital); the Sung emperor ruled from the city of Hangzhou on the Yangtze River Delta.

Both kingdoms enjoyed resources and luxuries that Mongols could scarcely dream of, but there were two things in particular about China that attracted Genghis. First, the Chinese had gunpowder that they used in hand grenades, bombs hurled from catapults, and cannons. Furthermore, the Chinese were fabulously wealthy. Silk, jade, gold, silver, diamonds, ivory—the palaces and temples of the Jin and the Sung were stuffed full of treasures.

But standing between Genghis Khan and this greatest of all prizes was the Great Wall, a serpent of stone, brick, and earthworks erected along the China/Mongolia border. Stretching 4,000 miles, the Wall was then and still is today the longest man-made structure on earth. At regular intervals the Chinese had erected watchtowers, barracks for troops, signal towers that were used to pass information quickly from one garrison to the next, and gates that gave access to the lands of the northern barbarians. It was through one of these gates that the Mongols entered China, although there is no consensus regarding the details. One story claims that the Onguts, a Turkic tribe who were allied to the Jin and defended a section of the Great Wall, were persuaded by Genghis to switch sides. Once they had pledged themselves to Genghis, the Onguts opened one of the Wall's gates and

the Mongols poured into Jin China. Another story says that it was an anonymous shepherd who, for some unknown reason, unbolted a gate and let the Mongols in.

Like the Huns, to whom they were probably related, the Mongols were terrors in the saddle. Their ponies were small, standing about 14 hands—about 56 inches high—at the withers or shoulder (by contrast modern-day horses stand about 16 hands, or 64 inches, high). They were a light, fast, hardy breed—and there were lots of them. Mongols bred their ponies on an epic scale so that each warrior owned six or seven. To keep the ponies fresh, it was a rule among Mongols that a pony could be ridden only one day in four. The speed and agility of the ponies, combined with the Mongols' extraordinary skill as archers, made them the most effective cavalry in Asia. In warfare the Mongols' signature strategy had always been a wide circling movement in which they rode swiftly around their enemies firing a storm of arrows—it was a maneuver that never failed to panic infantrymen.

Now that the Mongols were inside China, Genghis sent out four detachments to the four cardinal points of the compass, each detachment led by one of his sons. Following the invasion strategy that had worked against the

LIKE THE HUNS
TO WHOM THEY WERE
PROBABLY RELATED,
THE MONGOLS WERE
SKILLED HORSEMEN
AND ARCHERS.

Tanguts, the sons of Genghis killed the peasants, burned the crops, stormed the cities, and then sent train after train of food and valuables and slaves north to Mongolia. Any army foolish enough to emerge from behind their city walls to fight the Mongols was routed if not massacred. "Since the beginning of the world, no nation has been as powerful as these Mongols are now," one Chinese writer complained. "They annihilate empires as if they were tearing up grass."

In Beijing, the Golden Emperor Weiwang hoped a very large bribe would get Genghis out of the country and enable him to preserve some scrap of his imperial dignity. He offered the Mongol khan an immense quantity of gold, silver, and silk, along with 500 young men, 500 young women, 3000 horses, and a royal princess named Chi-kuo to be Genghis' wife. Genghis accepted the tribute and returned home to Mongolia—but not for long; Genghis was just giving his Mongols a breather before they made their final assault on China.

DISMOUNTING TO RULE

The steppe was littered with rawhide rope, once standard equipment among the Mongol riders but now discarded in favor of silken cords. With their conquest of the Jin Dynasty, the Mongols were swimming in silk. Every Mongol woman and child was swathed in silk sashes, robes, gowns, and shoes. The floors of their felt tents were covered with silk carpets; their beds were piled high with silk cushions and pillows. In every corner stood bolts of silk cloth, ready to be made into more clothes. There was so much silk that the Mongols used it to wrap and pack all the other treasures they had looted from the Jin.

Meanwhile, captive clerks, the mainstay of the Jin bureaucracy, stood beside each ox cart and camel caravan, itemizing the crates and chests and bundles of precious stones, gold and silver ornaments, porcelain bowls and vases, bricks of black tea, casks of perfume and incense and dyes, skins of fine wine, and trunks packed tight with fragrant sandalwood and precious cinnabar. Newly enslaved teenage boys loaded the loot into the wagons and tended the animals. Captured musicians and singers performed as the convoy began to move. And traveling with all the treasures was a large group, numbering

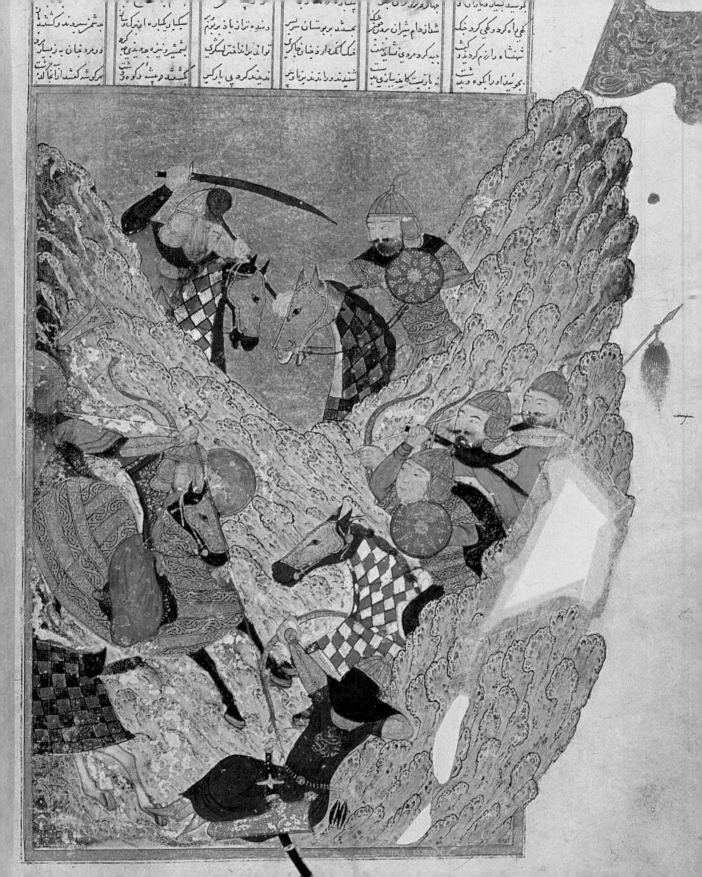

in the thousands, of physicians, scribes, goldsmiths, engineers, astrologers, gourmet chefs, tailors, and men of science who could make gunpowder—in other words, Chinese who possessed all the knowledge and skills the Mongols lacked but wanted desperately.

Early in the Mongol conquest it was an open question whether any Chinese, peasant or town-dweller, would survive. In the countryside, whole areas were desolate, the peasants dead or waiting to be auctioned off in slave markets. As for cities, the Mongols liked to boast they could level a place so completely that a Mongol pony could prance across the rubble without stumbling.

It was one of Genghis's prisoners, a nobleman named Yeh-lu Chutsai, who convinced the khan that the Chinese were worth more alive. As one of the countless administrators employed by the Golden Emperor, Chutsai understood how to run a government. Slaughtering the peasants meant no food at harvest time and no one to pay taxes. Killing all the inhabitants of a city meant no artisans to fashion the luxury items the Mongols had come to love and no technicians to make the gunpowder and siege engines the Mongols had come to rely upon.

"You can conquer China on horseback," Chutsai told Genghis, "but you must dismount to rule her." Genghis

was besieging the city of Kaifeng. By convincing him that the Chinese were much more valuable alive, Chutsai saved the people of the town.

The shift from massacring to administering, from destroying to hoarding, brought about changes to Mongol life. The Mongols had always been a nomadic people who traveled with their herds of ponies and livestock from one pasture to the next. The Mongol house was a yurt, a circular building built of wooden lattice covered with felt. Yurts were sturdy, warm, and relatively easy to set up and take down, but they were too small and offered no security for the vast quantity of spoils brought north from China. To keep his treasure safe, Genghis Khan authorized the construction of the first permanent Mongol buildings. The complex included an audience hall that resembled a Christian church—visitors walked up a long aisle to the dais where Genghis sat surrounded by his sons and generals.

The rest of the "palace" was actually a series of warehouses to store the wealth of China. Mostly likely it was in the yellow palace that Genghis Khan and his closest advisors planned their next campaign, against Russia and the Ukraine.

A FOURTEENTH-CENTRUY PERSIAN ARTIST IMAGINED THE MONGOLS FIGHTING THE CHINESE IN A REMOTE MOUNTAIN SETTING. IN FACT, MOST OF THE WAR TOOK PLACE AT CHINESE CITIES AND TOWNS.

THE GOLDEN HORDE: THE MONGOLS IN RUSSIA

THE MONGOLS HAD A GREAT KHAN, AN ABSOLUTE RULER with full authority over all the lands his people had conquered. In the thirteenth century, the years before the Mongol invasion, the Russians had no such centralized authority.

There were many princes scattered around the country, each of whom ruled over his own territory. Ranked below the princes were nobles who exercised a great deal of independence. And below the nobles were the artisans, merchants, shopkeepers, and free peasant farmers who met from time to time in regional assemblies to decide local issues by popular vote. That three-tiered structure of Russian society ended with the Mongol conquest.

After the first invasion in 1237, most of the princes and nobles were dead, in hiding, or living as refugees in Poland, Hungary, or Germany. The laboring classes, too, lost huge numbers of people, and many who had survived were now slaves of the Mongols. The old Russian model with the prince as a kind of chief executive who recognized the independence of his nobles and the democratic tendencies of the lower classes was over.

During the more than two-hundred-year-long period (1237–1480) that Russians call "the Tartar Yoke," the Mongols' autocratic administrative model dominated the country, and Russians adapted to living under strong, auto-

cratic, even despotic rulers. Long after Mongol power over Russia had been broken, men such as Ivan the Terrible, Peter the Great, and Joseph Stalin ruled as autocrats, according to the model introduced by the Mongols.

The Mongol conquest also forced Russia to find a new capital. Kiev, the largest city in the country, the cradle of Russian Christianity, the center of art and learning, a wealthy cosmopolitan city with links to the Baltics, the Black Sea, Constantinople, and western Europe, had been leveled by the Mongols. It was rebuilt, but Kiev never regained its former glory. Moscow became the premier city of Russia thanks to a series of able princes who learned how to manipulate the Mongol system to their own advantage. To this day, Moscow is one of the world's great political capitals, and Russians have a weakness for the autocratic leaders who dwell there.

RIPE FOR CONQUEST

Their wives wept and their children shrieked in terror, but the princes and noblemen of the city of Vladimir tried to disregard the noise. With their families and retainers and servants, they had barricaded themselves inside the Church of the Holy Mother of God. It could only be a temporary security measure. Outside a massacre was in progress.

TIMELINE

1237: THE GOLDEN HORDE, A MONGOL ARMY OF 120,000 MEN LED BY BATU KHAN, THE GRANDSON OF GENGHIS KHAN, INVADES RUSSIA AND THE UKRAINE.

DECEMBER 1237: MONGOLS MASSACRE THE INHABITANTS OF RYAZAN IN RUSSIA.

WINTER 1238: SUZDAL, ROSTOV, YAROSLAVL, MOSCOW, AND TWELVE OTHER CITIES AND TOWNS IN THE UKRAINE AND RUSSIA ARE DESTROYED BY THE MONGOLS.

Soon the heavy timbers that barred the church doors would give way and the Mongols would burst in and slaughter everyone in the sanctuary. But before that happened, the warriors of Vladimir wanted to become monks. Elbowing their way forward, shoving other men aside, these vengeful, lecherous, hard-drinking, hard-fighting Russians jostled to get close to their bishop or an abbot, or some other high-ranking cleric who would crop their hair and dress them in the black habit of a monk.

If they died in the religious life, these men believed, a lifetime of deadly sins would be wiped away and God would welcome their souls into the kingdom of heaven. But there wasn't much time. As the crowd of would-be monks jockeyed for position near the altar, the first dull thud of a battering ram striking the church doors reverberated through the holy place, and the women and children sent up a fresh wail of fear and dread.

The Russians were an easy target, ripe for conquest. Mongol scouts reported to their khans that every Russian town was at war with the town down the river, every Russian man skirmished with his neighbor. The scouts thought it unlikely the Russians could overcome their age-old habit of feuding long enough to unite and repel an invasion. And the scouts were right. Too proud to ask for help and only too glad to see old enemies wiped off the face of the earth, the princes of each Russian town and city stood alone before the Mongols, and each one perished.

The conquest began with a courteous gesture from Batu Khan, who claimed to be a grandson of Genghis Khan. He sent envoys to all the major cities of Russia, offering to spare them if their princes agreed to his terms: All the princes of Russia must acknowledge Batu Khan as their lord; they most open their towns to the Mongols; 10 percent of all property must be yielded up in tribute; and 10

TIMELINE

LATE MARCH 1238:
RUSSIAN RESISTANCE TO THE MONGOL
INVASION COLLAPSES.

LATE SPRING 1238: THE
MONGOLS FIND THE VAST MARSHLANDS AROUND
NOVGOROD IN THE UKRAINE IMPASSIBLE. THEY
RETREAT, AND THE CITY IS SAVED.

WINTER 1240: AFTER A DESPERATE
DEFENSE, KIEV FALLS TO THE MONGOLS.

1240–1480: RUSSIA AND THE
UKRAINE ARE RULED BY THE MONGOLS.

percent of the population must also be surrendered to serve as slaves or, in the case of strong, healthy men, to be trained as auxiliaries in the Mongol army. Insulted by such brazen demands, most Russian princes killed the Mongol envoys; at Kiev, Batu's emissaries were hurled off the city walls. Now that he had his answer, Batu unleashed a campaign of total war against the Russian people.

Most exposed were the towns situated on the steppes, the immense open grasslands that produced rich harvests and fed huge herds of livestock but also made Russia vulnerable to invasion. Rather than attack these easy targets, the Mongols turned into the forests where the towns were heavily fortified and the woods could shelter refugees. If they picked off the strongest Russian towns first, the Mongol chieftains reasoned, there would be no one to come to the help of the towns on the steppes. And following one of their favorite tactics, the Mongols decided to attack in the dead of winter, when the country's frozen rivers would serve as the Mongols' highways. Hunkered down in their log houses behind the thick walls of their towns, their granaries and smokehouses stuffed with food, the Russians did not expect a Mongol attack.

The first to fall was Ryazan, a city on the Oka River about 130 miles south of Moscow. On a frigid December day in 1237, the Mongols appeared outside the town. In what seemed like minutes, the Mongols hauled their catapults up to the front lines and battered down the town's walls. As the Mongols swarmed through the breach, the people of Ryazan looked for some place to hide. The Mongols pursued them through the streets and alleys of the town like hunters chasing down a herd of deer. The men they impaled. The women they gang-raped. The priests and monks they slaughtered like sheep, slitting their throats and piling up the corpses. The massacre went on and on until not a soul was

left alive. A Russian chronicler lamented that when the Mongols finally moved on, "No eyes [in Ryazan] remained open to weep for the dead."

Following the frozen rivers, the Mongols leveled the towns of Suzdal, Rostov, and Yaroslavl. When the inhabitants of Moscow—then a tiny settlement covering only a fraction of the area known today as the Kremlin—received word that the Mongols were riding in their direction, many people fled, including the bishop. The prince of Moscow remained, however, and perhaps because he did not run away, a considerable portion of the townsfolk stayed with him. It was a foolish, empty gesture, for the Mongols captured Moscow effortlessly, slaughtered the prince and his wife, as well as every man, woman, and child. Then they set fire to the looted, empty buildings.

At the Kolomenka River, a prince named Roman (his brother, Yuri, had been among the dead at Ryazan) assembled an army to drive out the invaders, but the Mongols swept over them like an avalanche. That day not a single Russian escaped "a bitter and violent death," as another historian put it.

A WELL-ORGANIZED INVASION

Under Genghis Khan, the Mongols had learned to approach warfare in a thorough, methodical fashion. In the summer of 1236, when the Mongol chiefs agreed to make their first incursion into Europe, they first sent out an advance team to survey the route the army would follow into Russia.

It was the job of these advance men to clear obstacles from the path of the Mongols, to build bridges over streams and rivers, to buy cattle and fodder from local farmers and keep them in way stations for the army, even to fence off the best grasslands so the Mongols could pasture their horses.

Weeks after the departure of the advance party, a long train of heavy oxcarts laden with the massive timbers of the Mongols' dismantled catapults and other siege engines set out for Russia. Some carts bore sacks of saltpeter and sulfur to make gunpowder, and naphtha, a highly flammable substance that produced a foul-smelling smoke—the Mongols burned it in battle to create a smoke screen for themselves and disorient their enemies. The Mongols had learned the uses of gunpowder and naphtha from the Chinese; now they would use these secret weapons against the Europeans. In battle, the Mongols threw hand grenades—gunpowder packed into small pottery balls—at the Europeans. They also packed gunpowder into large clay pots, loaded the pots into catapults, lit their fuses, and hurled these explosive shells against the defensive walls of cities and castles.

Last of all came the army itself—120,000 men under thirty-one-year-old Batu Khan, reputed to be the grandson of Genghis Khan. (There was some dispute about Batu's origins. His grandmother, Borte, Genghis' wife, had been captured by the Merkit Khan and kept a prisoner for some months. Soon after she was released, she gave birth to a son, Jochi, Batu's father. Genghis acknowl-

BATU KHAN AND HIS
GOLDEN HORDE BESIEGE
THE RUSSIAN TOWN
OF KOZELSK.

MARCO POLO

Marco Polo of Venice (1254–1324) was 15 years old in 1271 when his father Niccolò and his uncle Maffeo took him along on a trading mission to the court of the Mongol emperor, Kublai Khan, a grandson of Genghis Khan. Four years earlier, the Polos had visited Kublai at his summer palace in Shangtu, 150 miles north of Beijing. Kublai had befriended the Venetian merchants, permitting them to trade for silk, porcelain, spices, and other luxury goods they would carry back to Europe, and urging them to return soon.

Kublai Khan was one of the greatest of the Mongol rulers—not in terms of conquest (his invasion of Japan ended in disaster), but in terms of advancing civilization in Asia. Though a Mongol, he gave up the nomadic existence of his people and adopted the sedentary mode of life of a Chinese emperor. He was a patron of the arts and of learning in China. He preferred peace to war. And he encouraged trade with Europe, which explains why the Polos received such a warm welcome at Kublai's court.

When the Polos arrived back in Shangtu in 1275, Kublai took an instant liking to young Marco. Over the next seventeen years, the khan sent Marco on diplomatic missions throughout the Mongol Empire, from Tibet to Vietnam. When the Polos returned home to Venice at last in 1296, Marco wrote a book of what he had seen in China and other parts of the Mongol Empire. Even in Marco's own day, readers didn't know what to make of his stories of giant birds that could carry off elephants and of the bits of paper the Chinese used as money instead of gold and silver coins. If Marco Polo came home full of strange tales, he also came home rich, with fabulous jewels sewn into the hems of his clothing to conceal them from robbers.

In the fifteenth century, Marco Polo's book found an enthusiastic audience among explorers such as Portugal's Prince Henry the Navigator and Christopher Columbus, who read it eagerly and dreamed of finding a swift, direct route from Europe to the riches and wonders of Asia.

edged the boy to be his son, but most Mongols had their doubts; the Merkit Khan seemed the most likely father.

Jochi himself never believed Genghis was his father, and with each passing year the relationship between the two men grew more and more sour. When it was time for Jochi to become a khan in his own right by seizing the land of some hapless tribe, Genghis gave him only a paltry 4,000 men to do the job. This dearth of Mongols may have lingered on into Batu's day—when he prepared his army for the invasion of Russia, Batu was forced to recruit Turkic tribesmen to fight beside his Mongols. The sting of Jochi's dubious parentage plagued Batu. His cousins mocked him, saying that none of the other heirs of Genghis were as glorious as Batu, and they gave him a sardonic nickname, *Sain Khan*, the Splendid Khan.

BATU KHAN'S GOLDEN HORDE

The Mongol invasion of Russia followed the pattern that had worked well for them in Asia. They brought enough arms, equipment, and horses to last for

THE MONGOLS WELCOMED TRADERS FROM EUROPE, AMONG THEM THE POLOS OF VENICE——NICOLO, MAFFEO, AND MARCO, SEEN HERE TAKING THEIR LEAVE OF THE GREAT KHAN.

several years of fighting; there would be no brief campaign season followed by a retreat to the home country to rest and prepare for a fresh round of conquest next year. Batu's army would enter Russia and stay there until they had subdued every city and town. That is why they brought heavy tents to shield them from blizzards, as well as warm felt capes and sheepskin jackets for riding and fighting in icy winter weather.

Each man also carried his own set of essential supplies: needle and thread to repair his clothes; sacks of barley to feed himself and his horse, plus a feedbag and a little cooking pot. Each warrior kept his weapons—bow, arrows, and sword—in sturdy traveling cases. In battle, the Mongols used double-bowed Turkish bows reinforced with animal horn. The double-bend design gave these bows awesome firepower; they became especially deadly when the Mongol horsemen used their armor-piercing arrows mounted with three-inch-wide steel blades.

Mongols also carried long steel swords forged into a distinctive, gentle curve that made them more like a nineteenth-century cavalry saber than a scimitar. Some Mongols also carried lances with long hooks below the spear point. The rider used the hook to pull an enemy from his horse, then stabbed him. Since speed was essential to Mongol warfare, their protective gear had to be light. Mongols favored form-fitting oxhide armor to protect the upper body, a soft leather cap reinforced with iron bands to deflect sword blows to the head, and a leather neckerchief set with iron studs to protect the neck.

Women traveled with the army to cook the meals and also to provide sexual services for the men. More surprising was the presence of troupes of actors in Batu's army. After supper they performed well-known plays based on Mongol history and mythology, accompanied by ancient songs that everyone in the audience recognized and might join in singing.

Batu's army has gone down in history as "the Golden Horde." Some sources say that the name was derived from Batu's pavilion, which was made of cloth-of-gold. Others say it refers to the colors the Mongols assigned to the various compass points: north was black, south was red, blue was east, white was west, and yellow or gold was the center. But this direction-based explanation does not fit, since the lands Batu conquered were not in the center of the Mongol realm but far to the west.

THE FIRE IN THE SACRISTY

To the awful sound of splintering wood, the massive double doors of Vladimir's Church of the Mother of God gave way and a multitude of Mongols surged into the sanctuary. Like savage beasts they fell upon the defenseless congregation, killing men, women, and children without mercy.

Horrified by the sight, the city's prince, his wife, and the archbishop Mitrofan retreated into the sacristy, the chamber where the clergy kept their vestments and all the sacred vessels necessary for the Divine Liturgy. Once again they barricaded the doors. This time, rather than force their way inside, the Mongols heaped up wood and brush around the sacristy and set it ablaze. The prince and the princess and the archbishop and anyone else who had followed them perished in the inferno.

After the fall of Vladimir in February 1238, the devastation of Russia continued unabated. In the weeks that followed, the Mongols razed twelve Russian towns and slaughtered all their inhabitants. By the end of March, resistance in central Russia had collapsed; the entire region was in Mongol hands. It is impossible to tell how many Russians the Mongols slew—certainly the numbers run to the tens of thousands. And though the chronicles insist that the Mongols killed everyone in every town or city they captured, we know that is not true. The Mongols kept many slaves, some for their own use, others for sale.

They delighted in capturing Russian princesses and forcing them to do the most menial work, such as watering the Mongol horses. One Russian who saw it said, "It was strange to see those who had commanded servants doing the work of servants."

The sole holdout was the great city of Novgorod. If it fell to the Mongols it would be their greatest prize. Set on the shores of Lake Ilmen near the Baltic Sea, Novgorod was the commercial heart of central Russia. The city's merchants dealt in sable, fox, and ermine furs—the most expensive in Europe. Trade in such luxury items brought immense wealth to the city, but the Mongols never got their hands on it. Having subdued every other Russian city and town, Batu's Golden Horde was en route to Novgorod when the seasons changed from winter to spring. The frozen marshland around the city melted into a vast bog that was made that much worse by the heavy rains that fell all spring and into the summer. When they were about sixty miles from the city, the Mongols, sick of the wet weather and tired of hauling their horses out of the deep mire, turned around, leaving Novgorod unmolested.

With summer upon them, the Mongols took a break from warfare. This was the season when they scouted new areas for conquest, rested their horses, and forced the local peasants to plant, tend, and harvest crops for Mongol use. Led by Subutai, Genghis Khan's greatest commander and now the friend and supporter of Batu Khan, the Mongols rode south all the way to the Crimea on the northern shore of the Black Sea.

The warm climate produced grain and fruit in abundance, and the lush grasslands were ideal for raising cattle. The Mongols were assessing the Crimea's other possibilities when they encountered a group of unarmed Europeans. Since these men made no threatening moves, the Mongols did not kill them. The two groups could not speak each other's language, but very quickly the Mongols understood that these men were traders. The Mongols displayed their plunder and their Russian captives, and the traders bought whatever they liked best. This was the first recorded encounter between Mongols and Venetians; in a few years the Mongols would come to know very well another Venetian merchant, Marco Polo.

BATU KHAN'S TATAR ALLIES

The physical appearance of the Russians—their golden hair, blue eyes, fair skin—fascinated Batu Khan. They were unlike the Chinese, the Indians, the Persians, or any other people he had ever seen. If he spotted an especially striking Russian slave, he would have him or her brought to his tent so he could stare at the exceptional example of beauty.

Early in his campaign in Russia, his men spared the life of a young Russian named Oleg. Batu thought him so handsome he could not refrain from caressing his captive. As the khan began to stroke Oleg, the young man slapped his hands away. That broke the spell. Batu ordered his guards to take Oleg outside and kill him.

For their part, the Russians found the Mongols repulsive. One observer described them as having "lean and pale faces, stiff high shoulders, and short distorted noses; their chins are sharp and prominent, the upper jaw low and deep, the teeth long and few."

The Russians called the invaders Tartars. Today, because the name is believed to derive from the Chinese word *ta-ta*, meaning a barbarian from the north,

historians prefer to use the term Tatar. The Tatar homeland was northeastern Mongolia (now southern Siberia), near Lake Baikal. They were a Turkic tribe who spoke Mongolian. Under Genghis Khan many Tatar warriors joined the Mongol army, blending seamlessly into the dominant Mongol society. Yet for reasons that

THE RUSSIAN PRINCES PUT UP A HEROIC RESISTANCE, BUT THEY NEVER UNITED AGAINST THE MONGOLS. BATU KHAN PICKED THEM OFF, ONE BY ONE.

are not clearly understood, the Russians, Poles, Hungarians, and other eastern Europeans who fell victim to Batu's Golden Horde referred to the invaders as Tartars rather than Mongols. After the break up of the Mongol Empire at the end of the thirteenth century, those Mongols who remained in the Ukraine, Kazakhstan, as well as regions of eastern Europe were known as Tartars.

THE FALL OF THE CITY OF THE GOLDEN HEADS

Like Novgorod, the city of Kiev had survived the first onslaught of the Tartars or Mongols. Then in early winter 1240, Batu marched on Kiev. As the first rank of Mongol horsemen rode into view, the men of Kiev shut the city gates, which only made the Mongols laugh: "See how the piglets have gathered in their pen for the slaughter!"

Kiev was the chief city of southern Russia and the holiest place in the country. It had been the home of St. Olga and her grandson St. Vladimir, the first to bring Christianity to the Russian people. As grand duke of Kiev, Vladimir had filled his realm with churches and monasteries, and his shrine lay within the first church he had founded, the Church of Dormition of the Virgin. In the two centuries after Vladimir's death, Kiev had become a center of learning and high culture. The church interiors were covered with shimmering mosaics; hauntingly beautiful icons of the saints were arrayed before the altars, and the monastery libraries were filled with rare manuscripts and books. Even the Mongols were impressed—on their first view of Kiev, its skyline dominated by golden domes, they named it "the City of the Golden Heads."

The chroniclers of the time say that, in 1240, "clouds of Tartars" advanced on the town amid a roar of noise—the thunder of their horses' hooves on the frozen ground, the lumbering sound of the catapults being dragged into position, the battle cries of the Mongol warriors—that drowned out all other sounds inside Kiev. Nonetheless, the men of Kiev put up a ferocious defense; not until the Mongol catapults had made a breach in the city walls did they leave their posts. Meanwhile, frantic citizens huddled inside their churches, imploring the saints for a miracle. At one church, when no more people could squeeze inside, a huge crowd clambered up on the roof—so many that the roof collapsed, crushing everyone in the sanctuary below.

THE MONGOLS MASSACRED ALMOST THE ENTIRE POPULATION OF KIEV AND LEVELED THE CITY TO THE GROUND.

The Mongols killed every Russian they found, plundered the entire city, ransacked the tombs of saints and princes—including the shrine of St. Vladimir in the Dormition Church—then tore down the stone buildings and set fire to the wooden ones. When the Mongols rode away from Kiev, a dense pall of smoke hung over the pile of rubble that had once been a magnificent city.

The destruction of cities and the massacre of whole populations were not unknown in Christian Europe at this time, but nothing could compare to the devastation wrought by the Mongols. The invasion brought death and ruin and misery on a scale never before seen in Russia; with their invasion, the Mongols brought about the collapse of Russian society.

Russian society would scramble back, but by the late fifteenth century, when the Russians were strong enough to expel the Mongols from their land, Russia was a different place—more accustomed to centralized authority, more suspicious of outsiders, less willing to tolerate the old concepts of independence and democracy. In other words, Russia was becoming the nation it would be under the tsars, and under the Soviet regime, and to some extent, as it still is today.

SACKS FULL OF EARS:
THE MONGOLS
IN EASTERN EUROPE

I N 1096 AND AGAIN IN 1189, WHAT WE WOULD CALL AN
international coalition of western European armed forces united against a
common foe—the Saracens, who had had overrun the Holy Land and were
threatening to expand their conquest into the Byzantine Empire (in modern-day
Turkey) and then into Greece and mainland Europe. These coalitions, known as
the Crusades, had been initiated by the pope, the only leader whose authority and
influence crossed national borders and who could appeal to men to respond to a
crisis not as Frenchmen or Englishmen or Germans or Flemings, but as Christians.

In 1241, as the Mongols smashed every army sent against them in Poland,
Lithuania, Hungary, Transylvania, Moravia, Bohemia, Moldavia, and
Wallachia, neither the pope nor his archrival, the Holy Roman Emperor, made
a serious effort to galvanize Europe into action. Anxiety about the Mongols
stretched as far as Spain and England, but when barons and bishops sat down
with their king to discuss what must be done, they thought solely in terms of
their own realms, not of their neighbors'.

If the Mongols had kept advancing, they might have gotten as far west as
Dublin and as far south as Sicily, picking off the kingdoms of Europe one at

EVEN WHILE AT WAR THE
MONGOLS KEPT THE SILK
ROAD AND OTHER MAJOR
TRADE ROUTES OPEN.

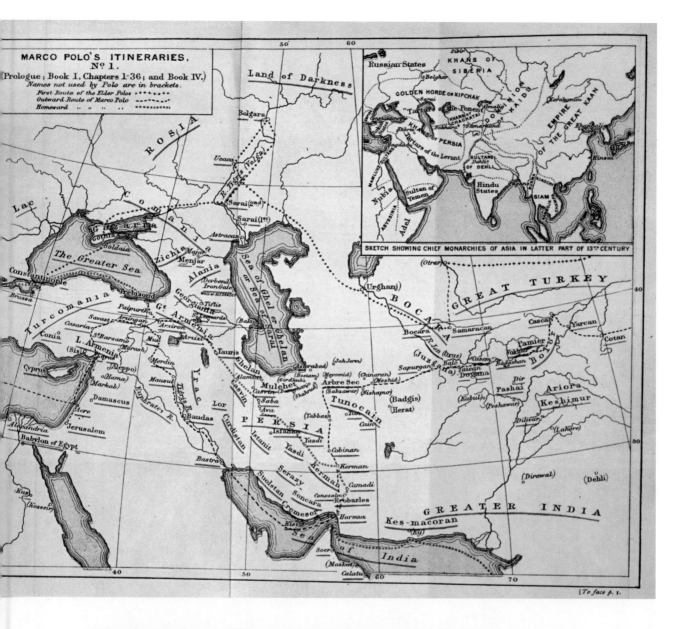

a time, because there would be no great European army to stand in their way. Like the petty princes of Russia, the nations of western Europe intended to pursue a policy of exclusive self-interest, no matter how suicidal.

This insistence on each country standing alone and pursuing its own individual policies—no matter what threat menaced the entire continent—would plague Europe well into the twentieth century, when within a single forty-year period European nations were torn apart by two world wars. Only

TIMELINE

C. 1239: BATU KHAN'S SPIES RETURN FROM EASTERN EUROPE AND REPORT THAT THE VARIOUS KINGDOMS ARE JEALOUS AND SUSPICIOUS OF ONE OTHER, LEAVING THE AREA VULNERABLE TO INVASION.

1240: RUSSIAN REFUGEES TERRIFY EUROPE WITH STORIES OF MONGOL BRUTALITY.

MARCH 1241: THE MONGOLS INVADE POLAND, DESTROYING THE TOWNS OF LUBLIN AND SANDOMIR, AND DEFEATING A POLISH ARMY AT CHMIELNIK.

APRIL 9, 1241: THE MONGOLS KILL 40,000 POLES, GERMANS, AND MORAVIANS AT THE BATTLE OF LIEGNITZ.

---

in recent years with the rise of the European Union has there been an attempt to present a unified front to challenges, and to find unified solutions to the continent's problems.

NINE SACKS OF EARS

The thick smoke from burning naphtha blinded the knights, stung their nostrils and filled their lungs, cutting off their air. Inside the dense, stinking cloud they could hear the clash of arms as the massed infantry from three nations—Poland, Germany, and Moravia—fought the Mongol horde hand to hand. Suddenly a Polish rider burst out from the billowing smoke shouting, "Run! Run!" The Polish cavalry broke ranks, uncertain what to do. Before their commander, Sulislav of Kraków, could call them back to order a large squadron of Mongol horsemen charged out of the smoke straight into the confused mass of Polish knights who turned their horses and deserted the field at a full run.

To counteract the Poles' retreat, Duke Henry the Pious of Silesia led his knights in a headlong charge against the Mongols. Then, out of the billowing cloud of naphtha, thousands more Mongols appeared; they fell upon Duke Henry's right and left flanks, then his rear, completely encircling the knights. Henry made a valiant effort to fight his way out of the melee, but Mongol riders surrounded him, dragged him from his horse, and beheaded him on the spot.

Elsewhere on the battlefield, the Mongols were testing a new tactic on the knights, bringing the knights' war horses down with their arrows, then skewering the fallen knights with their spears. For the Poles, the Germans, and the Moravians,

TIMELINE

APRIL 11, 1241:
SEVENTY THOUSAND HUNGARIAN TROOPS DIE FIGHTING THE MONGOLS AT THE BATTLE OF MOHI. HUNGARY'S KING BELA IV SEEKS REFUGE IN CROATIA.

FEBRUARY 1242: BATU KHAN SENDS ONE OF HIS COMMANDERS, KADAN, TO FIND AND KILL KING BELA.

SPRING 1242: THE HUNT FOR KING BELA IS CALLED OFF AT THE DEATH OF GREAT KHAN OGODEI. ALL MONGOL COMMANDERS ARE ORDERED TO RETURN TO MONGOLIA TO CHOOSE A NEW GREAT KHAN.

it was a day of carnage; it is believed that on April 9, 1241, as many as 40,000 Europeans fell at the Battle of Liegnitz in what is now southwestern Poland. Once

FOUNDED DURING THE CRUSADES TO PROTECT PILGRIMS TO THE HOLY LAND, THE KNIGHTS TEMPLAR HAD BY THE THIRTEENTH CENTURY BECAME ONE OF CHRISTENDOM'S MOST EFFECTIVE FIGHTING FORCES.

the naphtha smoke had cleared, the Mongols worked their way across the battle-field, slicing off the right ears of the European dead—they filled nine sacks.

Christian Europe trembled as news of the Battle of Liegnitz spread across the continent. If such a great army could be killed, almost to the last man, what would stop the Mongols from attacking Vienna, Paris, or Rome? Ponce d'Aubon, master of the Knights Templar in France, wrote to his sovereign, Louis IX, king of France, that every baron and bishop in Germany and Hungary, roused by the calamity, was assembling every fighting man they could find in a last-ditch effort to drive back the Mongols. "And if these be vanquished," d'Aubon told his king, "the Tartars will find none to stand against them, as far as your land."

Europe was saved, though not by the great German-Hungarian army. Within months of the victory at Liegnitz, as the Golden Horde advanced on Vienna, the Great Khan died in Mongolia. Batu Khan, as a member of the royal house of Genghis Khan, led his army back to their homeland to protect his interests and assess his chances of becoming Great Khan.

A DIVIDED EUROPE

One of the few survivors of the destruction of Kiev in 1240 was the Grand Prince Michael. As the Mongols massacred his people and desecrated the tombs of his ancestors, Michael hastened west, hoping to find safety in Poland.

In Batu's camp another Russian survivor of the destruction of Kiev, a nobleman named Dimitri the Galician, told Batu everything he knew about eastern Europe. Yes, there many churches and monasteries filled with gold, he said, but there were also well-defended walled cities, kings with strong castles and large armies, as well as several elite military forces—the Knights Templar, the Knights Hospitaller, and the Teutonic Knights, all fearless fighting machines unlike any other European knights the Mongols had ever encountered.

Two or three years earlier, Batu had sent agents or spies into eastern Europe to assess the state of the various kingdoms, and all the news they brought back was good. Poland was split into four large kingdoms, each one suspicious of and hostile to its neighbors. Although one king ruled over all of Hungary, the freedom of action he should have been able to exercise was severely limited by a pack of powerful noblemen and bishops who jealously guarded their own privileges even at the expense of the Hungarian nation.

THE ANTAGONISM BETWEEN THE KIPCHAKS AND THE MONGOLS DATED BACK TO THE REIGN OF GENGHIS KHAN—SEEN HERE AT PRAYER BEFORE GOING INTO BATTLE AGAINST KIPCHAK ARCHERS.

In the larger picture, the pope and the Holy Roman Emperor were locked in a perpetual power struggle over who would have supreme power in Europe. A few kings and nobles might unite against the Mongols, Batu's spies reported, but it was almost certain that all of Europe would not rise against him.

As Batu planned his move into eastern Europe, Poles opened their homes to the wave of Russian refugees and listened, incredulous, as the survivors gave their firsthand accounts of Mongol savagery. As the stories spread across Europe, the Mongols were painted blacker and blacker until, finally, they were transformed into genuine monsters—dog-headed creatures who ravished and then devoured Christian virgins. They were so foul, it was said, that after Mongols had finished eating a corpse, even vultures would not go near what remained.

Also fleeing the Mongols were tens of thousands of Kipchak tribesmen, along with their khan, Kuthen. A nation of warrior nomads, the Kipchaks had settled near the Black Sea in what is now southern Ukraine and southwestern Russia, but fear of the Mongols had driven them westward. In his palace at Pest on the eastern shore of the Danube River in Hungary, King Bela IV received the khan so graciously and demonstrated such solicitude for the traumatized Kipchaks that the khan pledged himself to an alliance with Hungary. Even more pleasing to Bela, the khan requested baptism for himself and all his people. It was one of the greatest mass conversions the Catholic Church had ever experienced.

Soon after the Kipchaks had become Christians, a letter arrived in Pest from Batu Khan. It was a warning to Bela to send back the Kipchak traitors for punishment or suffer the consequences. At least that is what the Kipchaks told the king. As the letter was written in Uighur, a language no one in Hungary could read but the Kipchaks, some Hungarians wondered whether in fact the letter was a secret communication between Batu and his Kipchak spies. One portion of the letter in particular made the Hungarians suspicious: Batu said that the Kipchaks, who had been a nomadic people, would "find it easy to escape" when he attacked. "But you who dwell in houses within towns," Batu added, "how can you escape from me?" Was that code, the Hungarians wondered, a little reassurance for the Kipchaks that they would not be harmed in the forthcoming Mongol invasion?

An Austrian archduke who had come to Hungary to help repulse the invasion decided that the Kipchaks must be treacherous. He cornered the Kipchak khan, decapitated him, and threw the head from a castle window. The moment the khan's head bounced on the courtyard pavement, the Kipchak-Hungarian alliance came to an end. The Kipchaks withdrew into the mountains where, rather than help the Hungarians against the Mongols, they became a bandit army that raided Hungarian villages and farms.

As the Kipchaks and the Hungarians severed their friendship, the Mongols were already on the march. Batu Khan divided his force into three armies. An army under Kadan, a grandson of Genghis Khan, swept through Poland. A second army under Kadan's brother Guyuk targeted Transylvania, Wallachia, and Moldavia in modern-day Romania. The main army under Batu and Subotai marched on Hungary. The commanders agreed to rendezvous at the Danube in early spring, perhaps outside Vienna.

THE MONGOLS ARRIVE EARLY

In the royal palace at Pest, the most experienced military men and the wisest bishops sat with King Bela, debating how to respond to the Mongol threat. They had time to plan carefully, they assured one another, because the Mongols were still on the far side of the Carpathian Mountains. At that moment the door to the council chamber swung open to admit a soldier, his face and clothes covered in road dust from hours of hard riding. He was the Count of Zolnuck, commander of Hungary's frontier guard, and it was his unhappy duty to report that the Mongols had crossed the Carpathians and were riding straight for Pest.

Even as Zolnuck was speaking to the dumbfounded royal council, sentries on the city walls spotted the advance guard of the Mongol army. Taken completely by surprise, Bela ordered the city gates shut and forbade any Hungarian lord to attack the Mongols until the king and his councilors had devised a plan for meeting the invaders.

The Mongol commander, Subotai, was just as cautious. Rather than attack Pest, he sent raiding parties throughout the countryside, hoping that the devastation would provoke King Bela to ride out with his knights. The king, however, kept his emotions under control—unlike Hugolin Csak, archbishop of Kalocsa. From the battlements of Pest, the archbishop could see towns and farms in flames, and the sight enraged him. Like many bishops during the Middle Ages, he had a small private army; now, against the king's

26

BOLESLAVS V. *Pudicus.* **27**

LESCVS VII. *Niger.* **28**

express command, he buckled on his armor and led his knights out to battle. Not far from the Danube, they spotted a small band of Mongol marauders. As the Mongols rode swiftly toward the forest, Archbishop Csak and his knights pursued them. This was their own country, yet the Hungarians followed the Mongols blindly into a swamp, where the muck and the vines entangled their war horses. As the knights thrashed about, the Mongols picked them off with volley after volley of arrows. Only three Hungarians escaped back to Pest—one of the three was Archbishop Csak.

In all likelihood, the Hungarians believed that they were facing the entire Mongol invasion force. They would not have known that to the north, Poland was already in flames. From the province of Volhynia in western Ukraine, Kadan and his army of about 20,000 Mongols had rampaged into Poland,

AT CHMIELNIK PRINCE BOLESLAV THE CHASTE OF KRAKOW TRIED TO TURN BACK THE MONGOLS. HIS ARMY WAS SLAUGHTERED, AND THE PRINCE BARELY ESCAPED.

destroying the towns of Lublin and Sandomir. At Chmielnik, a small army of Poles under Boleslav the Chaste of Kraków and Prince Mieszko made a valiant attempt to turn back the Mongols. In a fierce battle on March 18, 1241, the Mongols killed almost all the Poles. Mieszko fled west, while Boleslav headed south into the Carpathian Mountains. With their way now clear, the Mongols destroyed every town and every farm they encountered.

On Palm Sunday, they arrived outside the deserted city of Kraków; when word of Boleslav's defeat had reached the town every resident had packed up and fled west. The Mongols burned Kraków anyway. In the Romanian lands, Guyuk was following an identical policy, leaving a trail of smoldering towns and monasteries in his wake as he and his army drove westward to Hungary.

THE BATTLE OF MOHI

Wisely, Bela called upon his allies to join him before he set out against the Mongols: His younger brother, Prince Koloman, brought a force of Slavonian and Croatian troops; Duke Frederick the Quarrelsome brought an army of Austrians; a troop of Knights Templar arrived from France; and many Hungarian barons, as well as several archbishops and bishops, brought up their private armies. By April 4, 1241, King Bela had an army of about 100,000 men. As the Hungarians assembled outside Pest, they could see the Mongols in the distance retreating slowly. Bela gave the order to follow. Without ever going faster than a walk, the Hungarians shadowed the Mongols for six days.

On the sixth, night Bela and his army camped on a vast open plain called Mohi beside the Sajo River; the Hungarians and their allies were in an optimistic frame of mind—their scouts reported that the Mongols were gone, no doubt hiding somewhere in the Carpathians on their way back to Russia. But shortly after the scouts had made their report, a Russian, a slave of the Mongols, entered the camp. The Mongols had not run off, he said. The Hungarians' scouts simply had not gone far enough—the Mongol army was encamped just a few miles away, and they were preparing for battle.

The Hungarians were in a good position for a fight. The deep Sajo River flowed between them and the Mongols, and only a single stone bridge crossed it. Rising on each side and behind the Hungarians were steep wooded hills. It was a good, defensible position, but as an extra precaution Bela ordered all the luggage wagons arranged in a circle around the perimeter of the camp, making an improvised fortress. The king hoped to lure the Mongols into taking the offensive so the Hungarians could pick them off as they tried to swim across the river, or got bogged down at the bottleneck of the bridge. To guard that solitary access point, Bela placed 1,000 Hungarians under his brother Koloman and commanded him to defend the bridge.

In the Mongol camp, Batu Khan and Subotai agreed to divide their force—Batu would storm the bridge, while Subotai would follow the river to search for a place where his men could wade across. Before dawn, Subotai led his men downriver while Batu marched on the bridge.

Koloman repulsed the first Mongol assault on the bridge easily, but then the Mongols rolled seven catapults onto the field; in addition to the boulders, the catapults flung strange, terrifying explosive missiles at the Hungarians. This was the first time gunpowder was used in battle in Europe, and it had the desired effect—the Hungarians sprinted for the safety of their camp. Meanwhile, downstream, Subotai found a fording place and led his men into the hills above the Hungarian position. As Batu's horsemen charged across the now-undefended bridge, Bela's cavalry rushed out to meet them, a great thundering wall of armor and shields and lances. In response, the Mongols scattered, circling the knights and releasing a stinging rain of armor-piercing arrows into their ranks. With no archers of their own to return fire, and unable to engage the swift Mongol riders, the knights fell back.

Prince Koloman and Archbishop Czak tried to rally the knights for a fresh assault, but few were willing to face the Mongol arrows again. Only a handful of riders, and all the Knights Templar, joined the second charge. Once again the Mongol archers decimated the Hungarians. Prince Koloman was wounded, all the Templars were killed, and only a handful of men—including the lucky Archbishop Csak, made it back to the relative safety of the camp.

The loss of the bridge and the two failed cavalry charges unnerved the soldiers and dazed the king. As the Hungarians stood inside the circle of wagons, uncertain what to do next, Subotai's Mongols materialized on the slopes above and began firing flaming arrows armed with naphtha into the camp.

As pandemonium erupted inside the ring of wagons, the Hungarians saw something unbelievable. The Mongol riders who had surrounded the camp rode to one end of the plain, leaving open an escape route to the west, back to Pest, for the

SUBOTAI, GENGHIS KHAN'S MOST TRUSTED GENERAL, ACCOMPANIED BATU KHAN AND ADVISED HIM DURING HIS INVASION OF EASTERN EUROPE.

frightened Hungarians and their allies. Tentatively, a few men ventured out from behind the wagons and raced through the opening. No Mongol pursued them. Even the archers in the hills stopped firing, and now the entire army surged forward; King Bela with his wounded brother, Koloman, went with them.

Once all the Hungarians were in the forest, the Mongols closed in behind them. Frightened and frantic, the troops tried to run, nonstop, all the way to Pest. All those who collapsed from exhaustion, all those who stopped to rest by the way, all those stragglers who could not keep up with the main body of the army, the Mongols killed. Some men tried to hide in churches; the Mongols burned the churches down over their heads. Others sought shelter in villages; the Mongols killed the soldiers, killed the villagers, and then burned the villages to the ground.

King Bela, thanks to his swift horse, outpaced his troops and the Mongols. To save his own life, he left his brother Koloman behind. And while the remnants of the army hurried on to Pest, the king fled into the Carpathian Mountains to a remote monastery. When he arrived, Bela found the monks already had a royal guest—Boleslav the Chaste, fresh from his defeat at Chmielnik.

THE CHASE

By the time Bela's army reached Pest, only 30,000 of the original 100,000 were still alive. Prince Koloman, though dying, refused to remain in the city. It was a deathtrap, he told the barons, and they must evacuate the entire population to the west. But no one would listen to the dying prince. While his attendants carried him to safety, Pest prepared for battle. A few days later the Mongols arrived, overwhelmed the town, killed the inhabitants and reduced Pest to a scorched ruin. It is not known whether Prince Koloman heard the dreadful news before he died.

Between the battles of Liegnitz and Mohi, Poland and Hungary in particular were deprived of some of their strongest leaders and best fighters. Elsewhere in Europe, preachers and poets lamented the loss of "the flower of chivalry" in the eastern lands. The rumor spread that not a Christian was left alive in Hungary. A chronicler in Bavaria wrote, "The Kingdom of

THE DECLINE AND FALL
OF THE MONGOL EMPIRE

Genghis Khan died in 1227 and his empire passed first to his son Ogodei, and after the death of Ogodei to a succession of three of Genghis's grandsons. The last great Mongol emperor was Kublai Khan, who completed the conquest of China and founded China's Yuan Dynasty of emperors.

After Kublai's death in 1294, his heirs squabbled over who should become the next Great Khan. As none of the contenders had the political and military muscle to enforce his will, the Mongol Empire split into four pieces. Kublai's grandson Chengzong (died 1265–1307) received China as his domain. Duwa (died 1307), one of Genghis's great-great grandsons, became khan of the Chagatai region, a vast area in Central Asia that covered present-day Uzbekistan, Turkmenistan, and Kazakhstan. Noghai (died 1299), a great-grandson of Genghis, became khan of the Golden Horde, ruling over the Ukraine and Russia. The last portion of the Mongol Empire, known as the Ilkhanate, went to Baydu (died 1295) who, unlike the other khans, was only distantly related to Genghis. Baydu's territory included present-day Iran, Iraq, Afghanistan, Azerbaijan, Bahrain, Tajikistan, and a slice of Uzbekistan.

Although each of these four regions was immense, the Mongols no longer operated as a unified people. Dissension among the four khans became increasingly spiteful as each went his own way. The Chinese khan adopted the Chinese way of living. The Ilkhan converted to Islam and was drawn into the sphere of influence of the Muslim world. The Russians set in motion the uprising that would eventually free them from the khan of the Golden Horde. And the Chagatai khan would be conquered by Tamerlane. Genghis Khan's splendid empire did not last even a century.

Hungary, which began under Emperor Arnulf and has existed for 350 years, has been annihilated by the Tartars."

While Europe mourned, Batu Khan sent Kadan to find King Bela of Hungary and kill him. The Mongol spy network reported that the king had survived the flight from Mohi and was heading for the province of Dalmatia, in present-day Croatia, along the Adriatic Sea, where many Hungarian barons and knights had taken refuge. It seemed far enough from Hungary to be a safe haven, and even if the Mongols did get this far, the Hungarians could escape by sea—dreadful as the Mongols were, they had not yet learned how to sail.

In February 1242, Kadan caught up with Bela in Dalmatia, but the king boarded a ship and sailed to the island of Arbe, far off shore. Then Kadan coerced some Dalmatian sailors to carry him and his warriors out to the island. When he saw the boats full of Mongols bearing down on Arbe, Bela begged some islanders to take him to the fortress of Clissa back on the coast. Kadan followed him there, too, and now Bela rode to the strongly defended town of Spalato, a place where many survivors from his court in Pest had made their home. At Spalato, Kadan sent a Croatian prisoner into the town with a message, "Kadan, a lord of the unconquered army, bids you know that you will share the punishment of one who is not blood kin to you, if you do not yield him into our hands." Fortunately for the people of Spalato, Bela had left the town, hoping to find safety on yet another island, Tregir, also known as Trau.

Still Kadan pressed on, and Bela ran away again, this time to the island of Trogir. Weary of this game of cat-and-mouse, Kadan released his frustration by raiding a string of villages along the Dalmatian coast. He had assembled ships to take him to Trogir when a storm delayed their departure. Before the storm had abated, a messenger from Batu Khan arrived: The Great Khan Ogodei was dead, and all descendants of Genghis Khan must return to Mongolia to settle the question of who would be the next Great Khan.

It was fortunate for Europe and the future of western civilization that Ogodei died when he did. In Russia, Poland, Romania, and Hungary, the Mongols had not suffered a single defeat. If every kingdom in Europe had clung stubbornly to its "stand alone" policy, nothing would have stopped the Mongols from devastating the entire continent. Europe, like King Bela, escaped disaster by the skin of its teeth.

LESS THAN A CENTURY AFTER GENGHIS KHAN ESTABLISHED HIS IMMENSE EMPIRE, SQUABBLING BROKE OUT BETWEEN MONGOL FACTIONS, AND THEIR VAST REALM WAS BROKEN UP.

يهم على الشوك فواى الامير سيف الدوله حرص هؤلاء وطمعهم الكاد

آخرهم وعبى عساكره وسوى صفوفه ووقف هو واخواه نصر واسمعيل

تبه عيانًا ولا امر بعضهم بعضًا على افعالهم الذميمة واقدامهم على تلك الاعا

نبه وشعار الملاعبه لكنهم كانوا كثيرين العدد والعدد فوقفوا بازائه ومد الفريقان

واس من أكبر لي لا أراد أن

لظنهم انهم قوتون وان حضهم ضعيف فواطئوا بارجلهم اذناب الحيّات وقف

في نهب اتباعه وسلبهم فامر جماعة من عسكره بانهم يخاطون منهم فعلوا وق

وعمه بغراجوق في القلب فشاهد خصومه من اقدام اعلامه واقبال رايايه اه

الليلة وندموا فلم تنفعهم الندامة فلاجرم خرجوا من السلك في الثياب الملوّنة والك

BIBLIOGRAPHY

Aelfric, Abbot of Eynsham. *Lives of Three English Saints.* Edited by G.I. Needham. London: Methuen, 1966.

Ammianus Marcellinus. *Roman History.* Translated by Charles D. Yonge. Bohn, 1862.

Bede, the Venerable. *The Ecclesiastical History of the English People.* New York: Oxford University Press, 1999.

Bradley, Henry. *The Story of the Goths, from the Earliest Times to the End of the Gothic Dominion in Spain*, 5th ed. London: T. Fisher Unwin, 1887.

Brent, Peter Ludwig. *Genghis Khan.* New York: McGraw-Hill, 1976.

Buell, Paul D. *Historical Dictionary of the Mongol World Empire.* Lanham, MD: Scarecrow Press, 2003.

Bury, J. B. *History of the Later Roman Empire from the Death of Theodosius I to the Death of Justinian (A. D. 395 to A. D. 565).* New York: Dover, 1958.

Bury, J. B. *The Invasion of Europe by the Barbarians.* New York: Norton, 1967.

Campbell, James. *The Anglo-Saxons.* Oxford: Phaidon, 1982.

Chambers, James. *The Devil's Horsemen: The Mongol Invasion of Europe.* New York: Atheneum, 1979.

Clarke, Howard B. *Ireland and Scandinavia in the Early Viking Age.* Dublin: Four Courts Press, 1998.

Clover, Frank M. *The Late Roman West and the Vandals.* Brookfield, VT: Variorum, 1993.

Cross, Samuel H., ed. *Russian Primary Chronicle: Laurentian Text.* Medieval Academy of America, 1968.

De la Bédoyère, Guy. *Roman Britain: A New History.* New York: Thames & Hudson, 2006.

Douglas, David Charles. *William the Conqueror: The Norman Impact upon England.* Berkeley: University of California Press, 1964.

Doyle, Peter. *Butler's Lives of the Saints: July.* Collegeville, MN: The Liturgical Press, 2000.

Dudo of St. Quentin. *Gesta Normannorum: An English Translation.* Translated by Felice Lifshitz. The ORB: On-line Reference Book for Medieval Studies. www.the-orb.net.

Dvornik, Francis. *The Making of Central and Eastern Europe.* London, Polish Research Centre, 1949.

Fennell, John Lister Illingworth. *The Crisis of Medieval Russia, 1200–1304.* New York: Longman, 1983.

Ferrill, Arthur. *The Fall of the Roman Empire: The Military Explanation.* New York: Thames and Hudson, 1986.

Fletcher, R. A. *Who's Who in Roman Britain and Anglo-Saxon England.* Chicago: St. James Press, 1989.

Foord, Edward A. *The Last Age of Roman Britain.* London: G. G. Harrap, 1925.

Forte, Angelo, Richard Oram, and Frederik Pedersen. *Viking Empires.* New York: Cambridge University Press, 2005.

Freeze, Gregory L. *Russia: A History.* New York: Oxford University Press, 1997.

Gildas. *De Excidio Britanniae.* Translated by John Allen Giles. London: G. Bell & Sons, 1891.

Goffart, Walter. *Barbarians and Romans, A.D. 418–584: The Techniques of Accommodation.* Princeton, NJ: Princeton University Press, 1980.

Gordon, Colin D. *The Age of Attila: Fifth-Century Byzantium and the Barbarians.* Ann Arbor, MI: University of Michigan Press, 1960.

Gregory, Bishop of Tours. *History of the Franks.* New York: Octagon Books, 1965.

Griffith, Paddy. *The Viking Art of War.* London: Greenhill Books, 1995.

Haliday, Charles. *The Scandinavian Kingdom of Dublin.* Shannon: Irish University Press, 1969.

Hanning, Robert W. *The Vision of History in Early Britain: From Gildas to Geoffrey of Monmouth.* New York: Columbia University Press, 1966.

Heather, P. J. *The Goths.* Malden, MA: Blackwell Publishers, 1996.

Hill, David. *An Atlas of Anglo-Saxon England.* Toronto: University of Toronto Press, 1981.

Holman, Katherine. *The Historical Dictionary of the Vikings.* Lanham, MD: Scarecrow Press, 2003.

Hudson, Benjamin. *Viking Pirates and Christian Princes: Dynasty, Religion, and Empire in the North Atlantic.* New York: Oxford University Press, 2005.

Hunter Blair, Peter. *Roman Britain and Early England, 55 B.C.–A.D. 871.* New York: T. Nelson, 1963.

Isidore of Seville. *History of the Goths, Vandals, and Suevi.* Translated by Guido Donini and Gordon B. Ford. Leiden, The Netherlands: E. J. Brill, 1970.

Jones, Gwyn. *A History of the Vikings,* 2nd ed. New York: Oxford University Press, 1984.

Jordanes. *The Origins and Deeds of the Goths.* Translated by Charles C. Mierow. Princeton, NJ: Princeton University Press, 1908.

Kagan, Donald. *Decline and Fall of the Roman Empire: Why Did It Collapse?* Boston: Heath, 1962.

Kirby, D. P. *The Earliest English Kings,* rev. ed. New York: Routledge, 2000.

Lamb, Harold. *Genghis Khan: The Emperor of All Men.* New York: R.M. McBride, 1927.

Lasko, Peter. *The Kingdom of the Franks: Northwest Europe before Charlemagne.* London: Thames and Hudson, 1971.

Lenski, Noel Emmanuel. *Failure of Empire: Valens and the Roman State in the Fourth Century A.D.* Berkeley: University of California Press, 2002.

Liversidge, Joan. *Britain in the Roman Empire.* New York: F.A. Praeger, 1968.

Maenchen-Helfen, Otto J. *The World of the Huns: Studies in Their History and Culture.* Berkeley: University of California Press, 1973.

Magnusson, Magnus. *The Vikings.* London: Tempus Publishing, 2003.

McGovern, William Montgomery. *The Early Empires of Central Asia: A Study of the Scythians and the Huns and the Part They Played in World History.* Chapel Hill: University of North Carolina Press, 1939.

Merrills, A. H. *Vandals, Romans and Berbers: New Perspectives on Late Antique North Africa.* Burlington, VT: Ashgate, 2004.

Mitchell, Stephen. *A History of the Later Roman Empire, AD 284–641: The Transformation of the Ancient World.* Oxford: Blackwell, 2007.

Morgan, David. *The Mongols.* New York: B. Blackwell, 1986.

Morris, John. *The Age of Arthur: A History of the British Isles from 350 to 650.* London: Phoenix, 1973.

Mould, Daphne Desiree Charlotte Pochin. *The Celtic Saints.* New York: Macmillan, 1957.

Mummy, Kevin. "The Groans of the Britons: Towards the British Civitates Period ca. 406–455 C.E." *Ex Post Facto: Journal of the History Students at San Francisco State University,* 2002.

Nicolle, David. *Arthur and the Anglo-Saxon Wars.* London: Osprey Publishing, 1987.

Ó Cróinín, Dáibhí. *Early Medieval Ireland, 400–1200.* New York: Longman, 1995.

Perowne, Stewart. *The End of the Roman World.* New York: Crowell, 1967.

Potter, T. W. *Roman Britain.* Berkeley: University of California Press, 1992.

Ratchnevsky, Paul. *Genghis Khan: His Life and Legacy.* Cambridge, MA: Blackwell, 1992.

Robinson, J. H. *Readings in European History.* Boston: Ginn, 1905.

Schaff, Philip, trans. *Socrates and Sozomenus Ecclesiastical Histories.* Christian Literature Publishing Co., 1886.

Scherman, Katharine. *The Birth of France: Warriors, Bishops, and Long-Haired Kings.* New York: Paragon House, 1989.

Scullard, H. H. *Roman Britain: Outpost of the Empire.* London: Thames and Hudson, 1979.

Sergeant, Lewis. *The Franks: From Their Origin as a Confederacy to the Establishment of the Kingdom of France and the German Empire.* New York: G. P. Putnam's Sons, 1898.

Smyser, H. M. "Ibn Fadlan's Account of the Rus with Some Commentary and Some Allusions to Beowulf." *Franciplegius: Medieval and Linguistic Studies in Honor of Francis Peabody Magoun, Jr.* Edited by Jess B. Bessinger Jr. and Robert P. Creed. New York: New York University Press, 1965.

Smyth, Alfred P. *King Alfred the Great.* New York: Oxford University Press, 1995.

Southern, Pat. *The Late Roman Army.* New Haven, CT: Yale University Press, 1996.

Spuler, Bertold. *History of the Mongols: Based on Eastern and Western Accounts of the Thirteenth and Fourteenth Centuries.* Berkeley: University of California Press, 1972.

Swanton, Michael James, trans. *The Anglo-Saxon Chronicle.* New York: Routledge, 1998.

Taylor, Robert. *Life in Genghis Khan's Mongolia.* San Diego, CA: Lucent Books, 2001.

Thompson, E. A. *A History of Attila and the Huns.* Oxford: Claredon Press, 1948.

Thompson, E. A. *The Huns.* Malden, MA: Blackwell Publishers, 1999.

Thompson, E. A. *Romans and Barbarians: The Decline of the Western Empire.* Madison: University of Wisconsin Press, 1982.

Todd, James Henthorn, trans. *Cogadh Gaedhel re Gallaibh. The War of the Gaedhil with the Gaill, or, The Invasions of Ireland by the Danes and Other Norsemen.* London: Longmans, Green, Reader, and Dyer, 1867.

Vernadsky, George. *A History of Russia.* London: Oxford University Press, 1943.

Wacher, J. S. *The Towns of Roman Britain.* Berkeley: University of California Press, 1974.

Walker, Ian W. *Harold, the Last Anglo-Saxon King.* Thrupp, Stroud, and Gloucestershire: Sutton, 1997.

Wallace-Hadrill, J. M. *The Long-Haired Kings, and Other Studies in Frankish History.* New York: Barnes & Noble, 1962.

Ward-Perkins, Bryan. *The Fall of Rome and the End of Civilization.* New York: Oxford University Press, 2005.

Warmington, B. H. *The North African Provinces, from Diocletian to the Vandal Conquest.* Cambridge: Cambridge University Press, 1954.

Weatherford, J. McIver. *Genghis Khan and the Making of the Modern World.* New York: Crown, 2004.

Wernick, Robert. *The Vikings.* Alexandria, VA: Time-Life Books, 1979.

Wilson, David M. *The Vikings and Their Origins: Scandinavia in the First Millennium.* New York: McGraw-Hill, 1970.

Yorke, Barbara. *Wessex in the Early Middle Ages.* New York: Leicester University Press, 1995.

Vossius, G. J., trans. *Zosimus, New History.* W. Green and T. Chaplin, 1814.

PICTURE CREDITS

Front cover: Assemblée Nationale Palais-Bourbon, Paris, Giraudon/ The Bridgeman Art Library International

The pictures in this book are used with permission and through the courtesy of:
Bridgeman Art Library International: p. 6–7, 118, 179, Musée des Beaux Arts, Dunkirk, France; p. 18, Biblioteca Monasterio del Escorial, Madrid; p. 22, San Marco, Venice; p. 34, Galleria Borghese, Rome; p. 40, Palazzo Pitti, Florence; p. 40, 97, Bridgeman Art Library; p. 42, Louvre, Paris; p. 55, 69, 180, 196, 264, 275, 281, Bibliothèque Nationale, Paris; p. 56, 90, 94, 99, 104, 110, 125, 141, 145, 148, 151, 153, 166, 173, 176, 189, 198, 205, 214, 221, 222, 251, 278, 285, 289, 296, 298, 302–303, private collection; p. 59, Church of Notre Dame-de-Bonne Nouvelle, Paris; p. 61, Musée du Berry, Bourges, France; p. 63, Vatican Museums and Galleries, Vatican City; p. 72, Index, Barcelona; p. 75, Palazzo Barberini, Rome; p. 76, 115, 126, Musée Conde, Chantilly, France; p. 79, Abou-Adal Icon Collection; p. 84–85, New York Historical Society; p. 93, Santa Maria Antiqua, Rome; p. 108, Bradford Art Galleries and Museums, West Yorkshire, UK; p. 121, Castello Della Manta, Saluzzo, Italy; p. 129, Wallington Hall, UK; p. 133, Viking Ship Museum, Oslo; p. 134, 225, 272, 292, British Library, London; p. 139, Church of the Assumption, Oxon, UK; p. 154–155, Houses of Parliament, UK; p. 159, Huntington Library and Art Gallery, San Marino, CA, USA; p. 164, Royal Geographical Society, London; p. 185, Ministère des Affaires Étrangères, Paris; p. 192, Jamestown-Yorktown Educational Trust, VA, USA; p. 201, 240, Prado, Madrid; p. 208, Museu Civico, Padua, Italy; p. 211, Russell-Cotes Art Gallery and Museum, Bournemouth, UK; p. 228, Musée d'Art, France; p. 230, Bibliothèque de L'Arsenal, Paris; p. 235, Institute d'Études Slaves, Paris; p. 239, Central Naval Museum, St. Petersburg; p. 243, 291, Bibliothèque des Arts Décoratifs, Paris; p. 245, 256, Biblioteca Nacional, Madrid; p. 249, Vladimir Cathedral, Kiev
Historic Urban Plans, Inc.: p. 15
AKG-Image: p. 37, 44, 107
Alamy Images: p. 47, 51, 136, 219, Mary Evans Picture Library; p. 71, 255, North Wind Picture Archives
The Image Works: p. 48, 163, 170, 252, 268, Mary Evans Picture Library; p. 195, ND/Roger Viollet; p. 261, AAAC/Topham; p. 267, Werner Forman Archive/Topham
North Wind Picture Archives: p. 270

INDEX

Note: Locators in italics indicate illustrations.

A

Aachen, 120, 136
Abdurrhaman II, 194
Abydos, 256
actors, 73
Adrianople, Battle of, 16, 26, 27
Aed Finnliaith, 169–170
Aegean islands, 94–95
Aegidius, 123
Ælla, 109–110, 112, 138, 142–143, 147
Aesc, 101, 106
Aethelbert, 112–113
Aethelney, Isle of, 146, 150
Aethelred the Unready, 220, 221, 222
Aethelstan, 152, 178
Aetius, Flavius, 60–61, *61*, 64, 71, 83, 86, 101, 105–106, 123
Afghanistan, 300
Africa, 262. *See also* North Africa; *specific countries*
Africans, 198
Alammani. *See* Alemanni
Alans, the, 38, 43, *44*, 45, 48
Alaric, 9, 16–17, 20, 21, 26–28, 30–33, 82, 89, 90
Alaric II, 123
Alcuin, 132
Alemanni, 10, 124, 126
Alexandria, 10, 199
Alfred the Great, 143, 144–157, *145, 151, 154–155*, 221, 222
Algeciras, 199
Algeria, 80, 198. *See also* North Africa
American colonies, 233
Americas, discovery of, 8, 13
amethysts, 165
Amiens, 60
Amlaibh, 169. *See also* Olaf the White
Anastasius, 126
"Andredes Cester", 112
Andred's Castle, 112
Angles, 9, 13, 54, 100, 101, 105, 108, 110, 123

Anglo-Saxon Chronicles, The, 112, 131, 231
Anglo-Saxon royal line, 221
Anna, 250, 251, 256, 257
Annals of Fulda, 140
Antioch, 187
Apollonaris, Sidonius, 83
aqueducts, 15–16, 35
Aquileia, 31, 62
Aquitaine, 178, 182
Arabs, 200–201. *See also* Moors
Arbe, 301
Arbitio, 114
Arbogast, 27–28, 30
Ardennes Forest, 122
Arians, 74, 78, 80–81, 89, 115, 117, 200
aristocracy, 183
Arius the Heretic, 78, *79*, 80
Arklow, 11, 158, 171, 205
Arles, 199
Armagh, 158, 160, 166, 207, 213, 217
Armenia, 37
armies, private, 178
Arras, 64
Arthur, 106–109, *108*, 109. *See also* Aurelianus, Ambrosius
Arunulf, 299
Asia, 260, 262, 266, 280, 300. *See also specific countries*
Aslaug, 193
Asser, Bishop, 150, 152
Asturias, 201, 202
Atil, Rus, 252
Attila the Hun, 11, 12, 47–65, 83, 89, 106, 123
Augustine, St., 9, 78–79, 101, 112
Augustus, 95
Augustus, Romulus, *90*, 90
Aurelia, 60
Aurelianus, Ambrosius, 101, 106–109, 112. *See also* Arthur
Australia, 98
Austria, 16, 21, 120, 294
Austrians, 297
Avars, 120
Aventine Hill, 20
Azerbaijan, 300

B

Bactria, 38
Badbury Hillfort, 109
Baghdad, 12

Bahrain, 300
Balearics, the, 88
Balkans, 252
Baltics, 275
Baltic Sea, 149, 209, 236, 254, 275, 283
barbarians, 10. *See also specific groups*
in popular culture, 8–9
Roman's perceptions of, *72*, 73
Basil, St., 258
Basilica Aemelia, 20
Basilica of St. Paul, 21
Basil II, 202–203, 250, 254, *255, 256*, 257
Basiliskos, 91
Basilius, 32
Bath, 102
Batu Khan, 276–277, *278*, 279, 281–286, *285*, 290, 291, 293–295, 298, 301
Bavaria, 181, 299
Baydu, 300
Beauvais, 60
Begter, 263, 265
Beijing, 12, 263, 268–269, 271
Bela IV, 291, 294, 295, 297, 298, 299, 301
Belgium, 114, 120, 123, 124, 177. *See also* Gaul
Benfleet, 157
Beowulf, 110, 146
Berbers, 198
Bergamo, 62
Berkshire, 146
berserkers, 140–141, 218–220
Bertin, St., *179*
Besancon, 64
Bethlehem, 38
Bible, translation into Latin, 9
Biscay, Bay of, 202
Bishopsgate, 112
Bithynia, 241
Bjorn, 189–199, 202
Bjorn Ironside, 193
Black Sea, 202, 236, 241, 275, 284
Blathmac, St., 137
Bleda, 52, 53, 56–57
"blood eagle", 138, 142
"Blue Men", *196*, 196, 198
Bohemia, 288
Boleslav the Chaste, 256, *296*, 296–297, 299
Bonifacius, 77–78

Book of Armagh, 213
Book of Durrow, 135
Book of Isaiah, 50
Book of Kells, 135
books, 165. *See also* manuscripts
Borte, 279
Boru, Brian, 204, *205*, 206, *207*, 207, 210–217
Boru, Conaing, 210, 217
Boru, Cuduiligh, 215, 217
Boru, Donnchad, 213, 217
Boru, Gormlaith, 213, 214–215, 217
Boru, Mathgamain, 206, 210, 212
Boru, Murchad, 206, *207*, 215, 216, 217
Boru, Slaine, 213, 216
Boru, Tordhelbach, 210, 215, 217
Bosnia, 95
Bosphorus Strait, 16, 241
Boulogne, 182
Boyne River, 163
Brescia, 62
Bretons, 223–224
Brienne, Count of, 231
Britain, 10, 102, 123. *See also* Britannia; England; Ireland; Scotland
   Angle invasion of, 100, 108
   barbarian invasions of, 98–113, *99*, *110*, 128–143, *129*
   Christianity in, 109, 112–113
   Jute invasion of, 100, 101, 105–106, *107*, 108
   map of, *110*, *136*
   maps of, *110*
   Roman colonization of, 100–103, 105–106, 112–113
   Saxon invasion of, 100, 105–111, 112
   Viking invasions of, 128–143, *129*
Britannia, *15*, 110. *See also* Britain; England; Ireland
British Empire, 14, 98. *See also* Britain
Brittany, 109, 178
Brodir, 209, 214, 215, 216–217
Bulgars, 254
Burgred, 143, 147
Burgundy, 123, 124–125, 126, 175, 184
burhs, 152, 156
Buro, Cuduiligh, 210

Buro, Murchad, 210
Byzantine Empire, 16, 23, 120, 200, 202–203, 239–241, 246–247, 249–252, *251*, 256–257, 259, 288. *See also* Constantinople; Holy Roman Empire

C
Cabo Tres Forcas, 199
Cadiz, 199
Caesar, Julius, 91, 100, 101–102, 114
Caesars, line of, 90
Cain, 212
Callinicus, 57
Cambrai, 127
Cambridge, 142, 151
Camelot, 107–108
Campagna, 95
Canada, 98, 232, 233
Canterbury, 102, 112, 131, 135, 138, 152
Canute I, 220, 221, 222, 225, 226
Canute the Great. *See* Canute I
Cappadocia, 37, 39
Carlingford Lough, 169
Carpathian Mountains, 297, 299
Carpathians, 297
Cartagena, 74
Carthage, 69, 77, 78, 80, 88, 97, *97*. *See also* North Africa
Caspian Sea, 250, *251*
castles, 182–183
catapults, 279
cathedrals, 183
Catholicism, 20, 35, 78, 80–81, 109, 115–117, 123, 124–125, 247, 294. *See also* Catholics; Christianity; monasteries
Catholics, 69, 80–81, 96, 97–98, *129*, 200. *See also* Catholicism; Christians
Caucasus Mountains, 37
Cefalu, 187
Celestine I, Pope, 92
Celtic tribes, 101
Central Capital. *See* Beijing
Ceuta, 74, 77, 78, 200
Chagatai region, 300
Chalons, Battle of, 53, *55*, 64–65, 71, 83, 89, 123
Chararic, 127

Charlemagne, 120, 121, 122, 132, 136, 173, 177, 178, 181, 182, 184
Charles the Bald, *180*, 181–182, 185, 193
Charles the Simple, 174–175
Charnouth, 131, 138
Chartres, 174, 183, 186, 193
Chengzong, 300
Chester, 157
Chi-kuo, 271
Childeric I, 123
China, 8, 12, 260–273, 280, 300
Chippenham, 146–147, 150, 152
Chmielnik, 290, 296–297, 299
Christ, 78, 125
Christ Church Cathedral, 204
Christianity, 13, 35, 123, 136, 174, 190, 248, 299. *See also* Christians; monasteries; relics
   Arian sect of, 16–17, 20, 78, 80–81, 89, 115, 200
   in Britain, 14, 112–113, 146, 149
   Catholicism. *See* Catholicism
   Constantine's conversion to, 16
   conversion of Kipchaks to, 294
   conversion of Rus to, 248, 257–259
   Crusades, 288, 291, *291*
   Frank conversion to, 124–125
   in Kievan Rus, 237, 246–251, *249*, 254
   Orthodox Church, 247, 259
   reliquaries, 164
   in Russia, 275
   Saxon conversion to, 112
   Trinity, the, 78
   Viking conversion to, 130, 152, 177, 181, 203
Christians, 16, 23, 32, 69, 73, 156, 254. *See also* Arians; Catholics; Christianity
Chrysaphus, 58
churches, 136. *See also specific churches*
Chutsai, Yeh-lu, 273
Cinnaedh, 170
Cisapline Gaul, 114
Cissa, 112
City of God, 9
"City of the Golden Heads," the, *286*
Clare, 210

classical civilization, Catholic Church and, 35
Claudian, 43
Claudius, 102
Clissa, 301
Cloderic, 127
Clonmacnoise, Abbey of, 160–161, *163*, 169
Clontarf, Battle of, 215–216
Clothilde, 116, 124–125, *125*
Clovis, 116–117, *118*, 122, 123–127, *126*
Cogadh Gadhel re Gaillaihh (*The Wars of the Irish Against the Foreigners*), 210–212
Coifi, 113
coins, 105, 158, 171
Cole, Thomas, 82, *84–85*
Cologne, 60, 126, 127
colonialism, 13
Columbus, Christopher, 13, 280
Comgadh, the, 206, 215
commerce. *See* trade
Commodus, 19
Connaught, 206, 212, 214
Constantine I, 16, *22*, 23, 32, 78
Constantine III, 101, 103
Constantinople, 9, 11, 23, 49, 126, 203, 236, 239–241, *245*, 245–248, 256–257, 275. *See also* Byzantine Empire
Constantius, 73
convents, 35, 136, 156, 157, 165, 258
copper, 165
Corbie, monastery of, 178
Córdoba, 189, 194
Cork, 11, 158, 171, 205
Cornwall, 109, 135
Corsica, 88, 97
Côte d'Azur, 199
County Down, 169
Course of Empire, The, 82, *84–85*
Courtois, Christian, 91
Crecganford, 106
Cremona, 31
Crimea, the, 252, 257, 284
Croatia, 16, 21, 95, 291, 301
Croatians, 297
crucifixion, 73
Crusades, 187, 203, 288, 291, *291*
Csak, Archbishop Hugolin, 295–296
Cuaran, Olaf, 213

Cuthbert, St., 132, *134*, 135
Czak, Archbishop, 298
czars, 236, 259, 287
Czech Republic, the, 120

D

Dacia, *15*
da Gama, Vasco, 13
Dalmatia, 301. *See also* Croatia
Damascus, 12
Danelaw, the, *136*, 146, 152, 156, 157
"Danelog", *136*
Danes, 11–12, 120, 130, 138, 140, 142, 144, 147, 149–150, 152, 169–170, 174–175, 177, 203, 221, 262. *See also* Denmark; Vikings
Danube River, 252, 294, 295–296
d'Aubon, Ponce, 293
Dehli, 8, 12
Demandt, Alexander, *69*
Denmark, 130, 149, 175, 177, 181, 220, 221, 250, 262. *See also* Danes
Derry, 161, 170
Derwent River, 219, 220
Devon, 157
diamonds, 165
Didymus, 73
Dimitri the Galician, 293
Dnieper River, 237, 257
Don River, 237
Dorchester Manor, 130
Dorestad, 181
Dormition of the Holy Virgin, Church of the, 258, 286
Dorsetshire, 131
Dover, 102
dragon ships, 131, *133*, 133, 137, 157, 189, 190
drekar, *133*
Drevlians, 237–238, 242, 244–246, 253
Drogheda, Battle of, 168, 170
Dubh-linn, 160, 162. *See also* Dublin
Dublin, 8, 11, 158, 160–162, 168–169, 171, 204–205, 207, 209, 213, 215–217
Dudo of St. Quentin, 175, 191–192
Duwa, 300

E

East Anglia, 135, 138, 142, 144, 147, *148*, 149, 152, 157, 223, 229
eastern Europe, 12, 260, 288–301
Ebric, 215–216
Edeco, 58
Edgar (the Aetheling), 224
Edgar's Stone, 151
Edinburgh, 135
Edington, 146, 151–152
Edith Swan-Neck, *228*, 229
Edmund, St., 138, *139*, 142, 143, 147, 149
education, 136, 165
Edward, 147
Edward the Confessor, St., 220–223, *221*, *222*, 224, 226, 231
Edwin, 113
Edwin, Earl of Mercia, 226–228
Egbert, 131, 138
Egils Saga, 140
Egypt, 9, 10, 80, 199, 200
Eleanor of Aquitaine, 233
Elfrida, 147
Elias, St., 236
emeralds, 165
England, 8, 11, 66, 98, 101–103, 106, 109–110, 112, 128, *129*, 129, 178, 209, 214, 288. *See also* Britain; Britannia; British Empire
   culture of, 135–136, *137*, 140, 144, 146, 156–157
   literacy in, 146
   map of, *136*
   maps of, *148*, *225*
   Norman Conquest, 172
   schools in, 136
   unification of, 128, 130
   Viking invasions of, 128–143, *136*, 144–157, 175, 218–233
English Channel, 101, 103, 123, 135, 186
Epiphany, Feast of the, 147
Eric the Good, 203
Ermanarich, 38, 43
Essex, 135, 138, 142, 152, 157
Estonia, 234, 238
Etgal, 162
Ethelfled, 147
Eucherius, 30
Eudocia, 90
Eudoxia, 90

Eugenius, 27–28, 30, 54
Europe, 12, *15*, 260, 262, 275, 280, 288–301. *See also* Byzantine Empire; eastern Europe; European Union; Roman Empire; *specific countries*
European Union, 290
Eustochium, 33
Eutropius, 39
executions, 73, 74, *75*, 119, 138, 142, 143
Exeter, 147
Exploration, Age of, 13

F
Fabiola, 38
Fairhair Harald, 140
Fat Khan, the, 263. *See also* Targutai the Fat Khan
Ferrieres, monastery of, 178
field armies, 71–72
Field of Mars, 83
Findan, St., 167
Finns, the, 234
Fintan. *See* Findan, St.
flamethrowers, 199, 202, 241
Flaminian Way, 31
Flanders, 149
food, 88–89, 91
fortifications, 182–183
Fountenoy-en Puisaye, Battle of, *180*, 181, 182
Fourth Crusade, the, 203
France, 8, 53–54, *55*, 60, 64–66, 71, 114–127, 149, 156–157, *173*, *180*, 193, 199, 232–233, 293, 297. *See also* Frankish Empire; Gaul
Frankish Empire, 172–187. *See also* France; Franks
aristocracy of, 183
culture of, 178
map of, *185*
Viking invasions of, 177–178, 181, 182, 183–186, 199
Franks, 9, 13, 114–127. *See also* France; Frankish Empire; Gallo-Romans; Gaul
appearance of, 124
conversion to Christianity, 124–125
culture of, 124
Roman Empire and, 114–115, 117, 122–123

takeover of Gaul, 114–117, 122
Vandals and, 72–73
Vikings and, 140, 172–187, *173*
Frederick the Quarrelsome, 297
French Riviera, 199
Frigidus River, Battle of the, 17, 27–28, 30
Frisia, 100, 149, 156, 174, 175, 181
Fritigern, *24*, 24–25, 26
Fulford, 227, 228, 229
fyrd, 227

G
Gaiseric, 68, 69, 74, 77–83, 86, *87*, 87–92, 95, *97*, 97
Galahad, 107–108
Galicia, 202
Galla Placidia, 20
Gallienus, 21–22
Gallo-Romans, 19, 114–116, 117. *See also* Franks; Gaul
Gaudentius, Flavius, 60–61
Gaul, 67, 73, 92, 101, 102, 114–127. *See also* France
Catholicism in, 124–125
Frankish takeover of, 114–117, 122
map of, *115*
Vandal raid of, 72
Vikings in, 172–187, *173*
Gauzlin, 185
Gelimer, 97
gemstones, 165, 269
Genevieve, St., *59*, 60
Genghis Khan, 11–12, 260–275, *261*, *264*, *267*, *268*, *275*, 279, 281, 284, 291, *293*, 295, 300–301. *See also* Temujin
Gepids, 10
German Beck, 227
Germanic tribes, 19, 39, 67, 70, 80, 100, 117, 129–130. *See also specific tribes*
Germany, 10, 60, 100, 114, 119, 120, 124, 126, 127, 177, 181, 221, 274, 290, 293, 299. *See also* Gaul; Germanic tribes
Geza, 250
Gildas, St., 105, 106–107, 109, 112
Gilla Ciarain, 169
gladiators, 73

glass, 102
Glendalough, 163
Gobi Desert, 260
Godgisel, 68, 72, 74
Godwin, Earl, 222, 224, 226–227
Godwin, Edith, 222
Godwinson, Harold, 218, 220, *222*, 223–224, 229–230, *230*, 232. *See also* Harold
Godwinson, Tostig, 226
gold, 16–17, 102, 165
"Golden Emperor," the, 263, 268–269, 271, 273. *See also* Weiwang
Golden Horde, the, 276, *278*, 279, 281–282, 283, 293, 300
golden menorah, the, 90
Gonsalvo Sancho, 202
Gospel books, 136
Götaland, 23. *See also* Goths
Goths, 9–10, 13, *18*, 39, 43, 64, 65, 81, 90, 100, 103, 115, 123
conversion to Christianity, 23
fall of Rome and, 82
Huns and, 43, 48
sack of the Roman Empire by, 14–35
types of, 23
grain, 88–89, 91
Gratian, 31
"Great Heathen Army", 138, 142, 149, 151–152
Great Khan, 293, 300. *See also* Genghis Khan
Great Wall of China, the, 269–270
Greece, 13, 94, 122, 288
Greek, 203
Greek fire, *240*, 241
Greeks, 187
Grégoire, Henri, 66, 69
Gregory, St., 127
grenades, 279
"Groans of the Britains, The", 105–106
Guadalete, Battle of, 200
Guadalquivir River, 193–194, 199
Guinevere, 107–108
Gulf of Spezia, 197
Gunderic, 68, 72–73, 74
gunpowder, 269, 279, 298
Gurim, 175
Guthrum, 146, 151–152, *153*, 156
Guy of Pontheiu, 223
Guyuk, 295, 297

Hadleigh, 156
Hadrian's Wall, 68, 70, 100, 102, 103
Hadstock, 142
Halfdan, 131
Hampshire, 146, 151
Hangzhou, 269
Harald, 174, 181, *219*, 222
Harald Bluetooth, 250
Haraldskvaethi, 140
Hardrada, Harald, 218–220, 226–230, 232
Harold. *See* Godwinson, Harold
Harthacanute, 226
Hastein, 156–157, 189–199, *193*, *194*, 202
Hastings, Battle of, 186, 218, 221, *228*, 229, *230*
Helena, 246–247. *See also* Olga of Kiev
Hellespont, the, 256
Hengest. *See* Hengist
Hengist, 96, 100, *104*, 105, 106, *107*
Henry II, 233
Henry the Navigator, 280
Henry the Pious, 290
Herculanus, Flavius Bassus, 54–55
Hereford, 223
Herleva, 231
Hertfordshire, 103
Hippo Regius, 69, 78–79
Hispania, *15*. *See also* Spain
Hoelun, 263, 265
Holland, 100, 122, 156, 174, 177, 181. *See also* Frisia
Holy Grail, 107–108
Holy Land, 37, 38, 90, 288, 291. *See also* Jerusalem
Holy Mother of God, Church of the, 275–276, 283
Holy Roman Empire, 120, 288, 293. *See also* Byzantine Empire
Honoria, 53, 54–55, 60
Honorius, 20, 27, 30, 33, 73
Horik, 181
Horsa, 106, *107*
Howth, 215
human sacrifice, 254
Humber River, 135
Hungary, 16, 21, 39, 49, 115, 120, 250, 274, 288, 291, 293–299, 301. *See also* Pannonia
Hunimund, 43

Hunneric, 87, 90, 97
Huns, 9, 11, 12, 24–25, *37*, *51*, 81, 89, 106, 115, 270. *See also* Attila the Hun
    Alans and, 43, *44*, 45, 48
    appearance of, 39
    arrival of, 36–49
    culture of, 46, 48, 50, 52
    Goths and, 43, 48
    horsemanship of, 39, 41–42, 52
    lethal weaponry of, 41–42
    nomadism of, 46
    population of, 47–48
    Roman Empire and, 53, 56–57, 83
    skills of, 41–42
    slavery and, 48–49
    Vandals and, 67
Hyacinthus, 55

I

Iberian Peninsula, 188, 200–201, *201*. *See also* Portugal; Spain
Ibn Fadlan, Ahmad, 140, 238
ibn Zayid, Tariq, 200, 201
Iceland, 158
Igor, 236–243, 250
Ildico, 65
Ilkhanate, 300
illuminated manuscripts, 135–136
India, 8, 12, 13, 232, 233
Inishmurray, Sligo, 162
Iona, 130
Iona Abbey, 137–138
Iran, 300. *See also* Persian Empire
Iraq, 300. *See also* Persian Empire
Ireland, 8, 11, 101, 103, 149, 158, 160–171, 190, 204–217. *See also* Britain; Dublin
    books in, 165
    culture of, 164–166, 171
    map of, *164*
    metalwork in, 165
    Normans and, 172, 232–233
    slavery in, 209, 210
    Vikings in, 158–171, *163*, *164*, *166*, 204–217
iron mines, 102
Isidore of Seville, St., 74, *76*, 77
Iskorosten, 242, 244, 245–246, 250
Islam, 200–201

Isla Menor, 193, 194
Istanbul. *See* Constantinople
Italy, 9, 10, 53, 62, 95, 103, 114, 120, 181, 186, 280, 284. *See also* Roman Empire
    map of, *198*
    Vandal invasion of, *87*, 87, 88
    Viking invasions of, 197–198, *198*, 199
Ivan the Terrible, 275
Ivar the Boneless, 131, 138, 142, 211, 212

J

Japan, 280
Jarrow Abbey, 130, 137
Jerome, St., 9, 10, 33, *34*, 38, *40*
Jerusalem, 37, 38, 90, 186–187. *See also* Holy Land
Jews, 187, 200. *See also* Judaism
Jin Dynasty, 260, 263, 266, 269, 270, 271
Jins, 269–270, 271, 273. *See also* Jin Dynasty
Jochi, 279, 281
John, 32–33, 254
Jordanes, 57, 77
Judaism, 13. *See also* Jews
Julian, 200
Julius Caesar, 19
Justinian, 97–98
Jutes, 54, 100, 101, 105–106, *107*, 108
Juzjani, Minhaj al-Siraj, 268

K

Kadan, 291, 295, 296, 301
Kaifeng, 273
Kazakhstan, 300
Kenipolis, 94
Kent, 102, 106, 112, 135, 138, 157
Khasar, 265
Khazars, 234, 250, 252
Kherson, bishop of, 257
Kiev, 10, 11, 202, 234–247, 250–251, 277, *287*, 293. *See also* Kievan Rus; Ukraine
    destruction of, 275, 286–287
    map of, *252*
    natural resources of, 236
    Viking conquest of, 234, *235*

Kievan Rus, 234–249, 275. *See also*
    Kiev; Rus; Russia; Ukraine
    conversion to Christianity in,
        237, 248–249, 257–259
    culture of, 258–259
    map of, *252*
    Viking-Slavic dynasty, 259
Kildare, 166
Kipchaks, *292*, 293, 294–295
Knights Hospitaller, 293
Knights of the Round Table,
    107–108
Knights Templar, 290, *291*, 291,
    293, 297, 298
Koloman, 297, 298
Kolomenka River, 279
Korosten, 242
kow-tow, 263
Kozelsk, *278*, 279
Kremlin, the, 278
Kublai Khan, 280, *281*, 300
Kuthen, 294

L
Laeta, 31
Lake Baikal, 285
Lake Ilmen, 283
Lancelot, 107–108
Lancelot, Sir, *108*, 109
Latin, 9, 10, 35, 97, 109, 110,
    114, 115, 116
lead, 102
Lea River, 157
Leinster, 169, 206, 207, 209, 212,
    213, 214
Lemans, 174
Leo, Pope St., 53, 62–63, *63*, 82,
    89, 90, 92, *93*
Leo I, 91, 94
Leo the Deacon, 242–243, 249
Li An-Chuan, 266
Libya, 198
Liegnitz, Battle of, 290, 291, 293,
    299
Liffey River, 162, 215
Limerick, 11, 158, 160, 171, 205,
    206, 210–212
Lincoln, 102
Lincolnshire, 112, 226
Lindisfarne Abbey, 128–143
Lindisfarne Gospels, the, 135
Lindisfarne Island, 130, 132, 137
literacy, 259
Lithuania, 288

Lithuanian tribes, 254
Little Britain, 109
Lodvesson, Sigurd, 214, 215
Loire Valley, 156–157
London, 101, 102, 103, 112, 131,
    135, 138, 152, 156
Lothair I, *180*, 181–182
Lough Derg, 160
Lough Foyle, 169–170
Lough Owel, 161
Louis, Abbot of St. Denis, 185
Louis IX, 293
Louis the Fat, 186
Louis the German, *180*, 181–182
Louis the Pious, 174, *176*, 177
Louth, 163
Lublin, Poland, 290, 296
Luna, 197–198, *198*
Luna, Cathedral of, 193, 195–197
Luxemburg, 120

M
mac Cellaig, Lorcan, 166, 168
Maelmorda, 206, 209, 210, 212,
    213, 214, 215, 217
Maelmuad. *See* Maelmorda
Mael Muire, 169
Maelmurda. *See* Maelmorda
Mael Seachlinn, 161, 166
Maelsechnaill, 170
Magister militum, 114, 123
Magnentius, 114
Magnus, 226
Magyars, 234
Mainz, 60
"Majus", 194
Mal, 237, 242–244
Maldon, 152
Malta, 186
Man, Isle of, 149, 209, 214
Manchester, 102
Manchu, 269
Manchuria, 260
manuscripts, 165
Marcellinus, Ammianus, 43
Marcianople, 25
Margus, bishop of, 57
Maria, 27
Martel, Charles, 188–190, *189*
Martyrs' Bay, 130, 137
Matilda of Flanders, 231
Mausoleum of Augustus, 20
Maximin, 58
Maximus, Magnus, 103

Maximus, Petronius, 86
Maygars, 10
Meath, 169
Mediterranean Sea (and region),
    77, 88, 91, 122, 149, 188–203,
    192
merchants, 136. *See also* trade
Mercia, 135, 138, 143, 144, 147,
    148, 150, 151, 152, 229
Merkit Khan, 279
Merkits, 266
Mersey, the, 152
metals, precious, 165, 181, 237,
    269. *See also specific metals*
metalwork, 165
Michael, 293
Middle East, 262. *See also specific
    countries*
Mieszko, 250, 296–297
Milan, 103
Mitrofan, Archibishop, 283
Mohi, Battle of, 291, 297–299,
    301
Moldavia, 288, 295
monasteries, 35, 136, 144, 146,
    149, 156–157, 160, 162,
    164–165, 178, 182–186, 213,
    258
Mongolian Empire, 262–263, *268*,
    269–270, 280, 285, 288, *289*,
    291, 300. *See also* Mongols
Mongols, 11–13, 36, *267*, *272*,
    281, *293*, 293, 300, *302–303*.
    See also Mongolian Empire;
        Tartars; Tatars
    conquest of China, 260–273
    conquest of Russia and Ukraine,
        274–287, *285*, *287*
    in eastern Europe, *285*, *287*
    in Europe, 274–301
    horsemanship of, 270
    as a model for autocratic rule,
        275
    rule of, 271, 273
    warfare of, 279, 281–282,
        290–291, 298
monks, 136, 165, 182–185. *See
    also* monasteries; *specific monks*
Monreale, 187
Moorish Empire, 188–190. *See also*
    Moors
Moors, 120, 187. *See also* Arabs;
    Moorish Empire
    conquest of Iberian Peninsula,

200–201, *201*
Vikings and, 188–190, 198, 202
Moravia, 288, 290
Morcar, 227–229
Morocco, 74, 77, 78, 95, 188, 200
Moscow, 8, 12, 248, 275–279
Mount Badon, Battle of, 101,
106–107, 109–110, 112
Muhammed, 200
Mullingar, Westmeath, 160, 161
Munster, 165, 166, 206, 210, 212,
214, 217
Murchen, the, 269
Muslims, 200–201. *See also* Moors;
Saracens
Mynydd Baedon, 109

N
Naimans, 266
Naissus, 21–22
Nantes, 174, 182
naphtha, 279, 290, 291, 298
Narni, Umbria, 32
Nennius, 106–107
Nero, 73
Netherlands, the, 114, 120. *See also*
Gaul
Nicaea, Council of, 78, *79*, 80
Nicene Creed, 78
Nicholas of Myra, St., 78, *79*
Nieman River, 254
Nimes, 199
Ningxia Hui Autonomous Region,
265
Noghai, 300
Noirmoutier, 184
Norfolk, 112, 226
Norman Conquest, 172, 220, 223,
230, 232–233
Normandy, 130, 149, 172–187,
221, 224, 229
Normans, 130, 172–187, 218. *See
also* Normandy
Norse, 129, 130, 172, 177, 202.
See also Vikings
Norsemen. *See* Norse
North Africa, 69, 74, 77–78,
88–89, 95, *97*, 97–98, 117, 188,
190, 196, 198–200. *See also*
Algeria; Carthage
Northmen, 130, 172, 177, 181,
182. *See also* Norse
Northumbria, 112, 135, 138, 144,
147, *148*, 152, 226

Northumbrian Renaissance,
135–136
Norway, 11, 221, 226, 250
Novgorod, 236, 253, 277,
283–284, 286
Numidia, 80
nuns, 136

O
Ochubur mac Cinaeda, 166
Odin, 149
Odoacer, 19, 90, *90*, 90, 95
Ogodei Khan, 291, 300, 301
Oka River, 277
Olaf Cuaran, 169
Olaf the White, 161, 168, 169,
170, 171
Olaf Trygvasson, 250
Oleg, 236, 242, *243*, 250, 253,
284
Olga, St., 247, 286. *See also* Olga
of Kiev
Olga of Kiev, 234–247, *245*, 250,
254, 286
Olgass, 202
Onguts, 269–270
Onon River, 263
Orkneys, 149, 209, 214
Orleans, 60
Orre, Eynstein, 232
Orthodox Church, 247, 259
Ostia, 86, 90
Ostrogoths, 23, 38. *See also* Goths
Ota, 160, 161
Ouse River, 227–228, 232

P
Paderborn, 120
Padua, 62
paganism, 20, 32, 129, 149, 160,
161, 236, 257
Palermo, 187
Pannonia, 16, 21, 115
Paris, *59*, 60, 174–175, 186
Paris, Matthew, 262
Parthians, 19
Patriarch of Constantinople, 259
Patrick, St., 158, *159*, 160, *208*,
209
Paul, St., 33, 62, *63*, 73
pearls, 165
Pechenegs, 10, 252
Pelagius, 9, 10
Peloponnese, the, 94

Persian Empire, 12, 200, 262
Perun, 257
Pest, 294–296, 297, 299, 301
Peter, St., 20, 62, *63*, 73, 74, *75*
Peter the Great, 275
Pevensey, 112
Phocas, Bardas, 202–203, 256
Picts, 10, 68, 100, 101, 102, 105
pilgrims, 291
pirates, 132–133
Pisa, 10, 199
Placidia, 90
Placidia, Galla, 54, 55, 77
Pland, 293
Plautius, Aulus, 100, 102
Poitou, 177
Poland, 250, 256, 274, 288,
290–291, 293, 294, 296–297,
299, 301
Polo, Maffeo, 280, *281*
Polo, Marco, 280, *281*, 284, *289*
Polo, Niccolò, 280, *281*
Pontus, 122
popes, 35, 293. *See also specific
popes*
Porphyrogenetes, 257
Porta Salaria, 17
Portland, 130, 131–132, 138
Portugal, 188, 189, 200–201, *201*.
See also Iberian Peninsula
pottery, 102
Praetorians, 33
Principia, 21
Priscus, 58
Proba, 17, 20
Probus, 116, 122
Procopius, 88
Pskov, 238
public baths, 35
purple, 109
Pyrenees, the, 73, 74, 188, 189

Q
Quentovic, 182

R
Ragnachar, 127
Ragnar Lodbrok, 193
Rahman, Emir Abdul, 188–189
Ranvaik, 164
Ras Addar, 91
Ratiaria, Bulgaria, 57
Ravenna, 30
relics, 164, 166, 170